Cowboy Logic Continues

Homegrown insight on ordinary things

Ryan M. Taylor

To Morris -
Happy trails,
Ryan

Sandhill Communications

The publisher:
Sandhill Communications
5435 13th Ave. NE
Towner, ND 58788

Illustrations by Steve Stark
Edited by Kim Deats
Layout and cover design by Cindy Kittelson,
In Your Eye Graphic Design
Printed and bound in the United States of America by
Knight Printing, Fargo, N.D.
First Printing, 2004
Library of Congress Control Number: 2004097525
ISBN 0-9667756-1-9

For the Taylor Ranch crew –
my mother, Liz; my father, Bud;
my wife, Nikki; and my son, little Bud.
It's family that makes ranch life the good life.

Table of Contents

Introduction

It seems like just the other day that I was putting together the columns for "A Collection of Cowboy Logic." I checked the calendar and it was six years ago. If time flies when you're having fun, I must have been having an awfully good time.

What you have in your hands is most all the columns to leave my desk since the fall of 1998. For part of that time, I was still writing a column every week. The last few years, I've been writing one every two weeks. I hope they're twice as good. I know I'm twice as happy and half as stressed to only have a deadline every 14 days, instead of every seven!

A few things have changed since we printed that first book. The cattle market has gotten steadily stronger. Some might even say the prices in 2004 will allow us to live like other average middle-class folks! I hope it stays that way.

Not knowing if the cattle market was going to improve, I took a job off the ranch back in 1999 with a livestock pharmaceutical company to help pay some bills and get rid of some debt. I was still able to maintain the ranch and keep things going while I was collecting that paycheck, and I enjoyed my four years of learning new things and meeting new people in the animal health business.

But, I can say with certainty that I like ranching better than driving up and down the road 1,000 miles a week selling cow meds and horse drugs. One very good piece of fortune that happened while I was driving around the state is meeting the woman who would become my wife and the mother of our son. It was the best sale I ever made at an animal health supper meeting in western North Dakota.

In the introduction to my last book, I wrote about how I got into the column-writing business by winning an essay contest where I penned a few lines about my trusty horse, Dude. My column-writing notoriety led me to my job as communications director for a regional beef cooperative, my travels with that co-op introduced me to the man who would hire me on in the animal health business, the animal health job led me to the meeting where I would meet my wife. Yes, one thing does lead to another and I have to give all the credit to an aging gelding named Dude that I bought for $500 years ago. He's earned his equine retirement here on the ranch.

The stories in this book reflect on many things – courtship, marriage and fatherhood; off-ranch employment and travels; on-the-ranch wrecks and rewards; and the greatness of life on the Great Plains.

One reader wrote me an e-mail saying she looked forward to my "insight on ordinary things." I liked that phrase so much I used it in my subtitle.

I remember another letter I got in the mail from a reader in southeastern North Dakota who feared my job in the corporate world of animal health might lead to other things. He said, "Don't leave us with nothing to read out here because they will try to kick you upstairs in some big town. Life is more than money." He was right. There was talk of me climbing the corporate ladder into Kansas City, but I remembered his advice and stayed "out here." I've not regretted it.

I'll always remember the story written to me by a friend, reader and hospital nurse in Canada. She was assigned to a patient who had survived a 10-foot fall but could not speak, eat or move from the jaw down. His only communication was to blink once for yes and twice for no, and he could move his lips and eyebrows just enough to smile or pout depending on his mood, she said.

He was a 78-year-old farmer who had also owned some cows. She had a long shift ahead of her and was trying to figure out what would please him. She asked about television, sleep, music. Each query got the two blinks for "no." She asked if he'd like her to read from her new book, "A Collection of Cowboy Logic." He lifted the eyebrows and gave her a definite one blink for "yes." "Really?" she said. One blink, smile. She read aloud to him for about an hour, asking every 10 minutes, if he'd like her to continue. One blink, smile.

That's what keeps me writing and keeps me living "out here" where people like to read about ordinary things that they, too, have experienced and felt from time to time. And I think there'll be a day when we look back on our existence out here on the prairie, on the farms and ranches, and in the little towns dotting the countryside, and we'll say those ordinary things were really quite extraordinary in the modern scope of things.

So I'll keep writing. Thank you for reading. One blink, smile.

Clean country living

Delivery drawbacks

Pity to the parcel people

Oct. 12, 1998

If a package absolutely, positively has to be there overnight, and "there" is the Taylor Ranch, you might be better off just jumping in the pickup and driving it here yourself.

Getting in touch with other participants in the state, national and global economy has always been a bit of a challenge out here in the sticks, but it seems to be getting worse.

It all started with the U.S. Mail and rural delivery. On account of some bureaucratic mumbo jumbo about our ranch not being on an "established route," we drive seven miles round trip every day to get yesterday's newspaper.

Even though my father is disabled with Parkinson's, a veteran of World War II and a senior citizen, he can't get the same curbfront courtesy service that senior citizens in town and on established routes can get.

By the way, if a senator or congressman (that's you, Byron, Kent or Earl) has one of his aides reading Cowboy Logic for good ideas, here's one – get the U.S. Mail within a half mile of Bud Taylor south of Towner, N.D. It could make a great re-election campaign commercial.

"Express" delivery

We do get some deliveries right to our doorstep, but you never know if they're going to make it out either. United Parcel Service used to come out when they had a parcel to serve us with.

But now, they wait as many as three days for the parcels to pile up before they serve us with them. So if you send me a UPS package and it gets into the Towner truck on Monday, I'll be sure to have it by Thursday. You could just as well send it on a hot air balloon or a freight train.

This is where I have to hand it to the U.S. Mail. If someone a couple hundred miles away ships me some parts or repairs, the bill is in the mailbox before the package is in the yard. I hate it when the financial responsibility precedes the material satisfaction.

Another option for your package could be Airborne Express. I always know when I'm getting a package via Airborne. They call me up from the Cenex station in Towner and say, "Hi Ryan, we're leaving a package for you here at the Cenex." Great.

At least I know it's in the vicinity and I only have to drive 17 miles to retrieve it.

Mail in the muck

One delivery outfit I really do admire is Federal Express. They deliver 3 million packages a day to 211 countries with 619 airplanes, 143,000 employees and 41,500 vehicles. If they say it's going to be there, it'll be there.

That is unless you've just gotten 2 inches of rain on a country road that's been graveled with a conservative county commissioner's salt shaker.

That was the case yesterday. Not known for their handling capabilities on mud, a FedEx van nosed it in the ditch two miles from the ranch. The delivery gal walked that distance to the ranch in a drizzling rain.

I was gone, but our hired hand pulled her out with the 4020. No charge, of course. I'm sure she was cussing our address as she walked through the rain and the mud, but we really did appreciate her effort. She still got my package here closer and quicker than anyone else.

Workin' to the rhythm

Some work just requires the tunes Oct. 19, 1998

It's a well-established fact that music in the workplace is good for morale, and good morale means high productivity.

The fact that the Taylor Ranch has not yet owned a tractor with a radio may explain my general distaste for having to spend so much time on those rattling, clang and bang contraptions. But the driving force of impending poverty and the moral pressures of feeding a couple hundred cows through the winter keep me behind the tractor wheel, radio or no radio – morale or no morale.

But when it comes to any other kind of task, I'm tuned in and bolstering my on-the-job attitude.

Strategic stereo sound

Working in my office always requires some background music and I keep a 1976 model AM/FM radio on tap in the shop to help ease the pain of slipped wrenches and bloody knuckles. I've got the antennae hooked up to the sheet metal on the roof and that allows me to tune in most any station available in the free world.

I keep the radios in the ranch pickups in working order and try to make good use of them whenever possible. If the setting is just right, I can wing open the doors and enjoy the tunes from the pickup along a good quarter mile of fence.

I've often wondered if barbed wire can conduct sound. That way I could just wear a pair of headphones and attach them to a protruding barb as I go from post to post, stapling and clipping.

Dad has always frowned on my liberal use of the pickup batteries for musical entertainment. "You keep doing that and you'll be walking home someday," he warns. So, just in case, I park on a hill capable of rolling the rig to a start.

Busting a move

Music does have a way of bringing on some temporary, therapeutic rhythm.

I've always enjoyed a good two-step, waltz or jitterbug, but I seldom get out of control and really "bust a move" in public. However, in the pasture, around the yard or in the shop, you'd hardly recognize me as the modest country bumpkin I truly am. You'd think I was some choreographed hip hop dance machine.

It's not just fencing, wrenching and corral work that lends itself to sudden bursts of unexplained body shakes. I recently learned that house painting will bring it on as well.

This fall, I've been feverishly trying to paint the interior of a bachelor shack I built out in the west pasture. A paint roller with a 5-foot handle on it makes a dandy guitar when you're needing a break from the tedium of painting a million feet of wall with a 9-inch roller. I gave equal opportunity air time to all varieties of music – from Merle Haggard and George Strait to the Eagles, Green Day and Sheryl Crow.

I even strayed to the public radio station for a few Celtic melodies. At one point, I jumped off my painting ladder and did a little jig that I figured would look like the Irish hard-shoe dancer, Michael Flatley, in the Broadway musical, Riverdance.

Luckily, no one was there to watch because I caught a reflection of myself in the window and realized I looked more like the Beverly Hillbillies' Jed Clampett doing the Ozark stomp and clog.

Sometimes it's nice not having neighbors so close that they can see in your windows.

When you gotta go

Toddler tinkling is an urgent matter

Oct. 26, 1998

My brilliant, good-looking and well behaved 4-year-old nephew is progressing well in the eyes of his slightly biased uncle.

He's become a pretty good hand around the ranch with important tasks like petting the dog, steering the tractor and cheering up the grandparents. Plus, he recently cracked out on the rodeo circuit in the mutton busting.

He entered the sheep riding at the pro rodeo in Minot, N.D., this fall, and although he only made it 20 feet, he still got a ribbon and a T-shirt. I wasn't able to make it to the rodeo to watch him spur the wool, but I was still proud of the progress he's made in his actions at that rodeo compared to last year.

Boys' night out

Last year, I thought it might be nice to take my nephew to the Minot rodeo to see some buckin' horses, bullfighters and rodeo queens.

Maybe I was the one most interested in the queens, but, all the same, the two of us got strapped in our car seats and headed for the arena.

"Have a good time," my sister said as we were leaving, "and remember, if he says he has to go to the bathroom, he means he has to go right now!" I made a mental note of her warning advice.

We got to the rodeo and found a couple of open seats near the top of the arena. The lights went down for the national anthem. "Oh say can you see." My nephew gave me an urgent tap on the knee and said, "I gotta go pee!"

"Can't you wait a little while?" I asked. "No, I gotta go right now!" he said, crossing his legs and giving me that 3-year-old look of anxiety. I remembered my sister's warning and imagined the consequences of not getting him to the bathroom pronto.

I was torn between respectful patriotism and the fear of embarrassment. I took his hand and we started making our way past perturbed-looking people who were trying to be intent on our fluttering flag in the "dawn's early light."

I was doing my best to be reverent and apologetic as we made our way. When we got to the stairs, my nephew decided to jump down them two feet at a time. "Bang! Bang! Bang!" He might have been trying to imitate the bombs bursting in air, but my face had the rockets' red glare of embarrassment as I scooped him up and headed for the little boys' room. So much for reverence.

Near the bathroom, he discovered a video game that seemed more exciting to him than the rodeo action, and by the end of the night, he managed to keep me by that video game through all of the saddle bronc, most of the barebacks and a good share of the calf roping. At least he didn't care if the game had a quarter in it or not.

Good timing

A friend of mine from Iowa had a little boy with the same sort of urgency, but a better location for his potty break. They had gone into town to visit the banker in their small town, and, as they were leaving, the boy decided he had to go.

Before you knew it, his britches were around his knees and he was making a stream right there on the bank.

Was my friend angry or embarrassed? No, he just told his boy, "That's OK. I've always wanted to do that on this bank myself!"

Gone forever

A simple string could be the answer to averting losses

Nov. 23, 1998

I was nearly struck by two unimaginable disasters last week. I was sure that I had lost both my calving book and my Day Timer calendar.

Losing just one or the other would have been enough to completely shut down operations at the Taylor Ranch and Sandhill Communications, but losing both of them would have been worse than forced bankruptcy.

My calving book is way more than just calving stats. It's really a record of "a year in the life of the Taylor Ranch." Everything on the ranch that could be recorded is written down in there. Worst of all, there's no backup copy. It's one of a kind.

Usually, a calving book is pretty much all a rancher needs to get through life on the range. But, these days, maintaining a life on the range means capturing some crucial off-ranch paychecks, and that's where my Day Timer calendar comes in handy.

At the risk of sounding like one of those yuppie professional types, I don't think I could function without my Day Timer.

It tells me where I have to be and when for speaking engagements and mind bending conferences. It keeps track of my time and expenses when I'm out on the road for my new contract job with Fort Dodge Animal Health, and it has that all important "to be done today action list."

It also has all my important phone numbers. It's a sinking feeling when you're away from the ranch, realize you're about to be overdrawn and you can't find the phone number for your bank to request a quick advance on your operating loan. Those numbers need to be at your fingertips and ready for action.

Where are they?

Last week, I was sure I had left my Day Timer at the restaurant in Amidon, N.D., but I called them and they hadn't seen it.

I was assuming the worst, thinking I had dropped it in the snow somewhere or left it on top of the car when I was loading my luggage. Then I reached in the compartment on the door of the car and there it was. Life was back on schedule.

I was certain I had lost my calving book a couple days later. I looked in all my shirts, jackets, vehicles and other hiding spots. The vet was coming to preg check the cows and I couldn't even tell him with certainty what weekend I'd AI'd the heifers or exactly what day I'd pulled the bulls from the pasture.

I was crazed with the need to find that book. I felt myself slipping into a deep depression when I remembered the one shirt in my suitcase whose pocket I hadn't checked. Another mystery solved.

From now on, I'm going to take a lesson from the inventors of "soap on a rope" and the infamous "trucker's wallet." Those people are really on to something. It just makes good sense to have important things handy and on a tether of some kind.

I believe it's high time that someone introduce the "calendar on a cord" and the "ranch records on a rope." Just tie one end to your belt loop or your little finger, whichever one is strongest, and you'll never have that panicky, "oh no, it's gone forever" feeling again.

Just make sure you tie a good strong knot.

Prairie hospitality

A "come on in" attitude

March 15, 1999

"Come on in, I got the coffee on." It's a common greeting among rural folks addicted to the caffeine and conversation made possible by a few cups of the steamy brew.

Everybody I know will just about trip over themselves to get inside and huddle around the coffee pot. And we don't usually mind it if a few cookies or bars find their way to the table while we're sipping our java.

Of course, despite our coffee cravings and honest desire to sit, drink and eat with someone, we do have to turn down the host at least three times before it's considered polite to take them up on their offer.

"Oh, no, I really shouldn't stay for coffee." "Gosh, I really should be moving along." "You really shouldn't go through the trouble." "Well, I guess as long as you've already got it made, I could maybe stay for a cup or two."

Once we've rattled through our polite three-decline minimum, we'll shoot right past the one- or two-cup deal, staying for at least a pot or two.

We play the same little game when they bring out the pan of bars. "Oh, I don't need anything else. The coffee is plenty." "No, don't trouble yourself." "Well, maybe. As long as you've already got them cut up. I'll try one." Half a pan later, you can feel good with the fact that you gave them at least a couple of chances to save their sweets.

It's just a matter of good prairie manners. The only fear I have as a hungry bachelor with a severe coffee addiction and a real sweet tooth is that some young hosts or hostesses may not have learned about the standard three-decline etiquette.

It doesn't happen often, but, once in awhile, someone will take me seriously after one or two polite declines and there I sit, coffeeless and sweetless. So if your family is bringing in a new son or daughter-in-law who doesn't know the routine, tell them straight up about how this system works.

Abusing the system

Having been raised in a culture of free-flowing hospitality, I wasn't surprised to hear that even car thieves and jailbirds get invited in for coffee in North Dakota.

In case you hadn't heard, an inmate of the Barnes County Jail in Valley City broke free and hit for the countryside last week. He stole a couple vehicles, took some cash from an elderly couple and found himself at a farmstead in Ransom County.

The family at the farm did what most farm families do. They asked the fella to come on in and have a cup of coffee. I'm not sure if the convict did the polite thing and turned down the invite for coffee a couple of times, but he must have done what he could to blend in and keep their suspicions low. They never suspected that the fella was a felon. He told them he was a hunter with car trouble.

But after coffee, it was the farmer who ended up with car trouble. The farmer was going to give the "hunter" a ride, and the escapee kindly offered to start the farmer's car and bring it around to the front of the house. That was the last the farmer saw of his 1993 Ford Taurus.

The farmer was probably a little sore about getting his car stolen, but, as he told one reporter, "at least we didn't bring out the cookies, so we're not out that!"

Covert operations

Doin' the deal in a small-town parking lot

May 3, 1999

It was a rather dreary, cloudy day, but that was OK because I had a dreary, cloudy job to do.

No, I wasn't balancing my checkbook or tearing into the greasy guts of a tractor. I was on a food quest for the family. In the dark of morning, over coffee, I was instructed to do something that goes against the grain of most every cowboy I know. I was asked to go fetch some chickens for the ranch freezer.

Now, chickens are the arch nemesis of the beef industry, and it causes a rancher a lot of pain to eat so much as a drumstick. However, the head cook at our ranch can make that slimy old bird downright tasty.

I don't know if it's the seasoning, the coating or the way she fries it, but my mother can get the staunchest of beef eaters to pull up a chair and enjoy a couple pieces of her home fried chicken.

The fowl that springs forth from her frying pan bears absolutely no resemblance to those disgusting "pieces parts" that come out of the fast-food joints or the scraggly little chickadees that spend the week rolling around on the supermarket rotisserie.

Her's is the good stuff, and she claims that quality birds are the cornerstone of her success. She needed my dark car with the big trunk to make a run for her.

Chicken dealers

My mother isn't satisfied with those over-the-counter petite factory-raised fowl that come out of Arkansas. She likes a good-sized bird with the proper upbringing. And she knows where to get them – from the traveling chicken dealer.

She told me, "The chicken dealer's going to be selling birds in the parking lot down in Harvey today." I've heard of the shady deals made in the parking lots of big cities like New York, Chicago and Harvey. I didn't like the sound of it.

The chicken dealers pull into a parking lot, cut their deal and leave. The money supports their small religious sect and enables them to raise more chickens. It's a tidy little operation.

I was nervous, but I agreed to be the front man and go do the deal. I pulled into town looking for the parking lot and the people with the cold, dead birds.

I expected to find them in this one lot, but there was no action. I asked the proprietor where the dealer was and he sent me down the street to another parking lot. Maybe the deal is off, I thought. Maybe they were giving me the slip. Probably figured I was wired and armed by some radical beef group or something.

I went to the next lot. Nothing. I said to that proprietor, "Psssst. You seen the chicken dealer? He was supposed to be here at 11 a.m." He said, "Hey, cowboy, you got some bad information. That dealer ain't sellin' till noon."

I patiently waited. I looked around for people I might know. I pulled up my collar and put on a baseball cap to disguise myself from any cattlemen who might drive by and recognize me.

Then the chicken dealer pulled up in his van. I quickly got in line with a group of addicted-looking farmwives anxious to get their fix of fowl. "Give me two cases," I said, "and make it snappy, someone might be watching us."

They gave me the chickens all right, and I paid them their hush money.

Birds in hand, I sped down the road and I didn't stop until I could hear the sizzle of the waiting fry pan.

In a sinister sort of way, I was looking forward to seeing that chicken fry.

The tick of time

It's that time of year again

May 17, 1999

From the looks of the ears on my borderline border collie, Smokey, we're well into the wood tick season.

Smokey's kind of the bellwether that signals the advent of tick time on the Taylor Ranch.

When I'm in the tractor and Smokey's in the co-pilot position, I find myself passing the time with a little wood tick harvesting.

A quick pinch between the thumbs and forefinger, along with a rapid squeeze from my trusty pliers, and I can keep my dog relatively tick free until I remember to pick up his tick collar in town.

I try to keep ahead of the parasite problem, but some of the bugs will have a pint or two of the pup's blood digested before I get a chance to clean him up.

Sometimes, rather than give every tick the plier treatment, I go with the labor-saving method of execution by gas chamber.

My gas chamber isn't too sophisticated. A little unleaded petro in a mason jar is all I use. Those dirty, blood-thieving ticks don't even know what hit 'em when they expire doing the backstroke in the jar o' gas.

A word of advice, though. The ladies in the family aren't usually too impressed when you show them your jar full of squirming, dying ticks, and, whatever you do, don't stick that jar on the canned goods shelf in the cellar for a joke.

Some people just don't appreciate some species of our wild kingdom.

Creepy crawlies

After working on ol' Smokey's ticks, I begin to wonder if I should start checking my own ears.

I always seem to feel something crawling up my calf just thinking about those ticks.

Fencing is a prime wood tick gathering activity. And walking through the grass and trees fixing fence almost always yields a good crop of the little blood suckers.

I've had friends on professional fencing crews who could darn near fill their own mason jar gas chamber without even a dog to add to the collection.

I've been known to find a few myself, sad to say. And, when you feel one of those buggers crawling up your leg, you just do what you've gotta do to get a hold of him.

I once heard that the practice of mooning was inadvertently started by a fencing rancher in the heat of wood tick season.

Apparently, the rancher was fencing along a busy highway, felt a tick crawling up his thigh and, forgetting where he was, he dropped his pants right then and there to stop that tick's migration. As he bent over to grab the tick, he began to hear a few cars honk.

By the end of that day, teenagers up and down that highway were dropping their pants and signaling full moons from car to car, ticks or no ticks.

I can understand that pioneering rancher's sudden loss of shyness, though. It's always better to do whatever's needed to capture that tick in transport before he digs in and decides to stay awhile.

It always gets more complicated once they're attached. Rather than give the ticks a yank and risk infection, ticks in humans are backed out like a car from a parking spot.

Backing out takes rubbing alcohol or even a lit match, or, at worst, both. The latter is more like blasting them out than backing them out.

But we have to get those ticks out. After all, we need to save some blood for the new crop of mosquitoes.

Marooned

Fixin' a flat on the information superhighway

May 24, 1999

Cheerleaders of the information age proclaim that distance is dead.

For the record, I'd like to report that distance is alive and well on the Taylor Ranch.

Like most things in North Dakota, the vitality and health of distance is weather related. Six and one-half inches of rain in the last few weeks have taken out all kinds of roads, both the gravel kind and the information superhighway-type.

The gravel roads were first to go – washed out and overrun with water migrating from the high side to the low side. The road going south washed out just in time to make life miserable for all the ranchers wanting to get cattle to grass on the other side of the new gorge.

Luckily, our pastures were all within reach and didn't require a raft or any hoof-sized scuba gear. A lot of others in the neighborhood weren't so lucky. That little extra rain put another 16 or 18 miles on their cattle and the rigs that hauled them.

A couple other roads were saved by a load or two of small boulders the size of softballs. I guess money's so tight in our unorganized township that we're expected to crush our own gravel. In 10 or 15 years, we should have those boulders sized down to a pebble-sized road medium that's a little less rough.

Return to sender

The boulders might be a bit rough, but at least I can still get to town. My information superhighway didn't even get a load of rock when it washed out.

When the power went out for several hours in the middle of the night during a rain storm, I decided that sleep was more important than getting up and unplugging my computer.

By morning, the power had slammed on and off a half-dozen times and my computer's modem had slammed off for its last time. It kind of made a fella wish he'd gotten out of bed and pulled the plug and phone cord on the outfit.

I used the typical computer mechanic tactics to try to fix it. I turned the machine on, then off, then on – again. I took the modem out of its slot, then put it back in again. No luck.

Those on, then off, then on again methods usually work for computer repairs though. I once heard that a computer service guy was riding in a car with an auto mechanic when the car broke down.

The mechanic got under the hood, turned a few bolts and tweaked a couple of set screws but the car still wouldn't run. He asked the computer guy what he thought and he said, I got an idea – let's both get out of the car, then get back in the car, shut the doors and then try and start it.

Regardless of the logic on how to repair the computer, I found myself thrown completely off the information superhighway.

So if you've been trying to send me an e-mail for the last three weeks, I haven't been able to receive it. You can quit cussing me for being a rude, inconsiderate lout, now that you know of my technological breakdown.

Distance was dead, but it has risen.

I miss my e-mail, but I'm not quite as attached as the people in a survey that I read about. Given a choice of what they would want if they were marooned on a desert island, a large group said they'd want access to their e-mail.

Personally, I can think of a lot of other things I'd like to have access to on a desert island.

Move over coffee

Here comes something spendier

June 28, 1999

Ordering coffee isn't as simple as designating "cream or sugar with that?" anymore. Now, you have to designate if you want a cappuccino, espresso, latte, au lait or one of 47 obscure flavored syrups.

People love choices and the coffee world is giving us plenty to choose from. It's gotten to the point where you actually get a coffee "menu" to order from. You wouldn't think a simple shot of caffeine would require a full-page menu of options.

Something this complex usually only thrives in the big urban centers of the world. But, when I spotted a cappuccino machine at the Farmer's Union station in Sterling, N.D., and an espresso bar on wheels in Watford City, I knew that big-city coffee had invaded the countryside.

Purty tasty

I really can't make fun of these big-city coffee shacks too much because I'm a confessed addict myself.

I'm not quite sure why, but I'm a real sucker for sipping on a latte. It could be that I like the modern metropolitan feeling I get when I spend $3 for a cup of frothy java. When you live 17 miles from the cattle capital of North Dakota, you sometimes yearn to feel a little urbane.

But even more satisfying than the big-city buzz to my ego is the tickle on my tastebuds.

And I make sure there's plenty of taste to go around. The calorie-counting coffee drinkers will skimp a little and go "short" and "skinny." In coffee talk, that means a little bitty low-fat latte. Me, I get 'em tall and as fat as they can make 'em. At the very least, use whole milk. Half and half is even better.

They'll usually cost you the same whether you request some flavor syrup or not. So have 'em toss in a little sugar sweet hazelnut or raspberry. And don't forget the dollop of whipped cream to top it off.

If you're going to stray from the path of boiled black ranch coffee, you just as well really stray and head right down into the ditch of decadent desire.

Lingo au lait

Today's hip latte lover probably ought to be fluent in French to make an intelligent order at the cosmopolitan coffee café. Lacking any bilingual abilities, I do what most midwesterners do. Speak up and give it a lot of emphasis whether you know the pronunciation or not.

I give those French words my best Norwegian accent. Sometimes, I find myself stressing the syllables like my German Russian neighbors.

Being from North Da-KO-ta, I find myself sidling up to the coffee shack in cowtowns like Medora drawling out, "Give me one of them there caf-AY lat-AYS." Or, "on second thought, whip me up one of them es-PREZ-ers."

As odd as it sounds to hear a country boy ordering up fine French coffee, it looks even weirder when you see a 1976 three-quarter-ton pickup with barbed wire and fence posts dangling out of the tailgate, pulled up to the drive-up espresso shack in greater metropolitan Mandan. It's not everyday that you see $6 and a couple of "tall skinnies" trading hands through a side window that was rolled down with a Vise-Grip crank.

It's kind of like the cartoon with the four tough-looking, trail-weary cowboys sitting around the campfire clutching their hot tin cups. One of the ornery hombres looks to one of the others and says, "Hey, Slim, how's about another la-TAY?"

The barbering biz

Good haircuts and good atmosphere

July 5, 1999

There aren't many occupations that encourage family tradition anymore. Agriculture may be one of the last ways of life where sons and daughters make a real effort to follow in their parents footsteps and carry on the torch of tradition.

In Rugby, N.D., there's another way of life where the torch of tradition has burned for a father and his two sons for 142 years. The family name is Liming and the tradition is barbering.

That's right, 142 combined years of "lowering ears," trimmin' up the sides and cuttin' "whitewalls" around the ears of shaggy folks throughout central North Dakota.

On the chair

I speak from personal experience when I say time spent in Liming's Barber Shop was time well invested in a piece of fading Americana. And the haircuts were pretty good, too.

"You're next," Dwight would say, and I'd hang my hat on the hook in the corner and climb into a barber chair that Dwight's brother and father had bought second-hand back in the 1940s.

You knew you were in good hands when Dwight's scissors would start to sing. The Navy veteran was a decorated veteran of the barber business, too. His red barbering uniform proudly bore the pin designating him as "Barber of the Year, 1971-72".

Even without an appointment, you could usually walk in and get a cut without too long a wait. If you did have to wait, you could sit down and read from the selection of magazines that ranged from Sports Afield to U.S. News and World Report. Usually, you'd just sit and soak up the atmosphere and the conversation.

Liming's Barber Shop wasn't into Wal-Mart-style spacious square footage. I never took my tape measure along, but I doubt that place is wider than 12 feet at its widest point. Small as it is, you can still pack in at least three or four experts on everything from world politics to meteorological weather patterns to rural economic development.

If the chatter ever did lull, we could turn to the conversation pieces including the blown-apart shotgun in the corner (a quick lead in to gun safety), the model airplane bomber hanging from the ceiling (the intro to military policy) or the photos of Dwight driving his two-cylinder John Deere (a primer for a discussion on the high cost of new farm equipment).

The usual

I've had the same hairstyle – short, around the ears, parted from the right – since I was 8 years old, so we didn't have to waste a lot of time wondering how to style my skull. Just sit down, listen to the hum of the clippers, and watch the hair fall to the floor.

I suppose a young guy like myself ought to be getting his haircuts from some pretty gal in a beauty salon, if for no other reason than to feel a woman's hands massaging my scalp.

But beauty salons will probably be around for a long time. The good old-fashioned barber shop with its red, white and blue pole out front, and its old-time atmosphere inside, seems to be slipping into the pages of history. I don't want to miss out on this fading piece of small-town culture.

But things look good for Liming's Barber Shop. Even though Dwight and Neil Liming are retiring, fellow barber Milton Goodman has bought the business. My first haircut from Milt feels pretty good, and it looks like he's going to keep the same decor and atmosphere inside the shop.

Hopefully, I can keep growing more hair than I lose so I can do my small part to keep another old-time barber in business.

Starved for company

And hungry for a social feast

Aug. 2, 1999

The prairie is chock full of solitude. So much so that some folks would say it's downright lonely.

Living in a land where a lot of areas are measured in square miles per person, and not thousands of persons per square mile, makes for a small, but friendly, population.

It's the kind of population where people say hello on the sidewalk and wave to you on the highway. Sometimes we do it out of friendliness, sometimes we do it out of the sheer shock of seeing another human being on the street or a particular stretch of road.

We appreciate our solitude, but grow weary of the loneliness. And the difference between the two is often a pretty fine line. Sometimes it's just a matter of timing.

It's pretty easy to tell when we're having a lonely day. We'll tackle passers-by, make them talk, and, if necessary, tie them to the kitchen table until we're good and done with our visit. If we were dogs, we'd be wagging our tail when travelers drive in our yard.

I've witnessed a lot of these lonely day encounters out in the sticks of the North Dakota outback, and most all of them break down about the same.

Road stops

During our couple months of "warm enough to stand outside weather," there's the social phenomenon of road block parties.

This happens during those rare moments when we're not speeding along to put out the fires of the world. If we're going under 50 miles an hour and happen to pass a neighbor who's also traveling the speed of a rough-running field pickup, the two drivers can usually slow to a stop, hit reverse, jump out, lean against their respective rigs and commence to visiting.

Road block parties are cumulative events. When other folks drive up, they usually stop and join in. If traffic is particularly hectic, you might end up with four or five pickups all pulled over and joining in on the conversation.

The parties may not break up for an hour or more. It usually takes a road grader, a tractor with a really wide implement, or an impatient city person who can't get around the road block to scatter the participants.

Phases of farewell

Kitchen table company can last even longer than most road block parties, especially if both visitor and visitee are starved for company.

The stages of the on-site visit almost always follow a set pattern. After greeting the company at the door or in the yard, they come in to sit at the table and drink several pots of coffee and anything available that's loaded with sugar.

When the coffee and goodies are gone and the conversation hits a 10-second lull, the lonely visitors will ponder the thought of leaving. They may go so far as to push their chairs back, lean ahead and, if the momentum is especially strong, get up and stand in an interior doorway as they continue to visit.

They may walk a few feet to the next room or even get to the exterior door or stand on the porch, continuing to chat all the while. The next step is to stand in the yard for awhile, and maybe even stand by the vehicle.

The thought of leaving really takes form when the company actually gets in their car. Of course, they'll usually roll down the window and continue to visit for a few more minutes.

Finally, the vehicle is started and after a few gallons of gas are idly burned, the visit will actually end.

Unless, of course, the vehicle runs out of gas.

Canners and cutters

Puttin' up the airtights for winter

Sept. 6, 1999

Everyone has their own special talent in the kitchen. Mine is eating.

And every chance I get, I like to get into someone else's kitchen and put my talent to use. My mother still has enough sympathy for her bachelor son to let me put my feet under her table, and that's a good thing, because her kitchen is considerably more productive than my own.

My talent for eating is complemented by her talent for cooking. And, like many 67-year-old ranch women, she takes a lot of pride in her ability to fill up young cowboys and feed hungry cattle-working crews.

Her meals bring warmth to those cold fall days when the neighborhood crew gets together to wean calves, preg check cows or ship cattle to market. The best part of the meal, though, is the little piece of summer that comes in a jarful of home canned fruit and vegetables.

With summer on a slippery downhill slope, she's hard at work to capture the taste of summer in her collection of glass jars and tin lids.

Fruit gofer

Although I'm not much help in the kitchen, I do try and do what I can to help the season's canning project.

If she's canning tomatoes, I eat as many fresh tomatoes as I can to help reduce the workload. If she's canning Juneberries, I'll sit at the table and fill up on berries and cream to save wear and tear on the jars and lids.

My biggest contribution, though, comes with the canning of seasonal store-bought peaches and pears. My role is manager of raw material acquisition and transportation, or fruit gofer. I'm the guy who goes to town and gets the boxes of fruit, or lugs, as those of us in the business call them.

Lug is an appropriate term for the boxes because we spend a lot of time lugging them around – around the store, out to the car and into the house. Individually, they're not that heavy to lug around, but when you stack up four or five lugs in your arms, you really are lugging.

One family canner may only need a few boxes, but if a real bargain is found, I can end up acquiring and transporting a pallet or two of peaches and pears for the whole neighborhood. It's practically enough to warrant renting a forklift.

On the hunt

It takes a certain amount of know-how to find the biggest, best peaches in the store. I've paid my dues to learn the ins and outs of picking out peaches.

Peach lugs are all numbered with a secret code and the secret is to know that the lower the number the bigger the peaches. The bigger the peaches, the fewer to peel to fill the jar. The less peeling, the happier the canner. The happier the canner, the less likely they are to notice you inhaling the fruits of their labor a half a quart at a shot.

Unfortunately, it never fails that the low-numbered peaches in the store are always buried at the bottom of the stack way in the far corner. To get to the prime number 36 box at the bottom, I have to start tossing aside a slug of lugs.

As I'm tossing them aside, I sometimes put a few of the lugs in the carts of the ladies passing by. They think I'm a nice young man. I'm really just trying to get those number 60 pee wees out of the way.

If you like to eat peaches, you gotta know how to pick 'em.

Autumn sport

Fall hunting in the great indoors — Sept. 20, 1999

Winter must be on its way. Seems like everybody, man or beast, is trying to get moved inside this fall before the weather turns sour.

The muskrats are beefing up their huts, the badgers are doing a little interior decorating on their favorite holes, and I even did a little shingling and patched some holes and leaks around the ranch.

The flies have been hanging around the screen door waiting for a chance to sneak inside, and, while I'm busy swooshing flies away, a few mice have been slipping inside for a nice winter of climate-controlled housing.

I'm plumb happy to see most creatures doing what they can to make winter more comfortable. But I have to draw the line on the autumn antics of the flies and mice. They can find their own darn house. I don't especially care for their company.

Kill or capture

Ridding a house of these new fall tenants can be chore or sport, depending on your attitude.

When those black, sticky, miserable flies start moving indoors, I start plotting their demise. They get especially obnoxious this time of year, walking around on your food, sitting on your forehead and forcing you to knock yourself silly as you begin swatting and clobbering.

Being an old coyote trapper, I sometimes prefer to trap my flies on those sticky fly tapes and I set the swatter aside.

The wily ones don't fall for that sticky landing strip, though. They require the swatter, a quick hand or live capture. Using your bare hands to capture and swat the bugs is like using a muzzleloader instead of a high-power rifle in deer hunting season.

It gets just as tactical, too. Some primitive fly hunters use the theory that flies back up before they take off. Some quick calculations and a clap of the hands and that fly has performed its last back-off takeoff.

I like to stick with the concept of letting air go between my fingers, eliminating the "warning wind," allowing me to crush or catch with ease.

I used to enjoy live capture in the cup of my hand, but the escape ratio got too high. Nothing's more frustrating than stalking a renegade fly, catching him and then watching him fly free when you peek inside your hand to make a positive ID.

Quick and the dead

Mouse elimination is way more intense than ridding your home of a few insects.

Those furry little beady-eyed critters are enough to get some people standing on chairs and screaming at the top of their lungs. I prefer to accept the invasion in a more sporting manner.

My general response has been to set up a small trapline, and, although finding a mouse isn't quite as exciting as finding a big, silver coyote in a trap, it's still pretty satisfying.

The other night, though, I couldn't spend the time on a trap. I had to become a mouse hunter. One sneaky mouse ran by me and tried to give me the slip by jumping in a cardboard box with a newspaper sitting on top of it.

Immediately, I grabbed a whisk broom and began tiptoeing toward the box. Carefully, I snatched the newspaper away and BAM!, I thumped the little beady-eyed biscuit before he even knew what hit him. Yes, you can run but you can't hide.

He worked hard to get moved indoors for winter, but in the end, he was flung back outdoors by the tip of his tail.I left him on the front lawn as a warning to all mousekind – go find a pile of hay bales, or my house will be the last you see.

Bite the hand

So much for being helpful

Oct. 4, 1999

I can tell by the sound of the geese overhead that it must be fall. And with the geese come hunters and sportsmen from far and wide.

I'm a hunter myself. Although I've been a little overemployed the last couple of years to partake in a good grouse hunt or goose shoot, I still consider myself one of the gang.

I own more guns than I do pairs of shoes and, like some shoes, a few of the guns spend a lot more time on the rack than they do in the field. Yet, like a few shoe-crazy females, I was sure I "had to have" every one of those guns.

Most of my fellow hunters from the city can relate to my male yearning for more rifles and shotguns. But, unlike my city hunting cousins, I don't necessarily understand their yearning for the latest in new pickups and sport utility vehicles to take out into the mud and brush.

Hunt humbly

I would think that if a person's going to be hunting out in the boondocks, a well-used four-wheel-drive pickup with some "experience" would be a lot less nerve wracking to bounce around in and scrape the brush with.

A hunter with a head for hunting bargains would surely appreciate the value of a rig with pre-dented fenders, pre-scratched side panels and radio antennae previously torn off.

Much like wearing a camouflage coat out in the field, the conscientious urban hunter should drive a vehicle with "ranch camouflage" capable of blending in with the rigs of the locals.

When out in the sticks, one hates to stick out. And I would think that the game being hunted, who are used to seeing banged-up, bent-up ranch rigs, would fall for that camouflage. I'm sure it would be easier to stalk the animals in a 1978 Ford half-ton than in a 1999 Lincoln Navigator.

Stranger in need

No matter how new or old the vehicle, some hunters will eventually find themselves stuck in the mud while in the search for mudhens. Hunting isn't like getting a burger and fries; it's not a drive-up opportunity.

When this happens, ranchers find some guy in camouflage with a gun walking toward their house. They usually figure that, A) they're under attack by an invading foreign army, or B) they're about to be hit up for a pull from a hunter.

I heard a story from one rancher that started that very way. Stuck nearby, a hunter strolls in the yard requesting a pull. The rancher drops what he's doing, unhooks a tractor from its implement, then scouts up a cable and chain to pull him out.

He took the time to drive down to the mudhole and commences to pulling the fella out. All the guy can do is complain – pulling too hard, jerking the pickup, scratching the hitch. Well, someone should have told the guy that's how you get stupid stuck people pulled out of a hole.

There wasn't a lot of gratitude given for the rancher who took the time out of his day to get his tractor and his chains to pull the grouch out. The only recognition he got was an attorney who called him a couple days later and asked for his side of the potential lawsuit on how her client's pickup got damaged!

Nothing ever came of the situation legally, but if I knew what that guy looked like and I found him stuck on our land, I'd start up a tractor, drive down to his pickup, push it in deeper and thoroughly enjoy watching it sink!

Y2 worry?

Time for millenium bargains

Jan. 10, 2000

The world held its breath on New Year's Eve 1999, and when it came up for air it foolishly realized that the lungs still worked.

Some were quick to claim that the whole Y2K scare was a scam created by computer consultants wanting to cash in on two-digit-year fears. Others were just as speedy in claiming a victory for preparedness, their pre-doom investments had paid off.

I can see both sides of the argument. I wouldn't put it past mankind to spot an opportunity to fleece folks out of a few dollars to calm their fears.

Whether the computer fixers ever fixed anything or not was probably irrelevant. The important thing was that it made the computer owners feel better, pretty much a placebo effect. Kind of like giving a dying calf one of those home concoctions of milk, syrup, whiskey, coffee and ginseng – it may not help the critter, but it makes the giver feel like he did something.

But I can also see where maybe some of those investments really did keep us from a computer meltdown complete with power outages, bank runs and riots on the streets.

Like the neighbor who says, "I never fix my fence and my cows always stay in." He forgot that you fixed your fence fiddle-string tight, not only to keep your cows at home, but to deter his barbed-wireless beasts from coming on over.

We don't know if our cows would have stayed separate without the investment in posts, wire and shredded leather gloves. And maybe we'd rather have the boredom of seeing them in their pasture than experience the excitement of having to chase, sort and separate.

There is some satisfaction in – and here's the new word of the day – a "non-event."

Pick up the pieces

The chicken littles were recommending people stock up on bottled water, non-perishable food, alternative power and heat, and put aside some extra cash and precious metals.

I didn't give it a lot of consideration, but, in a way, I guess I was pretty prepared.

We still have a few pitcher pumps, and as long as there's a little water to prime them, you can still pull water out of the ground. The temperature on New Year's Eve was around zero, and most every food, including beef carcasses on the hoof, is non-perishable at that icebox temperature.

We all have a pile of old fenceposts and at least one old wood stove we could hook up. And as far as cash, gold or silver goes, I figured we've gotten along without it before Y2K, we'll just have to get along without it in Y2K.

But the lights didn't go dark, the fridges never got warm and the houses never got cold. Now, there's a few people sitting with more Spam, canned pork and beans and dried apricots than they'll ever possibly eat.

I heard a charity say that they'd be glad to take some of that fear food in and give it to their people who really live in fear of hunger, crash or no crash. That's a good idea.

Me, I have always wanted a portable generator for the ranch, just for those normal power outages, and maybe someone beside the computer consultants should benefit from the Y2K scare.

You can bet I'll be perusing the pawn shops and checking out the yard sales to see just how good the deals will get on excess electrical generation equipment. My standing offer is 40 percent of the price that was paid. Maybe 50 percent if you'll throw in a case of pork and beans.

Hometown hardware

A new void on Main Street

Jan. 17, 2000

One Saturday last winter, I walked into the Towner Hardware Hank. It was after 5 p.m., but Jerry was still there. He said it was either sit there or sit at home, and when you're a small-town store owner, one probably feels about the same as the other.

I needed a handle for a double-bitted axe. He asked if I wanted a manual or an automatic. I smiled and said, "I better go with the manual model, but I don't want one of those metric axe handles." He grinned back and said he could probably find me a standard.

Sure enough, Jerry had a double-bitted axe handle in the back of the store. He didn't have a whole bin full of them, but like most things in the Hardware Hank, he made sure that he always had at least one.

That was the nice thing about the Hardware Hank, you could find most anything you needed in there. A pipe fitting, a light switch, a can of varnish or even a toy for a visiting nephew.

It didn't have the expansive square footage of the do-it-yourself mega stores, but I'd have to admit that, albeit narrow, the Towner Hardware Hank was a pretty long store. It must have been at least 100 feet from stem to stern, and it'd scare me to know how many miles Jerry and his wife, Diana, put on in a day of leading customers up and down the aisles.

Most folks called this local hardware store the Hardware Hank, but a few us continued to call it the Coast to Coast, even after it changed affiliations years ago. We're the same folks that still call the Big T Diner "the Freez," even though it hasn't been a Tastee Freez for at least 15 years.

Like a burger at the "Freez," you could have your hardware "your way" at the Hardware Hank. If you just needed the middle part of a well cylinder because your end caps were still good, Jerry would spin off the caps on the new set, hand you the middle and say, "will that work for you?"

If you needed a box of rifle shells on the first day of deer hunting season, you could count on Jerry and Diana to have them on hand. There's a lot of big stores that think everyone in the world shoots a 270, a 30-30 or a 30-06. Jerry knew that some of us oddballs liked to shoot a 280 Remington or a 257 Roberts.

The Towner Hardware Hank, like all small-town hardware stores, probably lost its share of business to Menards, Home Depot and the other acres-of-everything super stores. I know I've strayed.

But although we may have strayed down the road 60 miles to shop in the super caves, we appreciated the selection, service and convenience we had in our little hometown.

I charged that axe handle at the Towner Hardware Hank on that Saturday. That's something you can do at your hometown hardware store.

But that night, I lost my line of credit. That's because we lost our hometown hardware store. It burned to the ground. And it's hard to imagine that another store will spring up in its place to serve a small town that's getting smaller with each new census.

But we're thankful that Jerry and Diana provided us with the hardware we needed as long as they did. And knowing the nature of insurance policies, I didn't think that the entire loss would be covered, so I sent them the $8.50 for that standard manual axe handle I charged.

Author's note: Towner did rebuild their hardware store on the same lot on Main Street. You can get most everything you need, plus world class small-town service from its new proprietors.

Achieving success

Graduates trudging uphill in search of eminence May 8, 2000

I'm supposed to give a little message to the senior class of Towner High this week. If I remember what my attention span was when I was that age, I'd say the key word in "little message" is "little," as in short, brief, get us out of here quick please.

The person who asked me to speak thought I could say a few things about living in the sticks of rural Towner and being successful in spite of it all. The first thing I did was check the definition of successful because I was sure I'd have to find her another speaker if it meant what I thought it did.

My American Heritage Dictionary defined one meaning of successful as having achieved wealth or eminence. I knew what wealth was and I hadn't achieved that, so I flipped to the "e" section to look up eminence. A guy with a limited vocabulary can spend hours in a dictionary just hopping from one word to another.

One definition of eminence was a rise of ground, a hill. Now I knew I could speak to the students because I was successful. I had achieved eminence. I had achieved a rise of ground.

On top

I've climbed Maggie's Hill. I've ridden horse to the top of Power's Hill. And not only did I scale Bald Butte, the highest point in McHenry County, I carried rocks up there.

And that brings me back to the subject of high school graduation in small-town North Dakota. In search of success, apparently through eminence and rises of ground, high school seniors have taken to the hills.

I carried rocks to the top of Bald Butte to help mark the grave of an Indian scout who was buried there by his cavalry colleagues out crossing the countryside. It helped me achieve eminence as I admired the view of the sprawling prairie, and it marked a piece of history.

As I travel across North Dakota, I see a lot of other people, especially graduating seniors, have thought it important to achieve eminence and mark their place in history with some rocks.

Driving toward Kenmare and Powers Lake, N.D., you can plot the success of each successive graduating class. The hillsides are records of white painted rocks laid out to read "79", "88", "92" and on and on. These seniors had achieved a rise of ground overlooking their hometown, they had achieved eminence that the rest of us are reminded of every time we look toward the hills.

The ritual was probably started by a farmer with a rocky field. Too poor to get a mechanical rock picker, he apparently appealed to the class of '72's desire for higher meaning.

What those students did after picking fields, painting rocks and going through commencement is hard to say.

My guess is that they moved and took jobs in Bowman, Rhame and Mandan, N.D., to help instill community pride with painted rocks on the sides of their civic buttes. One rock-toting grad must have gotten into bison ranching from the looks of a hillside rocky ranch sign between Harvey and Rugby, N.D.

At any rate, my revelation on how graduates can achieve eminence with rocks on the rural plains doesn't help me with my hometown audience. Sitting on flat, sandy ground, Towner graduates find themselves short of both steep hillside canvases and rocky artistic media.

I guess that's how painting the water tower got to be so popular.

The big 3-0

Another decade down the drain

July 31, 2000

I passed checkpoint three zero last week. My carefree youth, my energetic 20s, my days of a full hairline and bendable bones are gone, gone, gone.

Most people like to say they're 29. Ask them how old they turned on their last birthday and they smile and say, "I turned 29 again." Until last Saturday, I had it made. I was 29!

Now I either have to start lying or admit to the world my new "thirty something" age bracket.

Typical birthday

I always used to wish I wasn't born in the summer. In elementary school, the kids with birthdays between September and May got big parties, lots of attention and more presents.

Summer birthday kids got cheated. Sure our parents still tried to make us feel special, but it was nothing like telling a teacher and 20 other little kids that it was your birthday.

We all have birthday traditions like a white birthday cake and candles, cards from our relatives out East and birthday spankings with a light swat for each year. The spanking was probably the start of our yearning for youth – fewer years, fewer swats.

Kids with summer birthdays on North Dakota ranches have another birthday tradition. Yup, birthday haying. Ever since I was 10 or 12, birthdays meant raking, mowing, bucking, stacking or baling. Little John Deere was always invited to my birthday parties.

I didn't always put in a full day of haying, though, because my location and birthday timing meant another, funner custom. The North Dakota State Fair, always close by in Minot, always the last week of July.

Last year, I added one more birthday tradition. My recent move to a May/June calving season meant I had to pick a new day to turn out the bulls. I used to use June 20, a nice round number, or July 4, a memorable holiday. Now, my tradition for two years running has been to turn the bulls out with the cows on my July 22 birthday.

It's important to pick a day that's easy to recall so you can exactly estimate the start of your calving season. I've heard of fellas using the same logic to set their wedding days. No, not for gestation calculations, but for easy-to-remember anniversaries. Getting married on the first of the month or on a holiday like New Year's Eve makes for fewer forgotten anniversaries and more long-lasting marriages.

July 22 joys

So I spent my 30th birthday in the traditional way. I turned out the bulls, baled some hay and went to the state fair. I guess you could say it was a day of joy.

The bulls, I know, were quite joyed by the thought of joining the cows. I was quite joyed by the thought of not having to chase them back in or fix fence behind them for the next 60 days.

There's joy in getting some hay made for the long winter, and being outside under the sun on a green meadow holds lots of joys beyond the satisfaction of getting a job done. The fair meant the joy of seeing friends from around the state and enjoying a $3 cup of keg beer and a $4 hot dog.

And, with or without the joys, turning 30 meant doing some reflecting as I crossed into the fourth decade of my life.

I thought about where I was in the course of my life, and where I thought I ought to be. The two weren't very far apart. That's a nice feeling. Right then, I decided that reflection should come more than once a decade. So I'm going to do it every year. And maybe I won't feel the need to be 29 again and again and again.

Generosity in cow country

Philanthropy on the flatlands

Oct. 9, 2000

It's better to give than to receive. And North Dakota's done a good job of giving according to recent results of a "Generosity Index."

North Dakota came in ninth on the list of most giving states. Mississippi and other relatively poor states topped the list, while wealthy New Englanders, it was found, couldn't donate their way out of a paper bag.

North Dakota wasn't the only prairie state near the top. South Dakota came in third on the list published by the Catalog for Philanthropy. Dakotans don't mind helping others out. We're a culture of people who offer rides to joggers, push fellow motorists out of snowbanks and write checks to charitable causes, even if we are overdrawn because of poor crop or livestock prices!

New Englanders, who are quite a bit cashier than the Southerners and Dakotans near the top of the list, gathered together at the bottom of the list like Scrooge McDuck swimming in his safe full of coins.

It was a pretty solid trend with Connecticut and Rhode Island coming in at 45th and 46th and New Jersey, New Hampshire and Massachusetts in an eastern battle for dead last.

Truly generous

The Catalog for Philanthropy recognized our generosity by evaluating tax returns and comparing average adjusted gross income with average itemized charitable deductions. It's a good snapshot of a state's generosity, but I think there's even more to it.

Looking at itemized donations doesn't even take into account all the pancakes we've eaten at benefit breakfasts, the overpriced candy bars we've bought from sugar-peddling high school kids or the reams of raffle tickets we've scratched our name, address and phone number on, time and again.

In my family, we've been giving and receiving to beat the band lately. My mother contributed three quarters to the slot machine of a benevolent reservation casino and was rewarded $1,000 for her donation. It pays to contribute.

I gifted $10 to the North Dakota Red Angus Association in exchange for three risky raffle tickets last month. The payout wasn't too bad – I got a custom-built saddle worth a couple thousand more than the tickets in that deal. It really paid to contribute.

Finally, I was doing some work at a vet clinic last week, and when I left, I had a trained, purebred border collie cattle dog sitting next to me on the passenger side, compliments of the clinic. It's really nice to live in such a generous state.

Cow connections

It's hard to really know what makes North Dakota such a generous state. But one common denominator might be the cows. I won the saddle from a cattle association, I got the cattle dog from a cow vet, and the money that came out of the slot machine for my mother was probably put in there by other gambling ranch wives spending the proceeds from their bottle calves.

The cow connection has some merit. I'm convinced of its relationship with generosity because those same miserly states who finished last in the philanthropy lineup are turning to cows to improve their image.

New York City, Stamford, Conn., and West Orange, N.J., have turned to something called CowParade to raise money for charity. CowParade consists of a herd of fiberglass cows painted pretty by area artists. The bogus bovines spend a little time hanging around on the city streets, and after a few months, they're sold at auction to benefit local charities for children, the arts and education.

New York already raised $1.3 million when most of its herd went to market.

With cows like that, those Easterners might blast right past us poor, but generous, Dakotans with $700 cows and big hearts. Maybe we should let some artists paint on ours before we head to the auction.

Mail order's new order

The changing world of commerce Feb. 12, 2001

Plus shipping and handling. Four words that have always gotten stuff from the populated places to the unpopulated places.

Businesses can't always justify a retail outlet in every little ranching community, so us outbackers have gotten used to buying stuff from the cities that could keep a store and just added the outbound freight.

Even the great advances of e-commerce haven't changed that system of purchase and ship. E-businesses are just high-tech catalogs shipping goods to their customers. Their catalogs are probably a little more accessible on our computers than the paper ones were out in our outhouses.

While new e-stores emerge every day, one old catalog store has gone down for good. Montgomery Ward, pioneer of the mail-order business, gave up on its catalog back in 1985 and has now closed its doors completely.

Outback merchandising

Montgomery Ward got its start in 1872 with Mr. Ward's one-page catalog and its 163 items. Eventually, the Chicago merchant was shipping goods to all corners of the country, even Towner, N.D.

I have "Monkey Ward" to thank for most of the presents I found under a Christmas tree that was 25 miles from the nearest department store.

Montgomery Ward sold us a fridge, a garden tiller, a sleeping bag and a remote-control race car. They could do it all. They shipped the small things right to the ranch. The big stuff we picked up at their little catalog outlet in Rugby, N.D.

We looked forward to the thick catalogs that showed up in our mailbox for each season of the year. We'd peruse that catalog and earmark the pages, like kids these days cruise the Internet and bookmark their favorite e-store websites.

It was a simple system. They sent us the things we wanted. We sent them money. And cities like Chicago grew strong and tall because of it.

Routes reversed

Montgomery Ward may be a thing of the past, but the mail-order world they started continues to go strong. Maybe the new order of mail order will look at the rural reaches as providers and not just customers.

Goods could be gathered up in places like North Dakota and shipped to customers in Chicago, Denver, Seattle and around the globe. The middle of nowhere could be the perfect central location.

Right now I'm gathering up my calves for market. I'll sell them for a buck a pound, plus shipping and handling. That makes them about $1.05 in Kansas. But if they send me the money, I'll send them the calves. This year, cow country may grow strong and tall if the market doesn't fall apart.

I ship some Cowboy Logic books out from the ranch. I'm no Amazon.com but we distribute a few volumes. Last week, I shipped a goofy cowboy to Saskatoon, Saskatchewan, to speak at their cattle feeders banquet. The freight was high but the goods arrived in fine shape.

The catalog's a little thin right now – cattle, books, goofy cowboy speakers – but, you never know, Montgomery Ward started out with a single page.

I can hardly wait to start shipping to Chicago and bring some of those old catalog dollars back to North Dakota.

Creating smiles

Small-town dentist, big-time care

April 9, 2001

Anyone who says they look forward to getting a tooth pulled is probably a liar. But some folks around Rugby, N.D., have said they look forward to seeing the fella pulling that tooth, and they were speaking the truth.

I'm one of those people. Ever since I was a wee lad, I've been going to the corner of Second Avenue and Fifth Street in Rugby to see H.H. Vigeland, D.D.S. And I've always looked forward to the visit.

Harold Vigeland, or "Doc" as I call him and most folks with several letters behind their names, is one of those timeless characters in a person's life. I don't think he's changed a bit in the 20-some years I've been going to him for tune-ups on my teeth.

His office is one of those places you become so familiar with, you can imagine it in your mind with the slightest effort. The toys in the corner, the little fireplace, the fox hunting horses on the wallpaper.

You can see the table with the mind-bending games stacked on it. Some of them I never did figure out. You can hear the classical music coming from the speakers strung throughout the office. Doc was always faithfully tuned in to Prairie Public Radio.

It was a rather intelligent and cultural spot for a young ranch kid. Imagine a little Bach or Mozart coming across the speakers, some National Geographics and Readers Digest in the magazine rack and photos of Doc's travels to the Egyptian pyramids hanging by the chair where you sat with your mouth propped open.

The picture is completed by Doc's wife, Jean, smiling through the little cut-out rectangle in the wall of the waiting room. Through the rectangle you could see the office area where she managed the business, and the narrow counter at the bottom of the rectangle held the bowl of sugar-free candy that she would offer me as I left.

I always thought it would be better for business if they handed out sugar-loaded candy, but they were more concerned with preventing cavities than boosting business, I guess.

Dental devices

The small-town charm of the office was complemented by Doc's professional care. His care was considerably better than my options back at the ranch.

When I was losing my baby teeth, my mother's favorite line was, "Just let me look at it, I promise I won't pull it." I fell for it every time, and YANK!!!, she would have my tooth in her hand and I'd stand there awestruck with an empty new crater in my mouth.

Dad almost entered the dentistry field when an area old-timer asked him to pull his festering molar. He even a gave dad a brand new pair of pliers he'd been saving for the job. Everyone knows new pliars are as sanitary as if they were hospital scrubbed in disinfectant.

Dad looked in the old fella's mouth, and, spotting another gap in the row of yellow pearls, he asked, "How'd you get that tooth out?" When the rancher replied, "a dentist did it," Dad set down the pliers and told him to go see that dentist again.

So, untrusting of my mother's dental finesse and disappointed with my father's lack of experience, I opted to let Doc Vigeland work on my teeth. And that he did, until he retired this year after 55 years of providing dental care for me and many others.

Now I'm going to a big clinic with several dentists, multiple chairs and the sound of drills humming and spit vacuums slurping while doctors and technicians run about to keep everything on a profitable schedule.

It's good care, but a very different style of care compared to the clinic on the corner of Fifth and Second in Rugby.

I guess I'm just glad I got the time I did with Dr. Vigeland. I think of him every time I smile, chew or crack a sunflower seed. Me and my molars are going to miss his care.

Frontier History

Failing to understand, bound to repeat

June 4, 2001

Just when you feel like your part of the country is being ignored in the nation's newspapers, you see a dateline like "Fort Yates, N.D.," in the New York Times.

It's easy to feel forgotten when the country is focused on the energy crises in California and New York, the power struggle in Washington, D.C., and the usual social and environmental consequences of crowding too many people in too small an area.

And then, just when you fear that the rather unimportant food-producing, resource-bearing chunk of middle America has been completely forgotten, you see an article like, "As Others Abandon Plains, Indians and Bison Come Back," in the New York Times.

I'm always entertained by the theatrical interest shown by non-plains people in the fulfillment of the Buffalo Commons concept. They watch and discuss the emptying prairies like Romans watched gladiators get eaten by lions, or like Americans watched survivors survive on network television. One should not underestimate the entertainment value in personal destruction.

Timothy Egan, who wrote the abandoned plains piece, used some great terms of destruction in his lead. "In writing the obituary of the Great Plains, social historians have looked out at the abandoned ranches, collapsed homesteads and dying towns huddled against the wind in a sea of grass and seen an epic failure."

You can really paint a picture with words like obituary, abandoned, collapsed, dying and failure. I could almost detect him trying to lead the readers with those images.

Leaving the land

Egan accurately reported that 47 of North Dakota's 53 counties lost population in the last 10 years. More than 60 percent of the counties in the Great Plains qualify as what census takers in the 1800s called frontier – less than six people per square mile. Some, like Slope County, N.D., qualify as wilderness – less than one person per square mile.

He also detailed Slope County's designation as the "whitest county in America." Just three non-whites in a county of 767 and boasting a county seat, Amidon, with a population of just 25.

The whitest county hasn't been growing, though. The growth counties in the Dakotas, Montana and Nebraska were predominantly Native American. Three of the six counties that grew in North Dakota were counties with Indian reservations. Their population grew 20 percent.

And the buffalo have gone from a few hundred to better than 300,000. So the article declares that the plains are reverting back to the buffalo and the Indians.

I was amused by his statement that "bison…require no care to flourish." But the next sentence stated that a third of the nation's Indian colleges offered courses in bison management. Seems contradictory to teach management for animals that supposedly require no care.

After reading this upbeat article on my home where "empty homesteads and occasional schoolhouses litter the land, with caved-in roofs and grass growing where there used to be front porches," I was depressed, then angry and finally amused.

Sure, articles in the New York Times lead us to believe that "European agricultural settlement of big parts of the prairie may have been an accident of history," but I know that history, like fashion, does tend to repeat itself.

Maybe what's being repeated right now is the return of the buffalo and the native population. What changed that 100 years ago? It was the yearning of people from crowded, economically depressed areas to find new opportunities, a fresh start and some room to roam.

So I'm just going to watch the developments of Silicon Valley dot.com layoffs and the down days for traders on Wall Street and wait to welcome the next wave of homesteaders, who, I believe, will repeat the next chapter of frontier history.

An inborn fondness

Speaking on the greatest joys

Feb. 11, 2002

Several months ago, I was asked to speak at North Dakota's rural development conference.

They asked me to be on a panel charged with speaking on "the greatest joys of rural life." The topic was pulled from the words of the Future Farmers of America Creed, "for I know the joys and discomforts of agricultural life and hold an inborn fondness for those associations which even in hours of discouragement I cannot deny."

Rural economic development definitely sees some hours of discouragement as people try to create opportunities in areas hit hard by outmigration and diminishing infrastructure.

It was up to me and three others to remind conference participants of the great joys in rural life and help recharge the energies of those dedicated to perpetuating both rural life and rural joys.

Thinking assignment

It's good to get an assignment once in awhile that makes you sit down and think about why we live how and where we do.

What I came up with were three obscure metaphors of joy – tiger lilies, black and white photographs and summer sausage sandwiches.

To back up my obtuse ideas, I dug out some pictures. Most of the photos I found in a little album that I keep to show people where I come from. It's not unheard of for me to pull out those pictures and show a Chicago cab driver a few images of the Taylor Ranch while driving Michigan Avenue.

I have a great photo of tiger lilies growing wild on our hay meadow. They're actually wood lilies, but their beauty is striking. It's those beautiful things that are one of my greatest joys of rural life.

And it's not just tiger lilies, it's prairie roses, big bluestem grass, poplar trees, cottonwoods, hills, horizons, sunsets, baby foals, little calves and little children playing amongst it all. Beautiful things make rural life a peaceful joy.

My second great joy is black and white photographs. Not just any black and white photographs, but those old pictures that show my homesteading ancestors, the people and events that shape who I am.

When people move from city to city, taking different jobs and climbing the ladder to "success," you hear about them occasionally dropping out, telling their friends that they just need to "go find themselves."

I've never felt the need to go find myself, I know exactly where I'm at and who I am. And I've got some black and white pictures to prove it. What a comforting joy.

My last great joy was summer sausage sandwiches. Not many families get to eat together any more. I've had the joy of daily picnics, including summer sausage sandwiches, with my family out on the hay meadows all summer long. It's a joy to have real relationships with your family, built on quantity time, not just a few fleeting moments of quality time fit in between day care and bedtime.

It's a joy to work side by side with your father. And that's something that very few sons have been able to do since the industrial age began. It's those hours and hours of making hay, building fence, caring for animals and, yes, eating summer sausage sandwiches that give me a closeness to my father that is seldom found outside of rural life. What a special and healthy joy in a world full of angry young men, fatherless homes and bitter relationships between father and son.

Tiger lilies, black and white photographs and summer sausage sandwiches may not have made an immediate connection for everyone, but putting images and explanations to those obscure ideas was truly a joy.

Memorial memories

Small town cemetery soldiers

June 3, 2002

I attended the Memorial Day service in one of our local small towns last week. It's good to remind ourselves that Memorial Day is much more than another three day weekend, the start of summer tourism or the annual day to fire up the grill. It's about veterans and wars and remembering the soldiers who have died on our battlefields.

It was a nice, well-planned program in the high school gym. It came complete with a scant school band, who, I'm sure, struggled to get the kids back in during summer vacation. I smiled each time I heard a stray squeak or a misplaced honk and thought about the old days when I was contributing from the saxophone section.

We had local veterans marching down the aisle and presenting the flags. There were patriotic songs, poetry and speeches. We all sang the Star-Spangled Banner and prayed together. We drove down the street from the school for the ubiquitous church basement dinner and, preceding that, attended a nice ceremony at the cemetery to honor fallen comrades.

At the cemetery, veteran soldiers shouldered their rifles and fired the customary salute.

After the salute, the honor guard carrying the flags was given the command, "About left! Forward march!" It was a serious and dramatic moment as the ceremony was brought to a close and the flag bearers went to exit the cemetery.

The only problem was that one of the resurrected infantryman did an "about right" while the rest of the troop made an "about left." We tried not to laugh and spoil the moment as the lone soldier intently marched up the hill that his comrades were marching down.

Finally, someone gave the rather unmilitary-like order, "Ralph, hey Ralph, turn around!" We all relaxed, laughed and began to enjoy the comic relief as Ralph looked up, realized his mistake, smiled broadly and hightailed it down the slope to catch up with his band of brothers.

That's what I love about small towns and close-knit groups of familiar people. We can make mistakes, correct them and enjoy the humanness of the moment. I'll remember that Memorial Day service for a long time and think fondly of the day Ralph charged boldly up the cemetery hill.

More memories

The day Ralph went right brought back to mind my favorite stories of local soldiers, cemeteries and seven-gun salutes.

Our local color guard has some colorful and creative personalities. At the military sendoff for one fallen veteran, one of our shooters raised his carbine, pointed to the sky, pulled the trigger and…nothing happened.

Our man never skipped a beat and quickly covered the misfire and yelled "BANG!" He even kept a straight face. That's keeping calm under fire, or the lack of.

My favorite story is the one that's told about one veteran's funeral in our hometown that had all his family gathered around the gravesite for the burial service and military honors.

His mother, brothers and young nephews were gathered around. The mother sat in a metal folding chair under the canopy with her kids and grandkids close by.

The guard raised their rifles and fired a volley in his honor. Just as they pulled the trigger, the spindly leg of Grandma's chair broke through the turf and plunged into the soft soil beneath. The chair dumped Grandma forward and layed her out on the ground.

The young grandson saw it all, put two and two together and yelled out, complete with one of the newest words in his vocabulary, "The son-of-a-$%@*& shot Grandma!"

Yes, some memorial services will always be remembered.

The supper circuit

Fall fundraising time

Oct. 21, 2002

There's a chill in the air and a warmth in church kitchens near and far this time of year.

Yes, it's church supper season in my part of the world. It's an annual fall ritual and a mainstay of a congregation's fund-raising activities.

Sure, people could put an extra $20 bill in the offering plate on Sunday, but they'd rather trade $8 for a plate of vittles and donate $12 worth of food or labor to accomplish the same end.

Plus, it gives folks a chance to see their friends and neighbors from around the area. The Catholics raise a little money from the Lutherans, the Lutherans get to raise a little money from the Catholics. Somewhere inbetween you get to mix and mingle with Presbyterians, Methodists, assorted Evangelicals and even some hungry agnostics.

And, of course, no church supper would be complete during an election year without a full slate of local politicians. They're an easy sale for the meals, not to mention a lucrative target for some community raffle tickets and a chance at the church ladies' quilt.

Menu planning

The food is always good at these church suppers – swiss steak, turkey and dressing, roast beef, meatballs and, in Scandinavian country, the hallowed lutefisk.

I like it all, even the lutefisk. I can blame my Norwegian ancestors who put three-fourths of the blood in my veins for that.

Speaking of lutefisk, did you hear the story about the guy who had skunks move into his basement? The smell was really getting to him and try as he might, he couldn't get those skunks to leave.

He finally called the county agent, knower of all things both rural and domestic, to get his advice on ridding a house of the black and white-striped invaders.

The county agent instructed him to go to the store and buy 10 or 20 pounds of lutefisk and throw that down the stairs into the basement.

The fella did just that, and a few days later, the county agent saw him on the street and asked if his trick had worked.

He said, "Yeah, those skunks hightailed it outta there in no time flat, but now I can't get rid of all those Norwegians who moved in after them!"

Churches, however, are ready to handle an onslaught of Norwegians when they put lutefisk on the supper menu. They also generally arrange for good kitchen ventilation so they can attract the Germans, Irish, French and other various crosses in to eat a few meatballs and lefse along with the Scandinavians.

Tight scheduling

For whatever reason, all the church suppers in the area need to be scheduled within about a six-week period. It may be to accommodate the campaign season that boosts the ticket take every two to four years.

Having thrown my own hat in the ring for the job of state senator in my district, I can personally testify that getting to every church supper to meet constituents in a four-county area is a challenge.

One Sunday I ate a potluck dinner and two church suppers in a span of a mere four hours. Luckily, I'm a skinny guy with a hollow leg and I managed to take a polite amount of food at each meal. And one of the meals was even lutefisk!

Yes, local politics is a tough, brutal business. I'm at least glad that the missions of the church can get some funding out of it all. I may even go to those suppers next year when there isn't an election!

Freedom's answer

It's right to exercise your right to vote

Nov. 4, 2002

I haven't missed a chance to vote since I turned 18. I'm proud of that. A lot of Americans have seldom or never voted since they turned 18. I'm ashamed of that.

Some say there are people in Chicago who continued to vote even after they were dead! And others who voted several times. Seemingly pretty patriotic folks to have voted from the grave, or have voted so numerously, but I'm not proud of those activities either.

Voting is basic to the American experience. As one of the longest-lived democracies in the world, it's what we're all about. As Abe Lincoln said, "of the people, by the people, and for the people." That's a pretty succinct explanation of our system.

The Population Resource Center reports that 66 percent of people ages 65 to 74 voted in the 2000 election. That's the generation of my mother and father, people who've lived through the Depression, a world war and don't take their freedoms for granted.

Compare that to Americans in the 18-to-24-year category with a 25 percent voter turnout in 2000. What are we telling our children about the responsibilities of voting?

They get the job done in other countries. Our average turnout rate the past 10 years has been 45 percent. The United Kingdom, the folks we broke away from in 1776 so that we could create this democracy, has a voter turnout of 72 percent. My Canadian readers can take pride in beating us by 15 points with a 60 percent average turnout.

Off year

One of the challenges to American voter turnout is the difference between presidential election years and the off year congressional elections. The difference was 50 percent versus 35 percent turnout when comparing the 2000 ballot with the 1998 ballot. The 1998 congressional election turned out just 17 percent of the 18- to 24-year-olds.

That's why I was so impressed when I read about the Freedom's Answer campaign. It intends to make the 2002 election the largest non-presidential voter turnout election in American history, and it intends to get the job done with young people.

Appropriately, the Freedom's Answer campaign kicked off on Sept. 11 and it's charging high school students to help register their 18-year-old schoolmates, remind their neighbors to vote and serve as non-partisan poll workers on Election Day.

North Dakota is the only state that doesn't require voter registration – everybody knows everybody in these parts, and if they have an address they've been at for 30 days, that's good enough for us. But for everyone else who reads this column in the U.S., get registered, and if you are registered, please vote for the candidates of your choice.

It's nice to live in countries where you can draw the curtain and vote your conscience. No one can bully or intimidate you to vote any differently.

The other option

There are countries where voting is available but only if you vote the way they want you to.

Iraq had an unbelievable voter turnout – 100 percent, they said. Of course, there was only one candidate, Mr. Saddam Hussein. He barely squeaked in during the last election seven years ago with 99.6 percent. This year, he pulled in a whopping 100 percent of the hand-marked ballots.

I'm not sure if the campaign included more billboards, yard signs or radio and television advertising. My guess is it came down to a rigorous door-to-door effort from his gun-toting committee members.

Let's get more of our people to the polls, but let's do it freely.

Prairie home companions

Rush tickets and fast friendships

Oct. 20, 2003

I doubt I could name a single television program that I make any real effort to see every week. The spindly TV antennae propped atop the 16-foot corral pole by my house doesn't pull in much for habit-forming programming.

But every weekend for more years than I can recall, I've tuned in to my public radio station to listen to "A Prairie Home Companion" with Garrison Keillor, broadcast live from the Fitzgerald Theater in downtown St. Paul, Minnesota.

Yes, a radio show. A relic of days gone by when imaginative people could be entertained without having their eyes assaulted by multiple, rapid visual stimuli.

Every week, Garrison comes up with music free from the bonds of the Top 40, the news from fictional Lake Wobegon, Minn., and some subtle humor that comes at the expense of Midwesterners, Lutherans, Norwegian bachelor farmers and a few well-known politicians.

Hitting home

I guess the attraction to "A Prairie Home Companion" is the fact that I can relate to it. It hits a lot closer to home than trendy young people hanging out in Manhattan apartments, or doctors and nurses confronting emergency room crises or the reality shows that really don't pertain to my hope for reality.

I need hometown characters and regular guys. I can relate to the characters of Lake Wobegon, the bachelor farmers, those mild Lutherans and their white food. It hits home.

And last week, I hit a little closer to their home in St. Paul. I told my bride I'd like to take her on a date to go see a radio show.

The show had long been sold out, but there was a chance at something called "rush tickets" at the theater on the day of the show.

They went on sale at 4:15 p.m., but the box office attendant told me the line starts to form at noon for the limited number of tickets.

I figured it was worth the effort. I found a folding chair, filled my coffee thermos, grabbed a book and set up shop a little after noon. I was No. 8 in the wait for rush tickets.

Fellow waiters

I wondered what kind of people wait in line four hours to see a regular guy radio show? I should've known, they were just regular people.

There was Craig and Paula. Craig was a union carpenter, but before he started framing houses, he was a truck mechanic. His wife, Paula, worked for a paint company. Together, they liked to tap maple trees after the first hard frost and boil their own maple syrup.

There was Mike and Irene. Mike used to work at a feed mill, but after a few near misses with augers and silos and a fire that was allowed to burn a little too long for fear of raising the insurance premiums, he quit and went back to school to be an English teacher. This burly former feed miller liked poetry.

His wife, Irene, worked for a local software company. A good share of her co-workers recently lost their jobs when the company moved more operations to India. In an age of flag-waving patriotism, sending American jobs overseas for cheap labor seems pretty unpatriotic to me.

Irene had a sister who was a writer. She recently moved to a little town in western North Dakota thinking that the peaceful, small-town living would be good for the writing process. I told her she was right.

I also met Mary, Jean, Terri and Barb, an artist and North Dakota native, who gave me a ride to the coffee shop after our ticket purchase was complete.

The afternoon spent with wonderfully real people was perfectly capped with us all sitting right on stage with the performers in the rush ticket seating area. It was a great show.

Looking back, I'm glad the rush tickets weren't too rushed. The wait was worth it in more ways than one.

Bird's-eye view

Hawks take wing most anywhere

June 28, 2004

It's not often I find myself doing the same thing as folks in New York City on any given day. Our lives and our surroundings are a little different.

But after watching a piece on a Sunday morning news show, I discovered that New Yorkers and North Dakotans are both hawk watchers.

Granted, the locales are a little different. The New Yorkers were shown watching their hawk nest on the ledge of a trendy Fifth Avenue building in Manhattan. We used to monitor a hawk nest in a cottonwood tree in our east pasture.

My east pasture is a far cry from Fifth Avenue, but both places supported nests that were home to red tailed hawk families.

The New Yorkers have made quite a fuss over their nesting raptors. The birds are named, watched and photographed. There's a website, and a movie was made about the Central Park and Fifth Avenue hawk family. Postcards are available for sale.

Our hawks had more privacy in the east pasture. Not that they appreciated that fact. They figured our one or two visits a year to their nest were excessive intrusion.

Every year, Mom would load us kids in the pickup and take us out east to the big cottonwood tree to check on mother hawk and her little chickadees.

We'd lean a ladder against that cottonwood and take turns peering over the edge of the nest to look at the ugliest little critters you ever laid your eyes upon.

Mama and papa bird must not have thought those chicks were ugly. The way they screamed and dived and scared the daylights out of us little bird-watchers, I figure they must have thought a lot of those little fuzz balls.

I continued the tradition as I got older. When riding out in the pasture, I would park my horse next to the tree and, if it was the right horse, I could stand on the saddle and boost myself up into the tree to check on the chicks.

I never did lose the feeling that those hawks would like to pick me up by the shoulders and eat me for supper.

The wind finally blew that old cottonwood down one year, and the hawk family moved their roost to another nearby tree. This time, she built high enough to discourage little nest visitors.

Back on Fifth Avenue, the local hawk watchers have named the man of the family "Pale Male" for his light colorings and he's had a few different mates – First Love, Chocolate, Blue and, his latest love, Lola.

They've documented their nesting success, and a big day for Manhattanites is when the chicks jump off the ledge and commence to flying. Whenever someone else tries to jump off a ledge in New York, they usually have some firemen and a big tarp stretched out to catch them. Of course, they don't have wings.

I don't know if our hawk was a widower or if he had several wives. I don't think our male was too pale. Our red-tailed hawk was a pretty red rooster as I remember.

And although I thought our hawks were pretty interesting, you wouldn't catch me setting up a spotting scope and watching them 24/7 while they were hatching their nest.

But Pale Male and his offspring probably deserve the admiration of New Yorkers. First off, red-tailed hawks are pretty rare in the big city. And secondly, the website reported the diet of the Fifth Avenue hawks consisted of rats, mice and pigeons.

I've been to New York, and I'd say anything that eats rats, mice and especially pigeons, darn sure deserves some admiration.

On parade

Small towns turn out big for little parades

July 12, 2004

I love a parade. Just like the Boston Pops Orchestra tune says. It's hard not to, especially a good small-town parade.

I had the distinct honor of leading my community's Fourth of July parade this year. I guess the title they use is grand marshal.

Usually, organizers look for some sort of local dignitary to lead the parade. I'm not sure if I'm enough of a dignit, but I'm darn sure local, so I told them I'd be honored to carry the flag and serve as the grand marshal.

I was real impressed with the ranch gelding I saddled up at home and took to town to carry me and the American flag up and down the street. He's by no means a town horse, but he tolerated the people, the noise, the firecrackers and the flag flapping above his head like a seasoned veteran.

The float directly behind me played "Shake, Rattle and Roll" about a million times from the parade's start to finish. Luckily, my horse didn't do any of those things.

It was another nice fall day this summer for our Fourth of July parade. I saw quite a few blankets and jackets on the people sitting along Towner's chilly main street to watch the procession.

It was nice to walk my horse down the street and see men stand at attention and remove their hats when I passed with the flag.

Hats or no hats, it was nice to see so many people out lining the street. It was a pretty big parade for a town the size of Towner. When we were gathering everyone up, I was afraid the whole town was in the parade and no one would be left to watch it.

But we had an all-school reunion this year, so there were lots of alumni from out of town to help line the streets.

And a lot of kids lined the streets, too. They knew that as fun and lucrative as it was to be in the parade (kids riding their horse in the parade each get a dollar), it was also lots of fun to watch the parade and fill their pockets with candy.

Halloween is a pretty good holiday for kids and candy, but when it comes to total pounds of sugar, I think the parade collections will outpace the trick-or-treating.

People driving floats in parades learn early on to bring plenty of candy to throw out to the kids. Try driving down that street without some sort of peace offering for the little people and they'll turn on you like a pack of starvin' coyotes.

Drivers bring lots of candy and meter it out carefully so they have some left for the return trip.

Yes, in small towns, parades get two shots at the spectators. A lot of little towns are down to a two- or three-block main street, so it's customary to make a big turn around at the end of town and do it all over again.

You have to work to hold your crowd together after the first trip through. Seasoned spectators tell the confused out-of-towners, "No, wait, don't leave yet. They're coming back!" We like to think of it as an encore performance.

Sometimes a few cars get around the massive roadblocks (a piece of yellow rope), and a few undecorated late model cars and pick-ups get to feel like they're in the parade as they drive against the entries and the determined grand marshal working his parade back up the street.

Even with the encore return, small-town parades can go rather quickly, so if you plan on attending one yet this summer, get there on time.

Otherwise, all you'll see are road apples and candy wrappers.

Livestock levity

Take a reading

Cattle may be higher tech than we think

Nov. 16, 1998

We did a little practice weaning at the Taylor Ranch last week. Now that we've got that little warm-up completed, we should be able to really separate the calves from their mothers in earnest.

We never purposely have a practice weaning. It just always turns out that way when either the cows or the calves decide to break down whatever amount of fence necessary to get back together.

Some days, it seems like they're breaking it down faster than I can build it back up.

This year, I thought I had the corrals in tiptop shape and ready for whatever tricks the cows might have up their hide.

I like to keep the cows in for a few days until the calves quit bawling, and this year I put them in my Jurassic Park high-voltage holding area. It gives me some sadistic pleasure to know that even my most experienced fence crawlers will be greeted with 4,400 amps of unforgiving current when they try to make their escape.

However, I only had 90 percent of my holding area fully juiced. The other 10 percent of the perimeter was an old pole corral that I figured would be sturdy enough to keep the cows on the proper side. It turned out to be the weak link in the chain, the gateway to unwanted cow/calf mixing.

Stud finders

I recently bought a stud finder to help me locate the sturdy nailing points hidden behind the wallboard of my bachelor shack. It's a battery-operated thingamajig, and it works by sensing the density of the hollow walls behind it.

I didn't know my cows were so well equipped, but I'm pretty sure that they all had similar density sensors installed in their muzzles.

It may look like they're just dumbly walking along and sniffing the corral rails, but, in actuality, they're taking hundreds of highly sophisticated wood density readings.

I personally witnessed this phenomenon when I saw a couple of cows eyeing two sections of that pole corral. One section was made of old poplar poles cut here on the ranch. They were about as weak as a hollow-core trailer house door. The other section was built with pine rails bought at the local lumber yard. They were relatively new and quite a bit stouter.

They went straight for those hollow-core poplars and busted through them like a bunch of Class B basketball players crashing through a paper pep rally banner at a state tournament.

Harness the power

Next year, I'm really going to make sure I don't have to spend any extra time rebuilding corrals, resorting calves or regretting my life as a rancher. All I need is one traitor cow to cross the line and join my team for pre-weaning preparations.

If she'd only lend me the secrets of her muzzle, I would have a real advantage over the cow herd and their impending breakout. I could harness that cow's sensing power and have her pinpoint the weak spots in the corrals, then reinforce the exact areas that needed it and have a restful, worry-free weaning next year.

If it really works well, I might lease her out to the neighbors for their corral work. Batteries not included. And neither is the hay.

Feedbunk fatigue

Putting out feed with the one-man bucket brigade Dec. 21, 1998

Cattle feeding technology has come a long way on the Taylor Ranch. Yup, we've made the switch from steel buckets and have upgraded to a complete fleet of plastic pails to carry our feed.

Adopting space age technology like that isn't as easy as it sounds. You've got to have connections. Rounding up a full set of plastic pails is just as dependent on who you know as what you know.

In the old days, Dad was forced to grease his tractors and implements generously. It wasn't so much that he was trying to take good care of his machinery, he just wanted to empty out another steel grease bucket so he could clean it up and throw it in the grain bin.

Those steel pails had a good lifespan, but he still needed a steady supply to keep up with the cows and horses who'd stick their head in them, toss 'em around and stomp 'em into a wad of scrap metal for the sheer entertainment of it all. So the mower's got greased and the cows got fed.

But these days, ranchers need to really scout around to find a steady supply of plastic buckets. There just aren't many ranch supplies that come in big round plastic pails.

One look at our place and you'll quickly realize that we sure aren't going through that much paint, and I very seldom buy my pickles by the 5-gallon bucket. Thus, we end up bribing our friends in the house painting and restaurant business to get on their plastic pail waiting list.

I'm not one to reveal my sources, but I just so happen to have a direct contact deep inside the plastic pail cartel. Working for a large institution that uses high volumes of paint, sidewalk salt and various 5-gallon fluids, he regularly smuggles me the empties.

My neighbors are all extremely envious, even the ones with automated feed wagons. When they see my lineup of late model plastic buckets with their free-swinging handles and intact plastic hand holds, they kind of wish they hadn't put in their labor saving bunkline systems.

Balanced rations

Like many ranchers who saw the low cattle prices and low feed prices this fall, I weaned all the calves and decided to keep them at home for a while. If someone's going to feed some cheap feed to my cheap cattle, it could just as well be me.

At least that was my line of thought a couple thousand pails ago. Now that I've gone through a couple loads of feed and the cattle market has continued to slide south, it's probably about the right time to ship those calves out.

When I began the one-man bucket brigade feeding system, I had good intentions of getting the maximum gain out of the calves. But once I got up to 53 pails a day, I decided that a 2-pound gain would be better than a $2^1/_2$-pound gain if it meant carrying a single pail more of that optimum nutrition.

And it's getting to the point where I'm willing to let a real cattle feeder lose some money on these calves. My arms are getting longer, my checkbook's getting emptier, and for the right money, I'd not only sell you the calves, I'd throw in the plastic pails to boot.

Frigid fractures

Cold weather and calamities just seem to go together Jan. 11, 1999

There's nothing like a good cold snap to snap those things that were teetering on the edge of function and failure.

There are plenty of things teetering on the Taylor Ranch, and the recent mercury drops of 20 and 30 below zero were all the excuse that was needed to put at least a couple of them over the failing edge.

Breakout to the bales

Last Sunday morning, I was looking forward to a quick wrap-up on the chores so I could go to church and start the new year right.

The thermometer read a mere 20 below as I made my way to the water tank to see if there was anything liquid left under the tank's polar ice cap. Out of the corner of my eye, I saw a disturbing site – the entire cow herd had turned the winter supply of hay bales into a Sunday morning all-you-can-eat smorgasbord buffet.

Sometime during the night, they had realized how poor a barrier a barbed-wire gate is when a couple hundred cattle all decide to push at once. A good example of teamwork, but a poor example of good manners and dietary restraint.

It didn't look like I was going to make it to that nice, warm church service. Twenty minutes worth of yelling and waving at the cows to try and get them back into the feedyard did warm me up, but the cursing and anger was a poor substitute for a good calm sermon on the evils of swearing.

With the help of my 66-year-old mother and emergency cow chaser, I got the cows in and set myself to the task of rebuilding a stretch of fence that could have just as well busted down when it was about 60 degrees warmer. Apparently, the breakability of barbed wire and wooden posts increases greatly when the thermometer plummets.

Clickety clickety CLANK

The next day, the cold and the snapping continued. The morning mercury showed 30 below, a new low worth bragging about to the neighbors and anyone else who could sympathize.

Halfway through feeding the cows, I heard some discouraging sounds from under the hood of my usually mute 4020.

Click, click, click. I did my best to ignore the sounds and keep on feeding. I tried to mentally wish them away and I focused every positive biorhythm I had to try and improve the health of my failing green friend.

Despite my powerful positive thinking, the sounds progressed to a CLANK, CLANK, CLANK that even a mechanical pollyanna like myself couldn't ignore. I pulled the old girl into the shop and discovered that the water pump I'd heard screeching a little back in the warm days had taken this frigid opportunity to finally fail me.

I finished feeding with one of my trusty A John Deeres and a bale unroller that sported a manual winch made for guys like Popeye. The hard labor did keep me warm, but so would have the stove in the house if I'd have been finished feeding like I was supposed to be at that time of day.

But when I did get in the house, I took the time to think of how I could get around these breakouts and breakdowns that were plaguing me. I was considering things as radical as stronger fences and preventative maintenance when the weatherman on television gave me the answer I was really looking for – a warming trend.

Flocking sheep to market

Taking early retirement from shepherding

Jan. 25, 1999

It's a little-known fact that the Taylor Ranch has been home to a small flock of sheep the last several years. I guess I chose not to go public with that information to save everyone the effort of having to tell me all of those interchangeable Montana/North Dakota sheep jokes.

Like all old ranches, we used to have quite a few sheep roaming our range. But then our brains grew in, and we got out of the sheep business.

Undeterred by everyone's advice that I not get back in the sheep business, I bought 10 ewe lambs six years ago. The woolly little range maggots were to be the newest troops in my full-scale war with leafy spurge.

Got sheep?

The 10 ewe lambs were to be the seed for a hardy little band of grazers that would soon grow and prosper on our lush, yellow hillsides. I borrowed a buck from a fellow shepherd and made plans to keep every female offspring for flock expansion.

The plan began to remind me of the farmer who started with a bin full of flax, seeded flax every year and kept his own seed from the harvest for the next year's planting. Within a few years, he was out of seed. Within a few years, I began to fear that I might run out of sheep.

Between the coyotes, my poor management and the sheep species' inherited biological desire to die, I began to get worried about having enough critical mass for spurge reduction. To bolster the grazing numbers, I began keeping a few wethers too.

Well, for a variety of reasons, including burning hate, a lack of patience and a shortage of shepherding skills and labor, I decided to get out of the sheep business last week.

On Wall Street, they would call my decision one of "liquidating lagging assets (the sheep) and returning the focus to core competencies (cattle)." Like the Wall Street boys, I figured I didn't need to own the factory (the ewes) to reap the benefits (spurge control).

From now on, I plan to "outsource" my spurge grazers. The latest plan is to either buy cull ewes in the spring and sell them in the fall or contact rent-a-sheep for some custom grazing.

The last roundup

But, getting back to my marketing, I loaded up 24 "big sheep" and kept back 11 "little sheep" (lambs) to fatten up for that hot Easter market. As usual, by the time I got those 24 miserable critters loaded in the trailer, I was mad enough to sell them.

My "few wethers" had turned into 14 by sale day. Ten of those wethers averaged 202 pounds. No wonder I got so tired when I had to pick them up and throw them in the trailer one at a time!

I was pretty pleased with the proceeds from the sheep sale, but I was hoping that since I started with 10 ewe lambs, I could sell 10 ewes after six years of production. The trip to market began with 10 ewes, but it just wasn't meant to be.

When I pulled up to the sales barn, the attendant opened the door on my trailer, looked down and said, "You've got a dead one here." I looked at it, too, and realized there was no need for an autopsy. By examining those blank-looking eyes that were partially rolled back into that cavity where most animals store their brains, I knew the cause of death. It was a final crime of vengeance, another needless sheep suicide.

Bale feeder blues

Things might be bad, but can always be worse

Feb. 1, 1999

Sometimes, things that don't last can be frustrating.

But sometimes, things that do last can be just as frustrating. Sturdiness and strength are generally good attributes, but once in a while, you just wish something would break loose to save you the trouble of dismantling it yourself.

I've got some round bale feeders made of sturdy steel square tubing that could stand to give a little more. Especially when there's a 700-pound calf fully wedged between two of its jail-like bars.

Locked up

It's common to find a couple of 500-pounders weaseling in and out of my bale feeders as they strive to reach the finest middle morsels of hay. They'll rattle around and get stuck for a few seconds, but they're always able to free themselves.

So when I found a big, beefy steer locked up between his rib cage and his hip bones, I figured a little cajoling would soon have him free like his lighter-weight counterparts.

I pushed, pulled, shouted and squeezed. He wasn't coming loose. I tried tipping the feeder up to pop him loose. He returned the favor by trying to run me over. I dodged him like a matador in a Mexican bull fight. His next attempt was to knock me cold by throwing the feeder around. I chuckled at his weak attempt as the hurtling steel grazed my ear.

At one point the calf laid down and gave me that "I think I'm going to just bloat up and die" look. It was already getting dark, so I called in the troops – my cheery gray haired mother, a flashlight, a hacksaw and a sledgehammer.

I put in a new blade and hacked away at the steel bar with the intensity of an innocent man breaking out of Alcatraz. A couple blows with the sledgehammer and the steer pushed through to the inside of the feeder.

Displaying the best of his bovine intelligence, he jumped right through the bars on the opposite side. He squeezed his shoulders through, sucked in his gut, kept pushing and, in two seconds, he had himself in the exact same predicament.

Now I wanted to use the sledgehammer on the calf's head. My flashlight operator discouraged me from doing that, and I was soon hacksawing yet another bar in my once-flawless feeder.

Could be worse

The calf was soon free and now I had some welding to do. I was pretty disgusted until a friend cheered me up with the story of another rancher who had it even worse.

This rancher started the day by backing over a forked tree limb and puncturing the back tire on his feeding tractor. He walked a mile or two home and decided to push a little snow while he was waiting for the tire guy to show up. In minutes, he had the dozer blade curled up under that tractor.

He went to move some calves in the corrals and found his own version of a bale feeder disaster that made mine look plumb weak. His extra-large feeder had a couple of bales in it and the calves had eaten away at the bottoms, creating an impending bale avalanche.

When the bales did come down, they landed right square on the heads of two calves. The rancher found them there as dead as a couple of guillotined French revolutionaries.

Some days it just doesn't pay to get out of bed.

Slingin' season

Combating the spring's smear campaign

March 8, 1999

I hate to jump the gun, but it looks like winter will soon be beginning its downhill slide.

It won't be long now and we'll be simultaneously complimenting the sun and cussing the mud and the muck it creates. Cold weather definitely has its drawbacks, but, like good-quality electronics, chilly weather can make for "solid state" ranching with predictable hard surfaces to walk and drive on.

Ready to thaw

However, the other day, while I was trying to pick-ax my chute's frozen-solid state headgate to free-swinging freedom, I decided that a nice, warm thaw would maybe be a good thing.

A good thaw and I could toss my pick-ax aside. I don't know who's responsible for inventing the pick-ax, but I doubt that there's a more awkward tool known to man.

As clumsy as I am some days, I kind of hate to even swing anything that long and pointy. They're sharp enough and wicked enough to put cowboy shish kabob on the evening menu.

And cowboys aren't the only thing that can get damaged by a pick-ax. A friend of mine told me they can do quite a job on the back tire of an International "M" if you happen to run over one.

Usually, the only thing that gets damaged when I pick up my pick-ax is my pride. My poor pick-axing technique never fails to launch whatever I'm picking at right into my face.

From frozen mud and manure to chips of ice, you can bet that when I'm a pickin', I ain't a grinnin'. You really don't want your mouth open too much at all when the crap is headed your way. Sometimes I even shut my eyes when I'm pickin' and chippin'. If you really want to see a dangerous activity, just watch me swingin' a pick without my sight.

The sloppy option

I finally shortened up my pick-ax job by using a little boiling water to thaw out the frozen headgate. That's when I thought a good warming trend and a general thaw would make ranching a lot more enjoyable.

But, later in the day, after a little sunlight and some melting in the corrals, I reversed my opinion again. The thing about a general thaw is that the stuff getting thawed generally ends up on me. From the cuffs of my coveralls to the crest of my cap, I get covered with the once-solid crap.

A calf doesn't have to kick up too high in a warm corral to splatter a fella's face with a good shot of manure that was much less harmful in its frozen state. I can stand a little manure decorating my earlobes or highlighting my cheekbones, but I can't say that I like wiping it out of my eyes and I really don't care for the taste of it.

Some of that manure does have at least one redeeming quality, though. One time when we were doing some spring cattle work, I got a generous splattering of it on my lips and I just left it there.

My cattle-working companion for the day looked at me oddly and asked, "Aren't you going to wipe that manure off of your mouth?" I says, "Nope, it's good treatment for my chapped lips."

"Really," he says, "does it have some kind of healing and lubricating qualities for you lips?" And to that, I smiled and said, "Nope, not really, but it sure does keep me from licking them!"

Four legs up

The end of a legacy

March 29, 1999

I lost an old friend last week. She shall remain nameless. Of course, she was nameless in her life as well. She was always referred to by a number, No. T64 to be exact.

She was a black brockle-faced beauty. We found her dead with all four legs stuck straight in the air. It doesn't take much of a cow doctor to make a speedy diagnosis when every limb is pointed to the sky.

There was nothing left to do but pull her into a sand dune and invite the coyotes over for supper. I'm sure the coyotes were appreciative. They've been getting a little gaunt since I sold my sheep this winter.

A full life

It's not unheard of for a rancher to lose a cow or two in the winter. It's just part of the business. I've been luckier than most in the cow loss department, thanks to my knack for culling the old cows in the fall that don't look like they'll make the winter.

I guess ol' T64 should have gone down the road a few months ago. Of course, she made it through the worst part of the winter, when it was 20 below zero, icy and windy. It seems a real tragedy that she would choose to die just when the weather started to get warm again.

Age, however, was not in her favor. I don't know the age of all my cows, but I did know the age of T64. I knew this cow's age because she was one of the first cows I ever bought.

She was part of a group of 10 heifers I bought when I was 14 years old. I even borrowed the money from the bank to buy those heifers, preparing myself for a future life of cows, debt and interest.

T64 was the last of the 10. Kind of like Charley Russell's famous watercolor, "Last of the 5,000," give or take 4,990 head or so. And my cow was in a lot better shape than the bony blizzard-beaten longhorn in Russell's painting from an 1880s winter. But, all the same, we were talking about the last of a once-noble group of bovines.

Expiration date

I guess T64's time was up. I bought her as a calf in 1984 for 60 cents a pound. This spring, she would have been 15 years old and worth about 30 cents a pound. Fifteen ain't much for a human, but, for a cow, that's pretty agey.

A lot of progressive guys cull their cows at the age of 10, even if they're still producing a calf. So, a cow at 10 would be similar to a human at 65, both forced to retire even if they're productive. Of course, most cowboys don't quit ranching at the age of 65, so I figured my cows shouldn't have to quit ranching at the age of 10.

But, using that 10 and 65 ratio, ol' T64 would have been blowing out 97 and a half candles on her birthday cake this spring. I maybe should have let her retire a little earlier.

I like to think that T64 died on her own terms though. Laying on your back with your feet up and looking at the blue sky on a 50-degree March spring day in North Dakota isn't such a bad way to go.

As a matter of fact, if I make it to age 97, I might consider that a pretty good option.

Photo opp's

A well-planned shoot

April 26, 1999

I got the call early in the week. The Cooperative Partners magazine wanted to do a story about me, my eclectic career and my book, "A Collection of Cowboy Logic." They were aiming to take the angle of "hard-up rancher becomes struggling author."

Like any good publicity-hungry writer, I said, "Sure, that'd be great!" We did the interview over the telephone, but we had to get the photographs the old-fashioned way – with a camera and a photographer.

Cooperative Partners is one of those slick, glossy magazines, so they wanted some top-notch photos for the story. It would require more than a snapshot from a camera with a timer balanced on the hood of my pickup. Nope, this story was going to require one of those professional Minneapolis photographers with lots of film and a quick trigger finger.

The photographer called to set up the appointment. He had a couple other assignments in North Dakota and he was planning to get them all knocked out in a couple of days.

I gave him the directions to the ranch from the south. "Go north on a dab of pavement, then keep going on a whole bunch of gravel, be careful of the curves – they'll kinda jump out at you, turn on top of the hill – it's a real tall one by McHenry County standards, travel east a bit, then turn north again, go across the flat hay meadow, and turn into the ranch before you hit this low range of sandhills."

Surprisingly enough, he actually found his way into the place without getting lost. I met him at the car. He said, "Man, you're a ways out here." I returned his comment with the standard, "Well, it ain't the end of the world, but you can sure enough see it from here."

Staging the unstageable

The photographer was looking for some ranching shots. That was good since I had on my best dirty chore coat and my fashionable Elmer Fudd cap with the earlappers down on my chilly ears.

Since the story was going to focus on my writings about the lighter side of going broke, raising cattle and living on the prairie, I thought it would be good to find some photos reminiscent of my stories.

Luckily, circumstances obliged us with some of those very photo opps.

The weather wizard brought in some clouds and one of those classic 40-mile-an-hour North Dakota winds. Good, diffused lighting for the camera and the wind made us work quickly, saving valuable time.

Then a couple of my helpful bulls started fighting, tearing down their barbed wire corral, then continuing to tear down the cow's barbed-wire corral. The cows chipped in on the act and quickly ran for the hole in the fence. With the whole herd now out on the road, we had some prime photographic subject material.

The breakout was good, but the best shot came from a well-timed calving episode. A new slimy calf, a concerned mother cow and a rancher in his Fudd cap made for a photo that should be a real winner.

Of course, for the photo to be really reminiscent of my usual luck, the calf would have gotten stepped on by the fence crawling cow herd and died. Sometimes, though, it's good to get a picture of how things look when they go right for a change.

Those are the real Kodak moments.

The cow whisperer

Go ahead and whoopee-ty-yi-yo, but keep it down

July 19, 1999

Monty Roberts can have the official title of "horse whisperer" in the horse training world. Me, I'm working toward the title of "cow whisperer." Yes, I want to be the man who listens to cows.

Herding cows isn't quite as glamorous as training horses for the queen of England, and it may not be the material of a bestselling book, but, like horse whispering, it does lend itself to philosophies of "will you?" instead of "you will!"

My desire to become more of a cowman who moves cows, and less of a cowboy who chases cows, began with my move toward rotational grazing several years ago.

It's tough to get a big crew together to chase cows every couple weeks, so I had to figure out a way to move them that used more mind and less might.

Hyup, hyup, hyaaa!

I used to be as rowdy in the cattle pens as anyone, but somewhere along the line, I learned that louder isn't necessarily better. After figuring that out, I sometimes wish I could clip the vocal cords on all the cattle crews I work with, calming both the cattle and me.

But asking a cowboy not to yell at cows is like asking Luciano Pavarotti not to sing, not that cowboys sound anything like Pavarotti, but the level of commitment to expressing themselves vocally is about the same.

We all have our favorite cow-chasing quips. I'm personally partial to "Hyup cows, head up now, hyoo!" Other favorites include "hyaaa," "heyyyy," "aiyiyiyiyiyi" and the old classic, "yipyipyipyip," first used and made famous by a vocal cowdog.

Cowboys, like construction workers, like to whistle a lot, too. However, the whistle targets of big city construction workers are quite a bit more shapely than what a cowboy has to tweet towards.

If whistling and yelling aren't enough, we like to bang on the fence, clap our hands and jump up and down and flap frantically as we "coax" cows to their ultimate destination.

Smooth, dulcet voices

Cows "coaxed" with full-volume fright don't always make it to their ultimate destination though. They're usually the ones that'll bail over the fence, crash through the headgate, or turn tail and run directly opposite of the gate you were trying to get them in.

When I started becoming a cow whisperer, though, I found that cows were more likely to stay in the fence, walk up to the headgate and actually go through the hole you had them pointed toward.

I've learned, the hard way, that it's easier to rotate cows from one pasture to the next by riding my horse and not yelling myself hoarse.

Years ago, cattle knew what it felt like to have a wolf trot along by them, back and forth. Instinctively, they'd start moving away from that wolf with the hunger pangs and sharp teeth. A horse and rider going back and forth can move a bunch of cows in the same way. I'm not a wolf, but I play one in the pasture.

And if you're a man who listens to cows, you'll find out that there's not that much to listen to if you whisper while you work. Cows are a lot like kids. They'll bawl when you yell at 'em. Cow whisperers won't hear a lot of bawling and bellering.

And that's the peaceful and serene scene that cowmen were always looking for in their cowboy days.

Home for the holidays

Sending a bull back for Christmas

Dec. 20, 1999

My dreams of a brown Christmas were doused with 4 inches of snow this week, and the weather forecast calls for below-zero temperatures.

I guess it's time to admit that we will have a winter this year.

Admitting is the first step in the healing process, and after admitting the existence of winter, I figured I better act on it. It was probably time to bring in the cows and start supporting their bad habit of eating harvested forage.

We were preg checking the cows anyway, and as long as they were home to run through the chute, they could just as well stay home.

The big "O"

We run the cows through and gave them the home pregnancy test. Lacking the patience to wait around for something to turn pink or blue or whatever it's supposed to turn, we went with the old standby, rectal palpation.

The vet said we got most of 'em bred, and those who didn't got a big orange "O" painted on their hip.

The "O" was for "open," but I tried to make the cows feel better and told them it stood for "outstanding." Then I told them to go out and stand with all the other outstanding cows who were so outstanding that I was going to haul them to town, parade them around the sales ring and sell them to the most outstanding bidder.

All the "outstanding" cows got to stay home and eat some hay, along with the first- and second-calf heifers who were in need of a little pampering.

But even though I'd admitted the start of winter, I decided to send all the older cows back out to the east pasture to scout out some grass under a mere 4 inches of snow.

Running of the bull

After sending the cows back out to pasture, I decided it was high time to get a neighbor's bull out of one of our pastures. The yearling bull had fallen for my heifers and repeated attempts to coax him out were fruitless. He hadn't seen his homeland since July, and for the last month, he'd been in my pasture all alone.

He'd figured out the shortcomings of one impatient cowboy on an average horse in a pasture with an above-average acreage of trees and brush.

See the cowboy on the horse. Put your head up and run into the middle of the thickest bunch of trees. See the cowboy ride into the trees, get his face scratched and nearly poke an eye out. Run out of that group of trees and into the next closest thicket of impenetrable brush. Hear cowboy cuss.

Repeat that scenario four or five times and the patience of the impatient cowboy runs out. Bull wins. Heifers' 60-day breeding season becomes a 120-day extended honeymoon.

This week, I doubled up my efforts – two impatient cowboys on average horses. That way when the bull ran from one thicket to another, a reserve cowboy was ready to pursue while the first one got himself peeled out of the trees.

We tag teamed the bull that way for a couple of rounds around the pasture until we got him into the next pasture and the next heading due west, straight toward his homeland.

He even started to bypass all the trees. When he stopped in a gateless corner of the fence, I ran the horse at him, gave a war whoop and watched him make his own gate and head for his home.

We bid him a joyous new year, and as he left, I could swear I heard the bull beller a few bars of "I'll Be Home for Christmas."

Outnumbered

Short crews and long days

July 3, 2000

Big jobs planned an hour or two before they start usually turn into really big, really long, really drawn-out tests of strength and endurance.

I generally like to put a little planning and organization into major tasks like branding calves and working cows. But sometimes circumstances don't leave much time for that elaborate fluff.

For the last couple of years, I've been implementing a new calving strategy on the Taylor Ranch, one that fits in with my continual absence and always-working-off-the-ranch lifestyle.

I like calving in May and June, instead of March and April, for a couple different reasons. First, it puts me outside the norm of ranchers and I like doing things that others consider odd. Second, the odd practice has given me more live calves with a lot less labor, less disease and fewer calving problems. It's like raising buffalo, but with cattle.

But it has it's downside, too. Calving later means breeding later. And breeding later means trying to keep the bulls away from the cows longer. Which, in turn, means fixing more fence, chasing bulls out of the cows more often and learning more cuss words to address the bulls by.

My bulls aren't really into this whole late-calving idea. They've decided it would be alright to start breeding cows any time after June 1.

Last week, "da boys" decided once again to walk through a couple of fences and go visit the cows. So, I figured, why not brand the calves and work the cows while I'm busy sorting off seven ambitious bulls? Why not do it this afternoon?

Jobs a plenty

It's admirable to want to get things done. It's that go-get-'em attitude that employers find so worthy in ranch-raised job candidates.

Wanting to get things done is fine and dandy on an individual level, but spreading that enthusiasm to unknowing friends and neighbors on short notice is tough.

After a few phone calls and a little driving around, I was able to gather up my hired hand and a couple of busy neighbors to chase, sort, brand and work the small herd.

It wasn't a very big bunch of calves, but it was big enough for one team of calf throwers. The hired man and I took care of the vaccinating, castrating, implantinating, deworminating, dehornating and brandinating (basic jobs seem more medically high tech when they end "inating").

After we finished the calves, I let my weary neighbors go back to the weed spraying and fencing jobs they'd left to come help me. That left the hired man and me to run the cows through for shots and dewormer.

I gave him three or four jobs in the back moving cows from pen to pen and into the alley. I took on the headgate, the deworming, the two vaccinations and the tally book. It went slow but fast, dragging on at a furious pace.

It was probably frustrating for both of us to do a four- or five-man job. It absolutely reminded me of a story I'd recently read by Wally McRae, well-known Montana rancher, writer and poet, in Range magazine.

Sorting cattle with his dad, Wally found himself "multi-tasking," as the corporate boys say. The pressure got a little intense and Wally found himself yelling back at his dad's demands, "I'm doing the best I can. I've got three jobs: Hold the herd. Turn back. And hold the cut. I can't do it all!"

To which Don McRae calmly returned, "Keep moving, boy. Cows can't count."

A true piece of cowboy logic.

Making the shot

When the pressure's on — Sept. 11, 2000

Doctoring livestock has never been an easy proposition. The best we could do is enjoy the experience and find some element of sport in it.

It's that element of sport that explains the popularity of roping in the ranching community. Sure, you could find a way to corral a pinkeyed cow to give her some antibiotics, but closing a gate on a cow isn't near as fun as tying her onto a knob-headed horse with three strands of nylon.

I'm a poor roper and, subsequently, a poor trainer of horses to rope from. It doesn't stop me from doing both, though.

A few weeks ago, I had a cow with footrot that I was intent on doctoring. My horse is decent at bringing a cow into the corrals, but the cow wasn't too keen on the plan.

She played lame and wouldn't move out worth a darn. An easy target for my poor roping skills. But once I shook out my loop, she discovered super cow speed and agility as she loped across the pasture on her sore foot.

After a couple of "sighting in" loops, I tossed one on the cow as my high-headed, hard-mouthed horse went streaking past the target. I lost the tail of my rope but got the cow in a thicket of trees, dismounted, picked up the rope, dallied onto a poplar tree and trapped her in a cats-in-the-cradle web of rope and trees.

It was as good as a squeeze chute and I commenced to treating her with the finesse of a Beef Quality Assurance-trained technician. Subcutaneous administration of multiple 10-milliliter doses and all ahead of the shoulder. Both sporting and technically proper.

Spears and arrows

Not everyone enjoys being a poor roper of cows like myself. Still looking for a sporting angle for their doctoring chores, some ranchers have turned to antibiotic administering gadgetry that allows them to become medieval jousters or native warrior archers.

Essentially, we're talking about a long stick with a needle and syringe on the end of it, or an arrow-length stick with a needle and syringe on its end.

The idea is to run at a sickly critter with your jousting syringe and stick her when she least expects it. It's hard to imagine these things being used in accordance with Beef Quality Assurance guidelines. Jousting subcutaneously and getting multiple 10-mil jousts into an animal ahead of shoulder could be tough. I guess I'd rather be a poor roper with good injection technique.

Even more amusing than the idea of cow jousting is the vision of hunting one down with a bow and a loaded arrow.

I talked to one fella who borrowed one of these bow and arrow jobbers to doctor a sick buffalo. Yes, that's right, a sick buffalo. I could just envision this rancher in a leather breech cloth with a feather in his hair as he stalked the mighty pneumonia-plagued bison.

He said he got in close range, pulled back on the twine and ploop! He claims he's gotten better distance relieving himself off the back porch after two pots of coffee!

The arrow did get far enough to drop right into the buffalo's back hoof, though. And after inspecting the bent up $15 needle and squirting $25 worth of antibiotic onto the ground, he gave up his sick buffalo hunt.

He figured if natural selection got the bison this far in the evolution of things, it should maybe be left alone.

And maybe the evolution of cowboys should be uninterrupted as we allow ourselves to progress toward the use of squeeze chutes, headgates and maybe the occasional rope and tree.

Rock cow concert

Tractor diving and herd surfing

Dec. 4, 2000

I used to think my cows were country western fans.

Like their rancher owner, I was sure these mild-mannered, leather-wearing critters were into cry-your-eyes-out country ballads and the occasional up-tempo western swing tune. I figured they were cow/calf pair dancing, waltzing across the peaceful pasture in three-quarter time.

Little did I know. My two-stepping twangy country tuned Taurus turned out to be a herd of hard-rocking, slam-dancing radicals with punk rock respect for personal property.

I think it was the weaning process that really brought out their wild side.

Moshin'

Right after I weaned my calves last week, the gentle, quiet moo I was accustomed to turned into a roaring, deafening chorus of bellers. The crowd was chanting for some action and they were getting irritable.

I put the cows in a pretty good pen lined with some high-voltage electricity. I pulled up to the gate with my tractor and a couple of hay bales. The way they were rushing the gate, I realized that I was the rock star in this feeding concert.

It was well after dark as I pulled up to the mosh pit with my John Deere light show. I saw one cow push the electric wire against a steel post. A nice blue spark lit up the darkness. I smiled. Rock star ranchers take comfort in good crowd control.

What I really needed for complete control was some burly bouncers to push the crowd back while I drove through the gate. I finally screamed a couple lyrics at 'em like Gene Simmons of KISS. They backed off and let me through.

Once in, they really rushed my rolling green stage. I crept along, careful not to crush my fans.

I stepped out of the cab and pondered doing a stage dive. A little crowd surfing across the milling herd. Then I spotted that big cow with the gnarly horn and thought better of my urge to herd surf.

Instead of surfing, I stepped down into the mosh pit to take the twines off the bales. The raucous rockers moved me along and I worried that these body-slamming bovines were going to grind me into the bottom of the pit.

But being a savvy mosher, I kept my balance and maintained oxygen.

Slammin'

Having survived my cow's mosh pit, I thought my night's rockin' was over. I should've known that the younger generation was even more ready to mosh, slam, destroy and defy responsible ranch society.

Before the night was over, my newly weaned calves would slam dance right through my corral in an all-out effort to go back to moshin' with their mamas.

Early the next morning, I found the hole these punks had punched in the fence. They were out bellering at the top of their lungs with no respect for people in the neighborhood who were trying to get a little sleep.

Their friendly little slam dance had turned into a full-fledged riot. I was ready to call in the cops and let them go after these guys with some tear gas and rubber bullets. No cops would come to work over my cattle, so I pacified them with my own sorting nightstick and they gave themselves a little electric tazer treatment on the fenceline.

With the crowd finally controlled, I can only hope that those cattle start appreciating a two-step and some Merle Haggard pretty soon.

This ranch can't stand much more moshing and slam dancing.

Out of reach

Beaten by a bovine

Jan. 29, 2001

Sometimes you win, sometimes you lose. And, right or wrong, most of us like winning better. But losing teaches us what it takes to win someday.

I got beat last week. Not in a business deal against some shrewd man in a gray flannel suit, not in a sporting event against a human athletic machine, not even in a game of chance at a charitable gaming table.

No, I was flat out, hands down beaten by a cow wearing a black leather suit who was plenty athletic and not the least bit charitable in the game we played.

Cow crisis

I wheeled in to Rock Lake, N.D., to call on the veterinarian, satisfying my daily duties as a good drug rep for an animal health company.

I noticed the doctor's pickup parked along the road some distance from the clinic. I saw a trailer backed up to the clinic. Then I spied the reason for the vehicle left down the road.

The cow that was once in the trailer and once in the clinic was no longer in either. She was checking out the scenery on the north edge of town with a vet and a farmer in full pursuit. I could quickly see that what they needed out there was another person, like a cowboy drug rep.

We had as many as five people pursuing this critter at one time. Plenty of manpower, but critically short of a few needed tools, like corrals, fences and horses.

Tough neighborhood

Recently I was on the Internet doing some research on cattle statistics when I found a map of North Dakota's most concentrated cow counties.

A good share of the state's million cows can be found within 30 miles on either side of Interstate 94 between Jamestown and Dickinson, along with a jog up from Dickinson to Watford City, and an island-like pocket of cows in sandy McHenry County, home of yours truly. About half of North Dakota's cows inhabit one-third of our geography.

Things did get fairly blank on the map for cow numbers in northeast North Dakota, like around Rock Lake. Even the renegade cow had to travel 30 miles to get there so she could get loose in that town and refresh the local's cow identification skills.

As we were chasing that cow through the snowy fields outside of Rock Lake, I realized what it meant to be shy of cows in an area. It meant there wasn't a fence to guide her in or a corral to guide her into for miles around. Nothing but wide-open wheat fields and snow-laden acres of the Conservation Reserve Program.

Along with the general void of cows, corrals and fences, we were short on horses to borrow for pursuing and roping that cow in the wide-open country. The best we could do was pursue on foot, getting as close as 50 feet away with a 30-foot rope, breaking through the snow and hoping the cow would bog down in a deep drift. She never did.

So without a horse to ride, a fence to guide, or a corral to trap her, we gave up the foot chase and declared her the winner.

But I learned from my loss. Next time I see a cow loose by a vet clinic that's surrounded by open country, I'm going to keep driving until I find a horse to ride.

Rockin' or grazin'

What to do with those hills

July 2, 2001

Last weekend, Bottineau, N.D., will have hosted its annual "Rockin' the Hills" three-day concert, camp out and party. The guys I know who take it in say it's all about booze, babes and rock 'n' roll.

Earlier last week, I hosted a little range tour that I called "Grazin' the Hills." We had some weed (mostly leafy spurge) and some grass, too, man (mostly sand bluestem and prairie sandreed). For music, we listened to some chattering song birds and our concert goers were mostly ranchers and range scientists. We had a few rocks in our hills, too, but it was mostly sand and sandy loam.

Security needs were minimal to host the 50-plus people who attended Grazin' the Hills. One of the ladies from the Soil Conservation Service did help direct a little traffic and parking, but she didn't have to pack any pepper spray or a billy club to maintain order.

We didn't have a massive stage or elaborate sound system to belt out our message on grazing management and pasture rotations. We did have the standard little suitcase-handled speaker and microphone from the Extension Service, and the soil conservation folks did rent a 20-foot by 30-foot tent to keep our slush burgers and potato salad out of the sun.

Turnout was a little less for our event. Thousands and thousands of people will take in Rockin' the Hills. We had to settle for tens and tens of people for Grazin' the Hills. But those tens of people knew more about range management when they left than they did when they came. I bet most of the hard rockers couldn't tell a stand of blue grama from a bunch of little bluestem.

Both groups did probably learn a lot about "herd effect." Herd effect occurs when you concentrate large numbers of animals in a small area for a short amount of time. Followed by a good rest period, herd effect can have some real positive results on the range.

Herd effect helps concentrate the positive fertilizing effect of a lot of animals standing in an area urinating and defecating. Rock concerts try to get everyone in the latrine for those activities, but I bet there was still some ol' boys out in the trees completing the beer cycle outside of the confines of the john.

Put a bunch of cloven-hooved animals in a small area and their herd effect opens up the soil and improves the infiltration rate of future rains. It probably helps the ground soak up those concentrated fertilizers too.

I'm not sure what kind of improvement you'd get from thousands of tennis shoe and sandal clad rock 'n' rollers, but it's bound to break up the dirt a bit, too. Probably depends on whether they're wearing size 6 high heels or size 14 flip-flops.

The biggest difference between the herd of rock 'n' rollers at Rockin' the Hills and the herd of cattle at Grazin' the Hills boils down to money. It'll cost a rancher in my area $80 or $90 to summer a cow that'll go out there to nip the grass, open up the soil and spread its fertilizer.

The rock 'n' rollers were spending $70 a day each to stand around and do some of the same things. Financially, I'd say the cattle are a big loser.

Ecologically, we'll have to take a look at the Rockin' the Hills grounds in 10 or 20 years and see how the forage production is measuring up. Maybe we'll have to combine our tours in the future to inspect the results and be both Rockin' and Grazin' the Hills.

Might be the way to really get more people excited about the annual Soil Conservation range tour.

Meat meeting

Beefing up on beef knowledge

Nov. 5, 2001

I like learning. I guess that's why I was quick to sign up for the "Beef Starts Here" course put on at my alma mater, North Dakota State University.

Beef is an appropriate course topic at NDSU. My friends who couldn't get accepted into NDSU because of their lack of personality like to call my land grant school "The Cow College" or "Moo U." Since I admire and respect cattle, I consider the nick names a real compliment.

I hadn't taken a class at my endeared cow college since 1992. Now I was back on campus for a course patterned after the "Beef 706" courses in Nebraska and Texas.

It was sponsored by the North Dakota Beef Quality Assurance Program and the NDSU Extension Service and aimed to give us some insight on quality and consistency issues in the beef business and teach us about the value differences in cattle and carcasses because of those issues. The hope is that we'll find ways to increase the value of our cattle and carcasses once we've learned about those differences and issues.

My personal goal was to beef up my knowledge on the cuts of meat that come from a critter. That way if I was ever in the audience of the David Letterman show and was chosen to compete in the "Know your cuts of meat" quiz segment, I could ace the questions and drag home the big prize.

Lessons learned

My three days in Fargo, N.D., were well worth the time and investment. About a dozen of us took some time away from our cattle to learn about our beef. Instead of continually working in our business, we decided to spend a little time working on our business.

I learned lots of good things, like there ain't no good in an evil-hearted woman...wait, that's not what I learned, that's a country song.

What I actually learned was that my eyes aren't really good enough to look through a calf's hide and see the beef. Ultrasound machines can see pretty good, and a skinning knife works exceptionally well to get you down to the truth of the matter.

I learned that a critter can be worth a lot or a little depending on his quality (or lack of), his grid pricing premiums (or discounts), how he was managed (or wasn't managed) and how he tastes (if you can chew it, that is).

I spent a little time in a white coat with a sharp knife. I tried to be careful, especially around my fingers and the tenderloin. Fingers are worth a lot to a writer, and the tenderloin is worth even more to a rancher.

I learned to respect the folks who stand in packing plants with a knife so that I can sit on my horse with a pair of reins and consumers can sit at their table with a fork and a knife.

Finally, I learned about how muscle becomes meat. It has to do with pH numbers, acid and basic, and glycogen being broken down and being replaced with lactic acid.

It's some of the lessons in the meat locker that taught me what's going on with my legs when I run. Now I can go to the New York City Marathon understanding glycogen depletion, lactic acid buildup, and when I start feeling like dead meat after the 26.2 mile race, I'll know exactly what's going on.

Mysteries of the range

Unexplainable occurrences after the storm

Aug. 26, 2002

Aliens have attacked innocent, peace-loving cows on the Taylor Ranch!

Or maybe it was lightening, but I think the alien story has more commercial appeal. I've long wanted to make it into the supermarket tabloids, and I think the alien cow connection might get me there.

Last week, I was on the road for a speaking job when I got a phone call from the ranch crew back at home. One of our first-calf heifers looked like she'd had her last.

She was hanging out by herself with a stunned look on her face. Her hide was peeled back and burned looking from her hip bones back to her tailhead and down.

They described her condition over the phone and it didn't take me long to figure it out. "Did you see where those scoundrels landed that space saucer?" I asked. "Did they leave any other communication besides our scarred up cow?"

There were no burn rings in the pasture or odd-looking designs in nearby fields. No missing people or apparent alien abductions in the neighborhood. No local women carrying alien babies in their womb.

We did have an eyewitness account with ranch representative No. 067, but she wasn't talking. She was visibly shaken by the whole experience. Her usual calm, cud-chewing demeanor had changed to one of an angry Angus anxious to charge and mutilate approaching earthlings.

An apparent brain transfusion or mood-altering drugs administered by our outer space visitors.

Alien treatment

I treated 067's alien attack like I would any other ailment such as footrot or pinkeye or pneumonia – a rope and a syringe full of Biomycin.

I had to give her some supportive care, too. I hauled her home for easier access to feed and water and invested some time in maggot eradication.

These are the activities that make ranchers stronger than the average squeamish professional. Armed with a little Nolvasan solution, I got right in the heifer's scarred-up nooks and crannies and kicked those crawly little maggots out on their wormlike butts.

I reckon this is the kind of training that'll prepare me for the reality shows like "Fear Factor" and "Survivor." Put me on an island and ask me to do something really gross, and I doubt it could be much worse than a maggot-ridden heifer, a cow who hasn't cleaned her placenta or an advanced cancer eye.

The future for 067 is questionable, though. Somehow, those aliens drew up the ligaments on that cow's hind legs. Now her pasterns are tightened up and bent over and she's walking on her tippy toes. Not a good trait for a range cow.

Practical remedies

I've talked to a few people about my alien attack. A neighbor had one just like it. She lived about a year longer. He says it was lightening.

My veterinarian says he's seen three or four like it, from lightening, though. Euthanasia might be the best remedy, according to the doctor.

I guess I'll check my lightening insurance for the cows. If they'll pay more than the tabloids will for my alien story, I might have to cave in and admit the obvious lightening strike.

Otherwise, I'll be in the pasture with the photographer looking for Martian tracks and extraterrestrials with a taste for beef out hiding in the brush.

Got milk?

By the truckload and ready to blend

Sept. 23, 2002

Marie Antoinette is supposed to have said, "let them eat cake," when she heard the news that her people were starving. Uncle Sam looked at the cows hungrily walking the fencelines of the drought-stricken Great Plains and has said, "let them eat milk."

The U.S. Department of Agriculture is making available $150 million in drought feed assistance to cattle ranchers in South Dakota, Nebraska, Wyoming and Colorado. It's being doled out at a rate of $23 per cow via feed credits that they can use with their local feed dealer.

But before guys rush in to their local co-op to fill their pickup box with range cubes or supplement blocks they need to make sure they got milk.

Milk moustaches

That's right, milk in their feed. As a result of some other interesting programs, the government has warehouses stocked with 1.4 billion pounds of non-fat dry milk, one third of which is more than 2 years old and getting older every day. Now they've figured out a way to clean out those warehouses – give that milk away.

And they're giving it away by the truckload to feed manufacturers who must mix, blend or sprinkle their regular feeds with it and give it to ranchers who'll give it to their cows.

So here's the loop – cows give milk to dairy farmers who sell it to the government who then gives it to ranchers who then give it back to their cows, but not necessarily the same cows that originally gave the milk in the first place.

The news release I saw mentioned only beef cattle, heifers and bulls as eligible recipients for the milky provisions. Seems like a dirty trick that the dairy cows who gave us the milk in the first place won't be getting any of it back. Sheep, of course, are apparently not in need of the feed either.

But there's no use crying over spilt milk if you don't get any.

Borderline benefits

Feed manufacturers are trying to figure out ways to mix the milk in with their pellets, cubes and tubs of feed supplements, so they can sell it to their customers in the designated drought areas.

Droughts, like most weather-dependent phenomena, do not have abrupt and certain borders. Drought programs, however, like most politically dependent phenomena, do have distinct borders. According to the program's designers, the drought actually follows state lines.

So ranchers in Lodgepole, S.D., are in a severe drought and will get $23 in milky provender. But ranchers 14 miles north in Hettinger, N.D., are apparently not in a drought and will not get the assistance. Overhead flights of the region have failed to confirm this state line spector of dusty, dry browns on one side of the line and succulent, lush greens on the other.

But where it is green, like 442 miles from Lodgepole in Sioux Falls, S.D., state border definitions say they're also in a severe drought and should get some assistance.

The program is slated to run through Dec. 31, and administrators, feed manufacturers and ranchers, ought to have the details figured out by Dec. 30.

I'm sure it'll take some severe ironing to get the wrinkles out of this deal, but I am glad that assistance is being made available.

I just wonder if ranchers will be allowed to mix the surplus milk in their water tanks and let the cows slurp their way to nutritional balance. If so, it'd make a great new slate of "Got Milk?" billboard images.

Longhorns, long day

Some jobs are better done naturally

October 7, 2002

One sure way to add excitement to your everyday ranching routine is to trade in your no-horned cattle for a herd of Longhorns.

My herd of Longhorns is pretty small, just 10 head bought at a weak moment to raise some roping steers. Although it's a small group of cows, it's enough to make me really appreciate the genetic progress made in the other breeds of polled beef cattle.

I do like to see my Longhorns out in the pasture, standing on the hill, looking kind of western and nostalgic. The best place to admire those antlers is in a big pasture and from a distance.

Of course, cattle can't hang around a ranch just to be admired, so I had to think about getting them bred and reproducing their nostalgic selves.

Natural or not?

I put up with bulls on the ranch only because I have to. Fence wrecking, hole digging, gate bending, ornery buggers, their only virtue is that they do what they need to do for 60 days every summer to make a calf crop.

I contemplated the thought of adding one more of those surly pups to the bull battery to cover my 10 Longhorn cows. I have enough dislike for my polled bulls, I didn't think I needed to aggravate myself any more by adding a Longhorn or Corriente bull to watch out for during the 300-day off-season.

I decided I'd artificially inseminate my Longhorns to calve next summer.

There're decisions made in life that you question the sanity of even as you make them. Artificially inseminating Longhorns is one of those decisions.

It gets better, though. Not only did I decide to put these wide-antlered critters in the alley to breed, I decided to synchronize their estrous with another three trips through the chute for injections and an intravaginal progesterone insert.

So here's the deal – a Longhorn cow with 4 feet of antler tip to tip going down a 30-inch-wide alley not once, but four times.

And I've got to look them in the eye and explain the concepts of needles and injections, intravaginal units being inserted and exserted, and rectal palpation to facilitate artificial insemination to a prize Corriente stud. They looked at me with an expression that said they'd rather give me a rectal horn insertion.

Over an eight-day period, I did get the cows synchronized and ready to breed. On the ninth day, at precisely 29 hours after the last injection, it was time to breed.

My girlfriend and I had a church supper to attend, and afterward, I talked her into helping me run these critters down the alley. She gave me a look similar to the cow contemplating that rectal horn insertion, but she agreed.

The day was getting short, and by the time I started breeding the third or fourth cow, it was pitch dark without so much as a ray of moonlight. I used the pickup dome light to load the insemination wand and kept on breeding.

My girlfriend asked if I needed some light on the chute to finish the job. I realized, though, as I was elbow deep in the cow that it was pretty dark in there, too, and it probably didn't matter.

The task is done, but I think next year I'm going to look for a Longhorn bull.

Healing touch

Practicing patience with our patients

June 16, 2003

When it comes to my care of sick cattle, it's hard to tell if I'm running a hospital or a hospice somedays.

If it's a cow hospital, the patients are supposed to recover and get back on their four feet and resume grazing. Many times, though, it feels like I'm doing cow hospice, giving suddenly terminally ill bovines a chance to die in comfort.

I haven't had an alarmingly high number of patients this year, but one of my 90-pound birthweight bulls seems to be siring some 120-pound calves.

A couple of my more geriatric cows have laid down and stayed down while trying to have those big calves.

My first experience came when I found a cow down and out with a big, big baby halfways out and hiplocked. I helped her finish the job, pulling the calf that died a couple hours later, only to have her start prolapsing.

Prolapses are best dealt with sooner than later, and I put her womb back in place pretty quickly. She prolapsed again. I put it in again. She pushed it out. I pushed it back. Finally, after four or five tries, everything was as it should be. Except the cow was down and not looking like she'd get up anytime soon.

That began the process of carrying feed and water to her in the middle of a quarter section pasture. She'd eat and drink, but every time I went out there, she was flopped over on her side, making a real concerted effort at dying.

So I began some physical therapy, rolling her over onto her other side and helping her sit up square with the world and lay with her legs beneath her comfortably. This became a regular routine until she died. Chalk one for hospice.

I soon had another patient to work on, when another granny cow had a monster calf on her own but wasn't about to get back up. I rededicated myself to another project of cow convalescence.

She proved to be a little better patient. The big job wasn't carrying feed and water to her out in the pasture, it was keeping the other greedy cows away from her while she ate that feed.

Physical therapy with her was a bit more gratifying. Within a couple of days, I was able to get her to stand up if I lifted on her tail and propped myself up against her to act as her right hind leg. Eventually she got some feeling back in her own right hind leg and I was able to square her up and let her stand on her own for awhile.

She'd go down again, of course, but it gave me a little hope. Then, one day, she was gone from her "spot." Unfortunately, I found her down and out in a mud hole a little ways away, and a mud bath wasn't the kind of physical therapy she needed.

So I cleaned her up by transferring most of the mud to myself and got her back on shore.

I went out the next day, and there she was, gone again. No, the coyotes hadn't drug her off into the brush. She was up on all fours, limping and grazing and getting her own water. Chalk one for a successful hospital release.

Some you win, some you lose. But we try to save every one. It's a lesson we can put to use in our small-town businesses and schools, too. Because, sometimes, just when you think you'll be carrying feed and water to the patient until the day she dies, she'll get up and take off on her own.

And that's a pretty good feeling.

Injection infection

Getting on the receiving end of the needle

June 30, 2003

"Someone ought to give him a taste of his own medicine." That's the phrase you hear when we think someone should be on the receiving end of the treatment they're giving.

I reckon my cows have muttered that in cow-speak as I've poked, pilled and poured a variety of animal health products into and onto them throughout the years.

Last week, they finally gave me a taste of my own medicine.

Head-butting heifer

I had the most recent addition to the herd squeezed between my knees for the ritual ear tagging and a shot of "seven way" clostridial vaccine.

I was just fixin' to give Junior his injection when I saw something big and black coming at me from the corner of my eye. Mama and me met head to head, and when she hit me, my vaccinating hand flew toward my free hand and buried the syringe needle in the muscle at the base of my left index finger.

"Ouch, sweet pea, that really hurt," I told the cow. Or something like that.

At any rate, I pulled the needle out of my hand, stuck it in the calf and finished the job. Meanwhile, in less than 10 seconds my finger puffed up like a flesh-colored balloon.

I tagged another calf and read the label on the vaccine bottle as I drove home with my throbbing left hand. It read, "Accidental injection to humans can cause serious local reactions. Contact a physician immediately if accidental injection occurs."

I don't know who these physicians are that you're supposed to be able to reach in the evening, but I tried a clinic phone number and they routed me to the emergency room and the receptionist there told me to call my veterinarian.

I tried to explain to her that I was of a species that was supposed to use an MD, not a DVM, but I hung up and called a vet that I knew. When he found out who was calling, he recommended amputation. I told him I'd kind of like to keep the finger so I could cut it off with a table saw someday.

He said there was no imminent danger if I didn't actually inject the product, but he told me to keep an eye on it and see a doctor if it kept swelling or got discolored.

Bend over

It kept swelling, it kept hurting, it got red and splotchy. I gave it two days of cowboy stoicism and decided to stop in a clinic on my way through town.

The nurse practitioner was a little alarmed with my lack of treatment. I got a tetanus booster, an antibiotic prescription, an X-ray and a referral to a hand specialist.

Concerned with the neglected infection, she ordered a dose of injectable antibiotic that would go right to work. She told me to drop my pants and assume the position.

I looked at the needle (long), the syringe (huge) and its contents (cold and irritable).

I thought about correcting her desire to inject me in the hindquarter, letting her know that Beef Quality Assurance guidelines dictate that all shots go ahead of the shoulder. But the thought of her pinching my neck and putting that needle in there didn't appeal to me any more than sticking me in the rump.

So I just stepped up and grabbed a hold of the table, grinned, bared it and beared it.

Immediately, my finger seemed to feel better. It probably still hurt, but my hind end hurt more and it took the attention off my finger.

Cattle throughout my herd were probably smiling with revenge.

The cowboy way

Suited up

A once-in-a-lifetime investment

Feb. 22, 1999

I've discovered another sure sign of my getting old. Along with the receding hair line and prematurely graying follicles, I've proved my aging by going out and buying a suit.

Yes, an honest-to-goodness wool blend, three-button-coat-and-pleated-trousers kind of a suit. The last real matching coat-and-pants suit I had was the classy green denim ensemble my mother dressed me in for my kindergarten graduation back in 1976. Since then, I've exercised the normal farmer and rancher aversion to suits.

I have made the usual fashionable progression from brown corduroy to gray tweed to navy blue blazers, but they generally were worn with a pair of Wrangler jeans.

Now, however, I finally broke down and decided the time was right in my life to become a suit owner.

Timeless threads

Farmers and ranchers are not famous for spending a lot of cash on constantly updated wardrobes. When it comes to our Sunday go-to-meeting duds, our goal is to be buried in the same polyester blend suit we wore for our high school graduation – even if it is a sherbet-colored pink or lime.

So when I picked out my suit, I tried to choose something neutral enough to get me through 50 years of weddings, funerals and trips to the big city, and sturdy enough to last until my own funeral.

It's too bad I didn't have the suit several years ago when I was spending the better part of my summers as a professional groomsman, usher and Scripture reader. In the peak of my post-college wedding season, I read enough Scripture at the front of enough churches to qualify as a semi-ordained quack minister.

Although the rush of weddings is over, I figured it would be a good idea for me to have a suit for my next stage in life as a professional pallbearer.

Although I'm still pretty young for casket carrying, my family heritage indicates that pallbearing is a job that is sure to come my way. Dad carried out most every friend and neighbor he had. Luckily, he had that one good dark gray suit for his pallbearing uniform.

And that's about the only time he wore it. It got to where he could just check the inside pocket of his suit coat, pull out a funeral program and know precisely when he last wore that suit.

Cheap therapy

Buying a suit is a real ego-building experience that everyone should try, even if they don't need a suit. Walking into the men's store, I could tell by the salesman's brown nose and complimentary demeanor that he was working on commission.

I enjoy watching a good salesman in action and this fella was a pro. "That suit really looks sharp on you, sir. It's a good look for you. That fabric really hangs nice on your shoulders. It goes great with your complexion." I knew I was getting sold, but I was enjoying it.

By the time he got done with me, I would have bought four or five suits, but he let me off easy and just sold me the one. Like most cowboys, I'm sure that one suit is all I'll need. But the ego-boosting sales pitch probably will wear off a little sooner.

So the next time I get a little down on myself, I think I'll just go try on another suit or two. As long as I'm careful not to purchase, it'll be a lot cheaper than a psychiatrist.

6 billion and counting

Running the world's population through the gate   Oct. 18, 1999

The count is in. The herd of people on our little round ball flying though space has hit a new milestone – 6 billion living, breathing souls. That's double what we had in 1960.

The 6 billionth person was born in Sarajevo, Bosnia, according to the United Nations. The baby boy probably didn't realize he was so important in the scheme of the globe's population. He was probably just glad to have successfully crossed over from the womb to the world.

Add and subtract

I don't know who at the United Nations was in charge of doing the counting and making sure the baby in Bosnia was number 6 billion and not 5,999,999,999 and not 6,000,000,001, but my guess is that it must have been a team effort. Kind of like maintaining a running tally on a cow herd.

I can only imagine that they had a couple of counters at each maternity ward around the world. They probably had to post a couple at every morgue, too.

They must have had a good figure to start from, like 5,982,456,296. From there, it was just a matter of adding everything from the maternity counters, while subtracting everything from the morgue counters.

It doesn't sound much different than calving time at the Taylor Ranch when we were fighting the weather, scours and pneumonia.

Starting point

The trickiest part was probably discovering that starting point of 5,982,456,296.

The only way we can get any kind of large, accurate count on the ranch is to funnel the critters through a gate or a sortin' alley when they're in for branding, weaning or pregnancy checking.

That way we can step in and slow them down to somewhat of a trickle and have a decent chance of being within 10 percent of the actual count.

Having one person at the gate counting is usually good enough for less important tallies. Like, say, the counts we need for financial statements and our bankers. But when we really demand accuracy for things like sale day and loading the semi-trailers en route to the feedlots, we'll double and triple up our accuracy with two or three cowboy counters.

With three mathematical wizards standing at the gate, you often get three different numbers, but then you can at least take an average.

I know the people counters depend on mail-in census forms and door-to-door census takers, but I think they might learn a thing or two from the cow counters. They may think that we've witnessed the birth of our 6 billionth global resident, but I won't believe 'em until they've gotten a good human gate count.

To be really accurate, I think they'll need to post a few cowboys at the major traffic intersections and post a couple at the doors of the shopping malls. They'll be easy to spot, standing there with an intent look on their faces, moving their lips and wagging a crooked finger at the people and cars as they funnel by.

When it's all said and done, you'll see one cowboy say to the other, "What'd you get?" The other will say, "You tell me first!"

Finally, one will probably venture out and say, "Six billion and one," and the other lip mumbling finger wagger will more than likely say, "Uh, yup, me too. Let's go with it!"

On tap

Organized bleeding

Oct. 25, 1999

Sounds like the country is running short of a pretty important liquid.

It's not gasoline, although that's important enough to bring $1.40 a gallon, and it's not water, although that's important enough for some people to sue their neighbors in the more arid river valleys.

No, the shortage is in blood, something you can't pull out of the ground or siphon off of a river. The only way to get it is to talk a fellow human out of their personal supply one pint at a time.

Pass the pump

When I heard the news that one of the major cities in America was down to its last pint or two, I listened guilt-free.

Just last week, I had a spare moment while I was in Minot, so rather than head to the bar for a cold 16-ouncer in a frosty mug, I went to the blood bank to give 'em a warm 16-ouncer in a plastic bag.

It had been a while since the last time I gave blood, so I just went in and did it. I didn't even know that we were experiencing desperate shortages in the hospitals of a few cities.

I started donating blood back in college and I've tried to keep up the habit ever since. According to my card, I've given 20 pints to date. Not much for a rancher who likes to measure things in 5-gallon buckets, but it's a start.

I'm not sure why I started donating blood. I reckon I was probably walking through the Student Union when I saw someone giving away cookies and juice, and I probably didn't realize until it was too late that there was a catch.

Or it could have been that I just decided to finally make use of a liquid I had been letting trickle down my elbow and drip on the ground wastefully for years.

Rancher sap

Considering the dangerous shortage of blood that we face, it makes sense that we try and think of new ways to collect every drop that we can.

I know some guys who are deathly afraid of letting a nurse rub their arm with iodine and stick a sterile needle in a vein, yet they barely yelp when they rub mud and manure on themselves and tap their own veins with rusty barbed wire or a greasy sprocket.

The best way to get those fellas to make a donation to the blood bank might be to put them on an automated direct deposit system. Instead of talking them into going to town to donate, we would just make the best use we can of the blood they already let loose of out in the country.

Like collecting sap from a maple tree, we would just hang a couple of buckets off of the ranchers and catch as catch can.

I'd bet that on a good day of rolling up old wire you could catch at least a pint. A drip pan below the rancher when he's changing the pickup teeth on his baler should gather up another nice blood donation from the backs of his knuckles.

Granted, we might have to strain off the big chunks of various impurities and run it through some kind of purification process before we send it to a hospital.

Or, if purification proves too costly, we could just recycle it and use it as a low-cost option for other ranchers who come into the hospital. At least it'd help free up some clean blood for the other folks whose system probably couldn't take a few blades of grass or chunks of grease floating on the top of their pint.

Plumbing on the prairie

Rancher's home improvement skills honed on a windmill

June 7, 1999

Like the television show says, "It's home improvement time." Except, rather than being hosted by Tim "The Tool Man" Taylor, my show was hosted by Ryan, the foolish man, Taylor.

I've always been a fan of the "Home Improvement" show. Arrgh, arrgh, arrgh! They have some spectacular wrecks with the projects in their shop and it doesn't surprise me a bit that their main character's name is Taylor. It's a natural fit. The name, I think, is an old Celtic term meaning "walking catastrophe."

Ever since I was a lad, I've fancied myself a builder. I've ruined more good lumber and bent more nails than a lot of guys my age. Everything from trees to treehouses have felt the wrath of my poorly aimed claw hammer.

Mechanically, I've tried my hand at Go Karts and bicycles, and I've dismantled several small engines that have yet to be reassembled.

There is, however, one aspect of handymanship where my successes outnumber my failures – plumbin'.

A natural

My plumbing apprenticeship was spent with my father on the ranch's windmill and shallow well pump circuit.

I think I took to it because galvanized pipe is so hard to ruin. The threads are hard to strip and they're fairly hard to bend or break. I could practice all day with my pipe wrenches and do very little harm.

The wrenches were a big part of my attraction to plumbing. Since they were fully adjustable, two wrenches could do most everything you needed. The two-wrench system cut down on tool box clutter, and it greatly reduced the confusion of wondering which wrench to use on which pipe.

The work on the windmill and shallow well circuit could be pretty rough and no one would really notice. A leaky joint didn't cause a lot of trouble out in the pasture. And it didn't much matter if your poor planning resulted in a dozen extra unions, elbows and tees, just as long as the water eventually found its way to the tank.

Going interior

Having passed the pasture test, I decided it was time that I take my plumbing expertise indoors. To put my skills to the test, I decided to install some new plumbing in my McHenry County bachelor shack.

This was much finer work than what I'd received my training on. I decided to swap my galvanized pipe and wrenches for some plastic PVC, a hacksaw and a couple cans of primer and cement.

I went to work with confidence and gusto. I was really enjoying myself. I was smiley, happy, almost giddy. Of course, that could have just been a result of the fumes I accidentally snorted when applying the purple primer and all-purpose cement to the plastic joints.

The job was really coming together nicely. The white pipes and purple drip accents were extremely aesthetic. I thought they looked so good that I ran my pipes along the floor in plain view rather than try and hide them in the stud walls.

Like any good blue-collar tradesman, I drank a lot of coffee while I was on the job. So when I finally got the valves finished and the water routed to my new toilet, I had an immediate use for it.

And listening to the sound of the toilet flushing, it gave a whole new meaning to the term "job satisfaction."

Well wishes

Pre-winter water exploration

Nov. 22, 1999

I've always been a little pressed to get my fall work done. This year, though, my rate of progress has been so impressive that I'll soon be caught up with last fall's work!

We've got the hay hauled in, the cows gathered in close to home and at least one well ready to pump water for the winter feeding grounds.

I usually prefer to do well work in the middle of winter when it's 20 below zero and my wet, yellow, fuzzy chore gloves stick to the pipe like cockleburs on horse tails.

I maintain a higher rate of motivation when there's a big herd of thirsty cows crowding around an empty water tank while I'm down in a hole fighting with a couple of worn-out pipe wrenches.

Pipe pounders

This year, though, we actually found the time to do well work before the cows drank the last one dry. And it was even sunny and warm.

Well work in Towner, N.D., is probably done a little differently than in other areas.

Most of our water is coaxed out of the ground with a "sandpoint," a pointy pencil-looking piece of pipe and screen set 15 to 25 feet in the ground with a shallow well pump up top.

Bored wells on our place are really deep, like 45 feet. That's about 800 feet closer to the surface than some of my friends in western North Dakota, so I feel pretty lucky when it comes to the ranch's water.

We've bored a couple of wells on the place, but we still have a few sandpoints to water the cows in the winter.

We like the sandpoints because they fit into our "do everything the hard way" management strategy. Pounding in a new point is something you might need to do every few years as the old points plug up, and point pounding is good, "hard way" cardiovascular exercise.

Our point pounder weighs about 40 pounds and it can build muscle like a membership in Gold's Gym. Pounding pipe is like doing "reps" on a weight machine, and some wells take a lot of reps to get to the water vein.

Well wizard

The sandpoint for the cow's winter feeding grounds was down to a trickle last spring. I figured a shiny, new brass point would be the kind of proactive plumbing needed to get back to a full flow.

The hired man and I pulled up the old point with the loader and tried to get the new point and pipe stuffed down the old hole before it filled up with mud. We commenced to pounding and stopped when we hit the depth of the old point.

We were anxious to measure our success. We gave it the test – no water.

This is typical for my well work. Considering the wet year, we figured we must have gone too deep and missed the vein. We pulled it back up a ways. Another test – still dry.

I always figured any job worth doing is worth doing wrong two or three times. In frustration, we brought out my father, the well master. Dad's point-pounding days are over, but he knows as much about getting water with a sandpoint as he does about fixing two-cylinder John Deeres, and that's a lot.

He consulted his records on well depth, told us to start pounding again and to go down a little deeper. I can't say that we hit a gusher, but we found 5-gallon-a-minute water.

I think I'll start calling Dad ol' Jed. I just wonder how he is on finding some bubbling crude.

Double "O" Cowboy

The James Bond method of ranching

Dec. 6, 1999

It takes me a while to discover modern cinema culture. Last week, I saw my first James Bond movie.

I know Bond's been around longer than oatmeal, so I fully realize that I've been a little behind on the times. I think I waited too long to meet "Bond…James Bond," because the movie was not only entertaining, but it gave me lots of secret agent ideas for successful ranching.

Spy gadgetry

Bond, a.k.a. 007, had more nifty little devices than the gadget guru on the morning news.

You could never guess the uses of something that Bond was packing around by just looking at it. A watch wasn't just a timepiece, a jacket wasn't just something to keep out the chill, a boat wasn't just for traveling on water.

Bond's contraptions shouldn't be limited to spyie only. Like good tractors and pickups, I think ranchers should be able to buy the contraptions after they're used up and depreciated out.

The rocket-powered speedboat that he drove down the back alleys would be just the ticket for the swampy pastures where amphibious transportation is a plus.

Even better would be the wristwatch that shot out the string and hook that 007 used to swing away from a fiery explosion. Any gadget that can get you out of a tight spot like that would find some uses on the ranch.

It could even replace the time-tested lariat. The heck with swinging a loop overhead; just aim your watch at a renegade critter, push the button, and be ready to dally. It's one thing to lose a thumb roping, it's quite another to lose a whole hand because you forgot to dally your wristwatch cable.

The best secret agent apparatus in the movie had to be 007's ski jacket with the rip cord that inflated a big beach ball-looking thing with him safely inside. James Bond used it to save himself and Elektra, the beautiful industrialist oil heiress, from an avalanche.

Skiing to check the path of her pipeline, they got attacked by hybrid parachute snowplanes, and some more fiery explosions set off an avalanche. Lucky for them, Bond was wearing his special coat. He pulled the rip cord and – shazam! – they're instantly protected inside a big, inflatable ball.

Imagine the uses for that jacket when you're sorting cows and you find yourself about to be trampled in the gate. Just pull the cord, tuck inside the beach ball, and listen to the cows as they harmlessly glance off of it.

Or, you find yourself getting bucked off of a green colt and, in mid-air, you're able to pull the cord, inflate the ball and bounce away without even catching a hoof in the teeth.

Secret cowboy agent

I give 007 a lot of credit for having catchy gadgets to pull himself out of sticky predicaments. But ranchers have been pulling themselves out of losing situations for years without the high-tech advantage.

It's pretty easy to get away from danger with a titanium-plated, rocket-propelled, turbo-charged sports car with global positioning capabilities. I can't help but wonder how he'd fare with a '67 Ford half-ton pickup with two low tires and a bad clutch.

I think for the next James Bond movie, he ought to expand his horizons and do it rancher-style. I can hardly wait to see him on the big screen, trapped in a snake-infested Turkish dungeon with nothing but a fencing plier, some duct tape and a ratty-looking piece of orange plastic twine to make his escape and save the free world.

Now that would be a cliffhanger worth watching.

Carvin' up the Turtles

A hick and his snowboard

Dec. 27, 1999

Despite its downfalls, snow does have some redeeming qualities. Near the top of that list would be its ability to make a hill slippery, allowing for some gravitational winter recreation like sledding, skiing and, now, snowboarding.

In my youth, I spent plenty of time sledding down the ranch's sandhills, but, being a daring three-quarter Norwegian, I was soon tempted to strap a couple of boards to my feet and try going down the same hills upright and standing.

That got pretty wild. Especially since my skis were the extra-long, extra-skinny cross-country kind made for the flatlands, not the slopes.

There wasn't a lot of downhill stability in the oxford-looking shoes that were held to the skis by only the toes. I sprained an arm once using that set-up on the hills, but I was still determined to ski like my mountain-raised Scandinavian ancestors.

I finally tried some real ski slopes with chairlifts and groomed trails. I even went with genuine downhill skis, shorter and wider with rigid boots and bindings. Things went a lot better. No injuries and a fair bit of success at turning, stopping and getting down the hill in style.

Raising the stakes

Last week, I was in North Dakota's Alps, the Turtle Mountains, after a morning of chasing the cows out of the hay yard. I was ready to burn off some frustrated energy.

My traveling partner was game for a new challenge, so we decided to give snowboarding a whirl.

I went to the rental shop to get me a board. The fella who was fitting me had me stand with my back to him, then he shoved me forward and called me goofy. I just about went over the counter, popped him in the snoot and called him mouthy.

But what he had done was discover that I was right foot dominant so he could set up my snowboard. Left foot forward is regular, right foot forward is "goofy." In retrospect, the term was probably fitting.

I grabbed my newly borrowed board and headed for the bunny slope. Although the Christmas commercial for Wrangler jeans shows a cowboy riding up a mountain and snowboarding down, it's really not a natural activity for the majority of us cowboy types.

The best snowboarders are usually guys who grew up skateboarding or surfing. I've done neither. It's pretty tough to skateboard in the sand or on a gravel road, and, no matter how hard the prairie wind was blowing, I couldn't get the surf to pump hard enough on Smokey Lake to really hang ten and ride the never-ending wave.

But after an hour or two of falling down, I was getting the hang of having both feet tied together and pointed down a snowy hill on a slippery plank. And, although, I didn't have a goatee, baggy snow pants or bleach streaked hair, I was picking up on the snowboard lingo.

The slopes were killer and I was really stoked about getting the shred on and busting down the run. My lift ticket had only run me 10 bones, which left me enough cash for a few mellow ones down at the lodge.

By the end of the day, I had my goofy board carvin' up the hill. I made a caballerial, did a fakie to forward and come off the jump doing some flying squirrel air. It was sick (good).

Pretty soon, my boardin' buddies will be calling me Ryan "Big Air" Taylor.

But, for now, my friends on the flatlands ain't buying that story. They're just calling me "Full of Hot Air" Taylor.

Shock treatment

Stimulus and response

Jan. 31, 2000

A fella named Pavlov found fame with his idea of stimulus and response. Working with a dog, some chow and a tuning fork, he discovered the secret to the dog slobber response – a conditioned stimulus.

The idea doesn't really seem like rocket science. Any rancher who can jingle in cows (desired response) with an empty bucket (stimulus once conditioned by a bucket that actually held feed), could have come up with it.

We've latched onto the idea in the fencing world, too. Electric fences have taken Ivan Pavlov to the pastures.

A lot of us use electric fence for achieving that conditioned stimulus and desired response. Once we get the cows trained to know that touching the one smooth wire means getting jolted, we can completely ignore the maintenance of the fence, figuring that the cows won't need much more stimulus.

Human testing

In the past, I've used electric fence without much thought to what the cows were experiencing during the break-in period.

Sure, I've done the manly test of the electric fence. No digital readout gadgets, just grab that dang wire and let your senses test the juice. It might be the macho way to go, but I try not to make a habit of it.

Someone told me they knew a dairy farmer who used his electric fence for personal motivation in the early hours of morning. When he was feeling a little groggy in the a.m., he'd just grab the wire on the fence and let some rural electricity flow through him to get him charged up and ready to milk. Sounds effective, but I'd prefer a steamy cup of coffee and caffeine to get me going.

These days, though, I'm getting more and more practical experience with electric shock.

I get to spend a lot of time in hotels as I travel around the state, and last week I got my best lesson in conditioned response at a Bismarck, N.D., hotel.

I'd come into town on Thursday night for a Friday morning meeting. I was looking forward to a little cable television and relaxation in the queen-sized cot.

I stepped into the room and thought I'd just stepped into the Sahara Desert. My mouth got dry, my eyes got stuck in mid-blink and my lips cracked instantly as I entered a climate of zero percent humidity.

I dropped my bags, went to turn on a lamp and ZAP!, the static electricity just about brought me to my knees. I had to leave the room, so I went to switch the lamp off and – ZAP! – it got me again. I left with burnt fingertips.

I went outside to get some Chapstick for my newly cracked lips, and, sure enough, when I went back in the room, ZAP!

I didn't even dare touch the television. I grounded myself and the remote control and stayed a safe 10 feet away.

When I decided to turn in for the night, I had to get that lamp one more time. I braced myself, took my shock therapy like a man and crawled back under the sheets, vowing to never again touch that lamp, a newly conditioned response.

But I didn't have to worry about a lack of light in the dark room. There was a steady blue spark arcing between the hair on my arms and the sheets on the bed. A great natural night light.

And from now on, I'll have a whole new sense of compassion for those cattle in pastures with electric fence. But I have to admit that cows learn quicker than cowboys what not to touch in their surroundings.

Ski skijoring

Gettin' a pull across the prairie

Feb. 21, 2000

There's a new craze underfoot in the world of winter recreation. Skijoring.

I say that because in the last month I've heard the term twice, and that's a lot for a word I'd never been exposed to in the previous 29 years.

Skijoring is winter's answer to water skiing. It means "ski driving," and it involves an excitement-starved skier strapped to his sliding planks, a bungee tow rope and an animal mode of locomotion.

Who could conjure up a sport like skijoring? Norwegians, naturally, are the skijor conjurers. Long, dark winters help people think up sports like skijoring and cuisine like lutefisk.

I first read about it in a Wall Street Journal human interest article. Then, a friend of mine from Montana talked about watching a skijoring competition. The Journal story focused on dogs pulling people around on skis, but the Montanan said it was horses towing skiers near Bozeman.

Both modes of transport seem pretty unreliable to me. Maybe it's just the horses and dogs I associate with.

Hike and on by

Skijorers are at the mercy of their towers. The dogs are on their own. Except for the skier's commands of "hike" (similar to "mush" or "giddyup") and "on by" (meaning quit watering that tree Fido), the pups pretty well do what they please.

The horse skijorers are in the same unguided boat. Not so much as a rider to steer them down the trail.

We used to do a little skijoring in our neighborhood when we were younger. Well, maybe it was really sled-joring. The horse had a saddle and rider, and we towed a manned red plastic toboggan instead of a skier.

The rider added a malicious twist to our sledjoring. The goal wasn't a certain distance in a certain time. It was to peel the sledjorer off his sled as quickly and ruthlessly as possible.

As fast as he could go, turning as quick and as hard as he could, the rider would search out a nice hole or jump, or find a good patch of brush or thorny rose bushes to de-sled the hapless sledjorer.

I wonder if true skijoring has that element of surprise.

I doubt it, but it's probably a lot less damaging to its participants. Our sledjoring through the thorns scraped off a fair bit of skin, but it grew back eventually.

Around the ring

Real skijorers stick to trails clear of brush, but they will get in some jumps and smooth slalom turns.

I'd consider joining the sport, but I'm not sure if Smokey, my 17-pound border collie, could get me off the starting blocks. The horses on the ranch have got the power, but their guidance systems have something to be desired.

They hardly know the meaning of "gee" and "haw" like a good team of mules. Heck, they can barely neck rein.

Successful skijoring takes power, speed and control. I can think of only one animal that might offer each of those traits, especially if you keep a feed pail at the finish line.

Just like the picture on the sweatshirt I saw that proclaimed, "Ski North Dakota." It had a fella in a cowboy hat on a pair of skis, his arms out straight, hanging on to the tail of his trusty cow.

Born to build

If I had a hammer, I'd hammer all day

March 27, 2000

Ever since I was able to swing a hammer, I've liked "building stuff." I even aspired to be a carpenter at one point in my list of career goals as a 6-year-old.

My carpentry career got a big boost when my babysitter gave me a full-fledged set of half-sized tools for my birthday.

The tools had a bright blue coat of paint on them, probably to keep me from losing them. Even then, I had a habit of scattering my tools hither and yon.

The set had a little hammer, a little saw, a little of everything that a little boy would need to ruin a nice pile of lumber. I commenced to turning long boards into short boards and sawdust.

I built a birdhouse, a doghouse, a kid house. I couldn't tell if the birds appreciated my work, but my faithful canine companions, Waldo and Tommy, thought the doghouse was swell. At least that was my interpretation when I heard them wagging their tails inside the new abode.

The "kid house" was really a toolshed, because that was where I stored my new blue tools. I even built an attached lean-to that I called my wood shed, because that was where I stored my mutilated lumber and wood chips.

In retrospect, it was this rancher's very first shop. Or, in the terminology of psychologists and marriage counselors who study the male psyche, it was my first "man cave."

Young though I was, I still had the need to get out of the house and get away from my sister and mother for a while. I even nailed up a sign on my shed that proclaimed, "No Grils Aloud," which was my 7-year-old version of "No Girls Allowed."

Sacred caves, a.k.a. shops, are a real man thing.

Crackless corral

Before I built that toolshed, my only large-scale building project was a corral. But I launched into house construction realizing that it was exactly the same as building a corral except there weren't any gaps between the boards.

The toolshed was six fence posts and lots of corral boards – no gaps. I nailed it up and laid some plywood across the top to deflect the rain. Home building was a piece of cake, I decided.

I continued to hone my home construction skills out in the corrals. When I decided to construct some independent housing for myself on the ranch a couple years ago, I grabbed my fencing tools and deemed myself ready for the challenge.

I did weaken and hire a contractor to frame up the place and put on the siding and shingles. But I didn't feel too guilty about it, though. No worse than hiring someone to dig the post holes for a corral, I figured.

I still had plenty to do with all those bare stud walls and open rafters. Lots of insulation, drywall, wires, pipes, doors and trim to keep me and my blue tools busy.

The big job was drywalling and I figured putting up drywall couldn't be any worse than building a windbreak. Like horseshoes and hand grenades, close does count in the drywall biz if you know a good tape and texture man.

It took a couple of years, but I finished the house myself with the help of a few buddies. And it does look more like a house than a windbreak.

Not bad for an old corral builder who got his start with a little blue hammer.

Blocks and pieces

Learning life's skills

Jan. 1, 2001

Being useful takes years of training. Think about this the next time you run into someone you'd term "useless." It might be that person is just still in training.

This training starts young, too. I never realized how much so until I commenced to doing some gift shopping for the little people in our family.

My nephews, ages 6 and nearly 2, are just starting their useful training. Effective training takes good tools. Like the alphabet worm, the picture and letter cards, and the board games that trick you into learning how to count.

And when it comes to the building and engineering side of useful learning, you can count on Legos.

I gave the gift of Legos for Christmas this year.

The little scene on the box looked pretty cool. I wondered how difficult it might be to make those blocks look like that. I was reassured by the friendly reminder in the lower left corner that said "For ages 4 and up."

The Legos were the hit of the post-Christmas dinner playtime. We dug right into them and, though the 6-year-old was ready to start sticking things together, the 30-year-old uncle got stuck with the responsibility of deciphering the 32 pages of instructions to create the neat scene on the box.

Ages 4 and up. Yeah, right. We finally got it close to the cover photo.

Cabinet carpentry

Two days after the Lego training exercise, I was following up on a promise to my mother to get her running water and a drainable drain in the kitchen.

Actually, I started out saying I would fix her faulty faucet and old leaky sink, and it just got out of hand. It was like the children's song of the old lady who swallowed the fly, then swallowed a spider, a bird, a cat and a dog to get that fly taken care of.

Well I was going to fix the faucet, decided on a new sink, and a new sink needed a sturdy new countertop, and a new countertop needed a solid new cabinet base, and a new cabinet base ought to have matching wall cabinets, and "I don't know why she swallowed the fly."

By the time I got out of the home store, I had a trailer load of stuff and a receipt tape as long as my leg.

I went with the pre-fab boxed cabinets to save a little dough. I asked the clerks how hard they were to put together. They said a couple of ladies were in, bought a whole kitchen's worth and had them built in half a day.

I couldn't back away from the project now. They'd played the gender card.

And if two wimmen could build dem thar cabinets, by gawd, I could, too! Aarr, aarr, aarr!

I unpacked pieces, parts, screws, bolts and a set of directions from those cabinet boxes eerily reminiscent of my recent Lego lesson. If there were two ladies who put a whole kitchen set together in half a day, one must've been Martha Stewart and the other one Bob Villa's stunt double.

I stared at the finely printed directions until my eyes developed a permanent squint. I sorted DB's from V1's from R2's, and separated eight different screw types that were probably once separate before they mixed them up again into little plastic bags.

After a couple of false starts and some assembly, disassembly and reassembly, I got it all together. I thought my carpentry looked pretty fine.

Of course, I'm a carpenter who was trained on more Lincoln Logs than Legos.

Pictographs

Exercising our artistic flair

April 23, 2001

People like to draw. It's been a natural artistic outlet for us for thousands of years. Some time after standing upright and starting fire, we commenced to doing a little rock sketching.

I've always felt that link to my prehistoric past. I wouldn't say that I was ever an artist. But I was what my grade school companions would call a "good drawer."

A good drawer may conjure up images of a nice wooden box with two knobs in a chest with smooth gliding sides, but my being a good drawer had more to do with my ability to create pictures on paper that somewhat resembled their real models.

I haven't done a lot of drawing since my mother quit hanging them on the refrigerator with a sturdy magnet, but I do still dabble in doodling a little bit.

Sometimes I doodle to fight boredom, other times I doodle to satisfy my creative urge. And sometimes I apparently draw doodles to identify.

I had nearly forgotten that last artistic excuse until I freeze branded my replacement heifers this spring. I was reminded by an ear tag that I pulled from the ear of No. 747, a nice black heifer with baby blue identification.

I was pulling her old tag with her mother's number on it to replace it with her very own tag and new individual number. I looked at the old tag as I threw it in the pile and noticed that I had drawn a speeding jet airplane above the number.

Perplexed

I couldn't for the life of me figure out why I doodled a plane on that ear tag. Was I a little bored that day while I sat in the pickup putting the ink to the plastic? Was the calf really, really fast, like a jet plane? Did I smile smugly after I caught the speedster and fashioned her lobe with the sign of the jet?

I wondered if it was drawn to signify a sign from above. A passing plane on a clear day across the wild blue yonder?

It had me bamboozled for a whole day before I asked my hired man what he thought it meant. "Her number is 747, Ryan. Get it? Like the jumbo jet, the Boeing 747." Of course! So obvious it was a mystery.

I reckon I'd have made a similar drawing if I had a calf numbered DC9 or DC10. McDonnell Douglas deserves as much recognition in my pasture as Boeing does.

Cave doodles

I was reminded of my pictographic ear tag when I was in Billings last week for a bull sale and I saw the Pictograph Cave at the state park south of town. Prehistoric hunters had been hanging around this cave for a long time.

Either bored or creative, they chalked up some pictures on the back wall of their humble abode. Some looked like animals, some like spears and people. While I was standing there admiring their graffiti, a jet popped up from the Billings Airport and crossed overhead.

I thought about jumping off the trail and heading into the cave to draw one of my famous airplane sketches. But the park ranger was keeping an eye out for me, so I had to stifle my artistic urges.

I wonder if my ear tag will ever be admired by art and history buffs a few thousand years from now. I suppose it'll be part of the exhibition on prehistoric spray-painted water tower and rail car art.

Transition time

Wide brimmed fall fashions

Oct. 22, 2001

Walking out the door at the beginning of the day isn't as easy as it sounds. Especially if you're a cowboy. And it's fall.

It's a tough time of the year for guys who like to cover their cranium with a wide-brimmed hat. We're entering into that annual time of transition when we go to the hat rack on our way to the door and ask ourselves, "straw or felt?"

This isn't as easy to answer as you might think. It's not something to ponder half-heartedly like "paper or plastic?" or "can or bottle?" This is a serious question of protecting your noggin from the elements as we move into winter.

Dubious divisions

Some things in life have definite lines of division. The summer solstice, the Memorial Day start of tourist season, the beginning of earnest Christmas shopping on the day after Thanksgiving.

But the date for switching hats from the panama straw to the 20X beaver felt is a bit more ambiguous. You can't just cut if off at Labor Day and declare it felt hat season. And you can't make the switch too late in the season either.

I've seen some fellas still wearing their straw hat in the "country" bars in December. Of course, they're the same fellas you'll see line dancing and they get a confused look on their face when you ask them if they own any cows.

There's a double standard in hat etiquette. You can't wear a straw hat in winter, but you can wear a sweat-stained silver belly felt in the summer. That is, if you can take the heat and you don't mind a little sweat running down your brow.

And you don't want to be caught wearing that straw in November when it's 35 degrees. But if it hits 35 degrees in early April with a clear, sunny sky, it's admissible to break out that straw hat to show support for the warming trend.

Personal preference

For lack of any hard and fast rules on when to make the hat switch, I've come up with my own personal headgear calendar.

I can often go nearly all of September with panama, bangora or even palm leaf. But when we get a good killing frost and a skiff of ice on the horse's water tank, I start thinking about moving to the felt silver belly.

And by the time the first water pump has frozen and burst, I'm definitely in full fledged felt season. And I'll stick with it until at least May Day. If the sun is out and the sky is blue, I'll be delivering May Baskets in my summer straw regalia.

I don't know if the felt hats are really much warmer, but they are heavier and harder to blow off your head when the autumn winds start howling. Plus, a little less of that wind whistles through and chills your skull.

So I've made the transition. Of course, you'll only spot me in my felt hat when I'm traveling or going to town or taking in a meeting of some kind.

If you catch me out on the ranch, I'll be like all the other real cowboys, wearing my warm wool Elmer Fudd cap with the earlappers down and locked in position until April.

Trophy hunting

If you can't bag 'em, buy 'em

Dec. 3, 2001

Patience is a virtue, and it should be, because it takes an awful lot of time.

I guess that's why I've never bagged a real wall hanger when I've gone deer hunting. It's my lack of patience. I'm more of a shooter than I am a hunter. Shooting is a pretty immediate activity, but hunting takes some time.

Working and ranching doesn't leave me a lot of recreation time for things like hunting either. I usually devote about 15 or 20 minutes to my annual deer hunt. Sometimes I get one, sometimes I don't.

This year I got one. I saw a little four-point buck 20 minutes into this year's deer hunt, so I decided to finish the season. A nice bit of venison, but nothing to put on the wall and brag about.

It's that empty wall space and tight hunting schedule that had me tuned in to the radio when I heard they had some real nice antlers coming up for sale at the Napolean Livestock Auction.

Trophy antlers

The racks at Napolean Livestock weren't whitetails, they were Longhorns. They were on the docket for the Monday bred cow and heifer sale. It piqued my interest.

This would be my big chance to bag a wall hanger with nothing more than the high bid and a checkbook. No sighting in the rifle, no waiting in a tree stand for the big buck to walk by me.

Now some might say there's not as much beauty in hanging a Longhorn on the wall as there is in hanging a whitetail buck, but I beg to differ. I've seen them both, and I actually prefer the Longhorn. I appreciate the colorful cowhide, and I like those two long telescopic points.

I know the Cabela's hunting stores have some nice deer mounts for their customers to admire, but there're a couple of bars in Miles City, Mont., with taxidermied Longhorns that are even more impressive to my eye.

But, deer or steer, stuffed head mounts are more than mere decoration. They're useful.

Using your head

You can toss your hat up there to rest. You can make it into a game of "hat toss/ring toss" and go for distance, accuracy or style. Along with the hat, you can hang most anything – coats, ties, ropes, knick knacks, bricks – whatever it'll hold.

At Christmastime, you can put a Santa hat on your head mount. Something about a fuzzy red cap on a dead animal that really evokes the holiday spirit. At poker parties, fellas like to give the animal head a cigar to chew on. Make's 'em feel like one of the guys.

Considering the range of uses, I don't know how I've gone this long without the head of a dead animal on my wall.

So I bought 10 of those Longhorn cows that were up for bid at the auction barn. I was looking for some trophy mounts and there were some real wall hangers in the group.

They were pretty as a picture and bred to raise some nice ropin' steers next spring. They were young enough to raise me several more crops of ropin' stock. And someday they'll help me keep my hat off the floor.

But before they become a hat rack, I'll have to wait for them to complete their useful lives. Even domestic Longhorn wall hangers require patience.

I guess that's a virtue I'll still have to learn.

Making a meal

Trade show food trade

Dec. 17, 2001

They say there's no such thing as a free lunch, but there are a lot of free snacks in this world. And with a little planning and selection, you can make a lunch out of 'em.

I used to think a person could put together a fairly hearty meal by going to the supermarket when they're doing a lot of food sampling.

A little sausage on a toothpick by the meat section, some tiny squares of pizza in the frozen foods, crab spread on a cracker by the seafood and a taste of the cheese cubes in front of the dairy case.

A couple three laps and you've put together a pretty nice little meal. Of course, you might have to change up your appearance on the second or third lap to keep the gals with the toothpicks and napkins from getting suspicious.

A reversible vest and an extra beanie can do wonders to maintain your appearance as a new customer with a real interest in purchasing the food on the sample platter.

Buffet of booths

For the man who hates supermarkets, an even better meal can be rounded up at the winter trade shows, cattle conventions and ag expos.

I was just at the Range Cow Beef Symposium in Casper, Wyo., and it had as much grazing at the trade show for the cowboys as the Wyoming range had for the cows they owned.

Eight rows of booths made for a regular smorgasbord of snacks from the vendors all working to get a little quality time with customers to discuss feed, fence, feedlots, pharmaceuticals, corrals and all things cattle.

The fare wasn't quite as healthy as what you'd find in the supermarket samples, but the potential for high weight gains was there. Cattle producers appreciate performance.

One especially healthy animal health company had some dandy red delicious apples at its booth. You could snag some cashews and peanuts at another booth. That was about as nutritious as it got. From there on out, it was candy land.

Tootsie Rolls, Jolly Ranchers, Sweetarts and a surplus of chocolate, mints and holiday-appropriate candy canes. One feed company was conscientious enough to provide some Chiclets chewing gum for the folks to finish their meal. Always good to chew a little gum to help clean the cracks in your teeth and reduce decay.

Unlike the supermarket, you didn't have to feel sheepish about coming back to a booth two or three times to take advantage of the goodies. Actually, it was encouraged. It was good marketing to keep a customer at your booth for as long as possible.

It reminded me of my old coyote trapping days. A good set would put a lobo right into your trap. A good lure to bring them in range, some tasty bait on the other side of the trap, and a few small obstacles on the sides to put the little lamb-eater right where you wanted him.

Trade shows lure ranchers in from miles away. An attractive booth will bring 'em in range. A few mints and candy bars interspersed amongst the brochures to serve as bait and some table and chair obstacles to keep the customer immobile.

Once the trap is snapped, the rancher can learn about feed protein and mineral levels, vaccine disease protection, genetic performance data and the latest labor-saving feature on the new chute. If the pitch is good, it could lead to a purchase.

Maybe there is no free lunch after all.

Great American pastime

I took me out to the ball game

Aug. 12, 2002

I've never been much of a sports guy. Living way out in the sticks put serious geographical limitations on my high school sports career, and I kind of took to ranching and outdoor activities instead.

I think sports are great activities for young folks, though. They learn some good lessons about staying healthy and working with others, and it sure beats having them sit around eating cheese curls and playing video games.

If I could go back and be a sports guy, though, I think I'd be a baseball player. I reckon most cowboys would make that their second choice.

Smooth transitions

Going from beef to baseball could be a pretty smooth transition.

I'd still get to hang out on grasslands. Some years, the ball diamonds are a lot greener than the cattle pastures, but I could get used to it.

Unlike many sports, baseball players get to wear long pants and cover their heads. Some even wear long-sleeved shirts. What more could skin-conscious cowboys ask for?

It's bad for your health, but a lot of baseball players chew tobacco. So do a lot of cowboys.

Baseball players wear at least one leather glove to help minimize some on-the-job pain. Cowboys may start with two leather gloves to minimize fencing pains, but sometimes they'll finish the job with just one.

Cowboys don't get paid enough for what they do. Baseball players don't think they get paid enough either. One of them is right. We both enjoy what we do.

Baseball players need to be pretty versatile – hit, run, catch, slide, walk, steal, bunt and make lots of split-second decisions. Cowboys spend years learning a little bit about everything. They may not be able to do it all, but they try.

Live comparisons

Recently, I got to see some major league baseball in person and make a couple more observations.

Baseball is about statistics, meaningless data and copious notes. Just like what you find in a rancher's little red calving book.

When I watched the Minnesota Twins play the Kansas City Royals last week, I tried taking official notes just like the program showed.

Mientkiewicz hit a single in the bottom of the fourth inning so I wrote a "1B" in a little box and drew a line on the bottom right of a little diamond. But he got the first out, so I wrote a little "1" in the same box along with a "6-4", because the out came when the shortstop (6) threw Cuddyer's grounder to the second baseman (4). Cuddyer got an "FC", a fielder's choice.

I hadn't taken such intricate notes since No. 136 got bred by the yearling Charolais (1C) in the first cycle and gave birth to a bull (B) on April 1 (4/1) with a calving ease score of 1 (no assistance) and a calf vigor of 1 (nursed immediately). Just as many notes in about the same size square.

Announcers filled me in on Cuddyer's batting record when players whose names started with “M” were on first in the fourth inning. Dad told me how many times No. 136 had bull calves in April and the percentage of them that lived to see May.

I got to see a guy get hit square in the chest with a speeding baseball. He laid on the ground for a while, but he got up and made it off the field.

I’ve been kicked in the chest by some cows, but I got up and made it out of the corral.

We both grimaced through the pain and thought about our next at bat, or our next calf crop.

We both think the next one will be a home run.

All thumbs

But none of them green

Sept. 9, 2002

I’m a cattle raiser. A stock grower. That means growing anything else – crops, gardens, lawns, flowers, trees – is as foreign to me as black dirt and regular rains.

Visitors either admire or ridicule the lawn around my house. Some are shocked and appalled by what they consider a sparse, unkept, weedy patch of plants.

Astute ranchers and range managers, however, see the real value in my native range yard. They nod approvingly as I point out the nice stands of big bluestem, blue grama, prairie sandreed and lead plant in the stand. They appreciate my not seeding pesky non-native invader species like Kentucky bluegrass.

They agree that good native plants like I’ve got ought to be grazed, not mowed, and that commercial fertilizer and a lawn sprinkler would be insults to such proud old plants accustomed to cattle manure and sporadic rains.

So I’ve let my native range flourish, stimulated only by the occasional grazing of the saddle horses and a few yearling steers. I think it’s the best yard for miles around, and it is (the only yard).

I was so encouraged by my success in lawn care that I decided to get into gardening.

Vegetable diversification

Along with my native grasses, I like home-grown tomatoes. I like ‘em so much that I thought I ought to grow a few of my own this year.

I was at the greenhouse this spring buying some tomato plants for the real gardener in the family, my mother, when I was struck by the idea of getting a tomato plant for myself.

I bought Mom the little plants that came in six-pack trays. I knew her thumb was green enough to make them prosper. For myself, I decided to get the super-duper, half-grown and ready-to-bloom model sold by the eaches not the sixes.

I think it cost something like $2.99 for that single plant. I dropped off Mom's little plants and brought my Big Boy back to my house.

I started my gardening off by leaving him on the porch for a couple weeks in the sun and the wind. He got watered occasionally and managed to live through the ordeal.

I finally decided to give ol' Tom the tomato some room to roam. I broke up a corner of the native range in the yard and prepared my garden site.

Looking at the fine yellow sand in my garden spot, I felt a pang of generosity and put a half a bag of potting soil down so Tom could spread his roots in a little richer environment.

I put a couple of pepper plants next to Tom to keep him company when I was gone. I should've put in an automatic sprinkler, too. But Tom waited patiently for the rain and my occasional water can.

The peppers didn't last long enough to keep the tomato company or steal any of his water, though. One day, my horses got a hankering for some Mexican grazing and clipped my jalapeños to the ground.

Now it's harvest time. Tom is working hard to beat the frost, and he's doing everything he can to support the three small vegetables, or fruits, on his vines.

My three little tomatoes look rough, scarred and thick-hided, but they're survivors. And that's a key trait for plants in my lawn and garden.

I have my knife, salt and pepper ready to go. When I figure in the jumbo starter plant, the half bag of potting soil and the decoy peppers, my little tomatoes will have cost me about $5 each.

I'm going to savor every bite.

Skunked

Expanding homestead security to striped invaders — Nov. 18, 2002

Some wild critters are cute. Some are plumb disgusting. Some could be cute, but they just can't get past their disgusting side.

A couple of weeks ago, I went out to the pump house in one of our pastures to fiddle with some valves, replace a piece of tubing and make sure the well wasn't freezing.

I opened up the little door, stuck my head inside, reached for the valve and heard a little scurrying right below my nose. I looked down and there were two little beady eyes looking back at me. It looked like a black and white kitty, except it wasn't a kitty.

I jerked my head out of there quicker than quick and somehow kept from knocking myself out on the door frame.

Luckily, my new skunk friend stayed calmer than I did and didn't do its thing and spray me down. I gave him some room, left the door open and decided to postpone my work.

When I came back, he'd vacated the premises. I sealed the door and decided to do my job another day when I had more time. A few days later, I was back again, I opened the door a little slower, and there he was. I was skunked again on my water work. Next time, I decided, I would not be run off by this smelly scoundrel.

The next time I went to the pump house, I was packing heat. Sometimes, I don't know why I own a 357 Magnum six-shooter. Then I'm threatened by something dangerous like a skunk in my pump house and I can justify the purchase.

I put my back against the wall and inched toward the door like a Chicago drug agent. I flung open the door, pivoted, leveled my piece and yelled, "Freeze, lowlife!" Lucky for the skunk, he was gone. Maybe he was tipped off by a mouse who spotted my approach.

Finally, I got inside and got my work done. While I was in there, I nailed some tin over the little hole that served as the skunk entry, making the shack safe for entry and smelling sweet.

Smelly tales

Ranch country is ripe with wild animal conflict. Wolves pulling down calves and ripping them apart for supper, coyotes killing lambs just for fun. Mountain lions jumping horses from tree limbs and peeling the meat from their bones.

These are the conflicts that make the papers. We don't get to read many stories about the common conflicts between ranch dogs and porcupines, garden-robbing raccoons, or the skunks that usually go head to head with the ranch wife.

Mom, the head of homestead security here on the ranch, has a zero tolerance policy with skunks. She doesn't like the way they smell and she doesn't want them spreading rabies on the ranch. Plus, it makes her mad to have skunks out robbing the nests of our local hard working bird mothers.

She thinks skunks are way more despicable than they are cute. I should have had her covering for me when I went to work in that pump house.

Yes, skunks are one of the prime reasons my peace-loving, old, gray-haired mother keeps a rifle behind the door.

And, take note, skunks of all kinds, she knows how to use it.

Bath time

A good dirty cleansing

Dec. 2, 2002

I remember when the cowboys in the old westerns would come into town after the big cattle drive and they'd treat themselves to a nice, hot bath to wash off a few layers of trail dust.

For years, I enjoyed a nice soak in the bathtub before we got modern and put a shower in my house. It's always a good idea to get a little of the ranch washed off of you before you head to bed.

If it's the wet season, there's usually some mud to be washed off, too. I found out in California, though, that there's also some mud to be washed in.

Mud to soothe

Last week, my fiancé and I were out in California visiting my brother and seeing the sights around San Francisco – the Golden Gate Bridge, cable cars, Chinatown, the redwood forests.

After all that, we decided to take a little drive up Napa Valley to tour the wine country. Coming from an area where it's a struggle just to get grass to grow most years, it's amazing to see land where they can grow grapes, olives, oranges, lemons or any other seed you happen to drop on the ground.

We threw out the anchor in Calistoga, Calif., and decided to call it a night. I was ready to hit the hay when I was told that Calistoga was famous for its hot mineral mud baths and that we were scheduled to go get one.

Now, I've been in mud and I've been in a bath, but I've never been in a mud bath. I always figured there needed to be some separation between the two – first get dirty in the mud, then a little later get clean in the bath.

And whenever I've gotten muddy before, I've never paid anyone for the privilege. Most times, I'm working in mud in the hope that it'll pay me. Not so in spa country.

Folks there have figured a way to get people to pay for the chance to sit in a tub of mud – a mix of clay, peat and hot mineral waters. The sales pitch says the mud bath relaxes muscles and joints, cleanses your body of toxins and impurities, and leaves the skin soft and renewed.

I reckoned none of that could hurt, so I gave it a shot.

Toxins be gone

The staff mentioned several times that we should "feel the toxins being slowly released from our bodies." I had a couple of bubbles make it to the surface in my mud bath, so I guess there were some toxins being released, but that's probably not what they were referring to.

I'm actually surprised that any of the locals would have any toxins to release. The stores and restaurants were chock full of organic this, natural that and free range the other thing. Maybe it was all the urban exhaust they were inhaling and the freeway traffic stress that needed releasing.

At any rate, I survived the mud bath and the herbal mineral hot tub and the hot blanket wrap and the Swedish massage and the steady stream of soothing ocean wave sounds coming from the speakers. Yes, life is tough for a traveling cowboy on the California range.

I'm plumb anxious now to start up my own mud bath spa next spring when the rains come and the corrals start to melt. I'll just have to figure out a way to market the extra ingredients like cow manure that spa goers will find in our mud baths.

Water worries

Water, water everywhere – but the faucet

April 7, 2003

I'm lucky to live in an area where finding water is pretty easy.

Water witches would die broke in my neighborhood. No one around here would pay money to have someone locate water when all they need to do is stick a pipe and a sandpoint in the ground 10 to 20 feet.

Water witchers' forked sticks and wires would be in a constant bend as they walked atop our abundant water-bearing sands. It's about as challenging as hunting buffalo in my neighbor's feedlot. It's pretty hard to miss.

Finding the water may be easier than a lot of places, but it's not completely effortless.

Across generations

Ranch plumbing and water well skills aren't born, they're passed on from father to son.

About every three years, Dad and I would end up replacing the plugged sandpoint that provided the water for my parents' house. The point was in the basement – a basement with a 6-foot ceiling and a couple of 6-foot 2-inch cowboy plumbers trying to pull 24 feet of pipe.

But, 4 feet at a time, we'd pull the old pipe, then screw on the new sandpoint and try to head her back down the hole before it filled in.

Soon, though, it was pounding time. Our point pounder was fashioned from a piece of 2-inch pipe and a section of tractor axle. It weighed about 30 pounds, but seemed like a ton.

For whatever reason, our basement sandpoint was the hardest pounding point on the whole ranch. And it plugged up a lot quicker than any other point on the place. We just put up with it. We had to. It's hard to move a basement.

About 10 feet of that pipe drove real hard. We'd only gain an inch for every 50 licks with the pounder. Slow going but fine bonding time for a father and son.

Satisfaction was ours when we hit water. We'd head upstairs to a hero's welcome as the water pressure returned and the ringing in our ears subsided.

EZH20

Somewhere along the line, I decided to have a few wells dug on the ranch and I traded in our plugged-up, hard-driving sandpoints for submersible pumps and underground pipe going from site to site. The water was still easy to find, the dug wells were just 40-foot deep and could put out all the water you'd want from their 4-inch casings.

All the water you want, that is, unless the underground pipe freezes when the frost sinks in the spring. That's what happened this spring when the running water for my house quit running, walking or even crawling.

It wasn't a terrible hindrance, though. Living down in the state capital for the legislative session, I was only home on weekends and I could haul water for my coffee for two days a week. Flushing the toilet took a couple more gallons hauled from the ranch. A fella flushes a lot less when you have to haul the water.

After a few weeks, I figured I better come up with another water source while I waited for the frost to leave. It was back to the pipe, point and pounder, and the skills my father taught me.

Before I'd even finished pounding the point, though, my water started running again. The mere threat of an alternative water source must have motivated my underground pipe to melt itself free. Now I'm back to taking long showers and flushing that toilet whenever I please.

But, considering the fact that there'll be a woman moving into my house soon, I should be a responsible newlywed husband and complete the project to have some back-up water in place. You know, so she can wash the dishes and mop the floor. Or is that so she can take a bubble bath while I wash the dishes and mop the floor?

Herding hypertext

Going global on the range April 21, 2003

Give a man a fish and he'll waste an hour. Teach a man to fish and he'll waste an entire lifetime. That's one version of the saying anyway.

Likewise, give a man a website and he'll waste a couple hours telling his friends where to find it. But teach a man to build and maintain his own website and he'll waste a lifetime fiddling around with it, uploading images and updating text. Same concept.

I've had an e-mail address ever since Al Gore invented the Internet, but I've never had my own website. I had a high-tech cowboy friend of mine from South Dakota put a little information about my book on his website, www.ranchers.net, but it was his information corral; he just let me use it to round up a few stray customers.

I couldn't understand why he took such an interest in having a website, but now I know because another friend of mine made the mistake of teaching me a little bit about creating my own home page.

In an instant, I was fully tangled up in a worldwide web.

Homepage on the range

My friend, Tom, is an Internet addict. Like most addicts, he likes to spread his addiction to others. That way he has someone to carpool with for Webaholics Anonymous meetings.

Like most bad habits, it started rather innocently. We sat down at my computer and he helped me register with a free web server. Then we copied his web page over to my newly assigned address.

He then began showing me how to customize it with my own words, pictures and links with something called HTML.

I always thought HTML stood for "hate mail," and, as a columnist, I never went out looking for hate mail. Fan mail, yes, but hate mail really bruises the ego.

It turns out that HTML actually stands for "hypertext markup language," and it's the set of codes, or tags, that puts the pictures, stories and annoying advertising messages up on your screen when you're surfing the web.

It all looked Greek to me, but I was comforted by the fact that my web-savvy buddy didn't understand the symbols either. So it's kind of like any other technology. Don't question it, just use it.

I was swimming around in a sea of "href", "<a>", " " and "<br>". I just looked for places where Tom had typed in something like "Tom" and I replaced it with "Ryan." Leave the "href" and "<br>" where they be.

Time waster

There was instant gratification. Change a word, upload a different photo, go to view the website, and there it was! It was like learning to read or write all over again.

I was as happy as a kid with a new toy on Christmas, and, in what seemed like a fraction of a minute, I looked up at the clock and realized two hours had gone by.

This might be a bad season to be picking up a new addiction. I need to be putting tags on my calves, not tagging codes in my HTML file.

But, you know, if I had one of those digital cameras, I could take pictures of all my calves and put them on my website. They wouldn't need eartags. Me and the whole wide world would recognize them from their pretty little mugs plastered on my website. And it would only occupy my whole year instead of a couple months during calving season.

Yes, it is a tangled web we weave. And I'm afraid I've tangled myself right up in it.

Go see "Seabiscuit"

A movie that's worth the trip and the ticket

Aug. 11, 2003

I don't often make blatant commercial endorsements in my column. That's more for radio personalities selling air beds and acoustic wave radios before they get to the rest of their story.

But this week, I'm crossing over to make an unsolicited, unpaid endorsement of the movie "Seabiscuit."

All I hope is that maybe I could get one of those movie review quote lines, like "Two thumbs up! Ebert and Roeper.", "Nothing can stop this story from putting a lump in your throat. David Ansen, Newsweek.", or "'Seabiscuit' is two hours of gloriously beautiful filmmaking. Joel Sigel, Good Morning America."

After this column, I hope to be able to go to the "Seabiscuit" website and see my review, "A movie that's actually worth the $7! Ryan Taylor, cheapskate rancher and author of Cowboy Logic."

My audience is those folks out on the farms and ranches who might make the 50 or 60-mile drive into the city to see a movie just once a year, so a lot is riding on that single evening of cinematic entertainment.

When these folks get burned and have to sit through a loser of a movie, they may swear off of theaters for three or four years. I'm here to tell them that "Seabiscuit" is a safe bet and a decent date for you and your haying partner.

The line up

When my bride and I were looking at the movie posters, it was an easy decision for me – only one of the posters had a horse on it.

When in doubt, go with a western or a horse movie. Another way to spot a good movie is to look for a good story. Anyone looking for a good story in "Seabiscuit" won't go home disappointed.

And nothing makes for a better story than a true story. As one of my reading friends says, "Fiction is the maggot of society." "Seabiscuit" is the kind of non-fiction that reassures us of the value of real-life stories.

So we passed over the contrived movie stories of bad boys, tomb raiders, extraordinary gentlemen and the wedding of previous "American Pie" movie characters, to watch a piece of history about a too-small horse, a too-big jockey, a too-old trainer and a too-dumb-to-know-any-better owner.

Of course, any movie of the big screen, fiction or non-fiction, good plot or bad plot, would have been better than the sad collection of brainless reality shows that we could have watched on television that night. Reality TV may qualify as non-fiction, but it's also non-entertaining.

Classic lines

The movie's producers would promote this as the movie's classic line, "You don't throw a whole life away just 'cause it's banged up a little." It's a good line, and it strikes the theme of the movie and its characters, but for the ranchers and horse folks out there, I preferred some of the horse trainer's words preceding that.

I'm paraphrasing, but he said something like, "every horse is good for something…he could be a cart horse, or a lead horse, or he might just be kind of nice to look at."

I don't know of anyone who likes horses who can't think of one they kept around the place just because it was kind of nice to look at. To me, that line alone was worth the $7.

It gave me the justification of knowing I wasn't the only one who felt that way.

Coffee with a cause

It's more than a caffeine in a cup

Jan. 26, 2004

Morning coffee has always been a ritual for me. A regular, somewhat ceremonial part of my mornings.

Get out of bed, rinse the pot of yesterday's coffee, fill the pot for the morning's brew and turn up the heat for perfect percolation. I'm still a blue-speckled enamel pot on the stove burner kind of guy – no filters, no glass carafes, no hissing and spitting machines.

I like my coffee strong. I don't want to see the bottom, or even the sides, of the cup when it's full of my black brew. It doesn't bother me if it's so thick a spoon can stand up straight in the middle of the cup.

Of course, my cup doesn't see many spoons. No cream or sugar for this cowboy. Our range cows are too hard to milk, and I prefer to get my sugar fix elsewhere.

I do need a spoon to get the coffee grounds out of the can and into the pot, though. I like an oversized tablespoon, and I take the definition of heaping to new, physically challenging heights.

My spoon resides in the red 3-pound coffee can when it's not in use. At least, the can used to weigh 3 pounds at one point in history, and it used to be a can.

The 3-pound can has only weighed 2 pounds 7 ounces for a long time now. Subsequently, our horses have seen a corresponding shortage in their morning oats. A coffee can's a coffee can when it's out in the barn.

And now, it's not even a can. It's more of a container now, and it's made of plastic. It doesn't look nearly as rugged. I'm not sure how it'll work in the shop for holding nails, pole barn spikes and fencing staples. Plus, the jury's still out on its adequacy in the barn's feed room.

Cool beans

With my traditional tin can gone, it was a good time to make a coffee change. When my wife brought home a little bag of coffee beans from a meeting of our congregation's church ladies, the change made sense.

It was more than changing from big cans of ground coffee to a little bag of beans. This was coffee with a conscience. It's called Equal Exchange coffee and it said it was committed to paying a fair price to the farmer, trading directly with democratic cooperatives, developing long-term partnerships and supporting sustainable, shade-grown farming practices.

It made me proud to be a mild-mannered Lutheran, knowing that our church ladies were selling and brewing fair trade coffee at our after-church fellowship. I could enjoy a cup of joe and know that small farmers in Latin America, Africa and Asia were getting a fair shake on the deal.

It maybe isn't the cheapest coffee on the store shelf, but, as a food producer myself, I like the idea of people being a little more concerned about the livelihood of the folks who grow their food than they are about the weight of their wallet.

The heck with falling prices. I'd like to know that my food, clothes, shoes, furniture and gadgets were made by someone making more than 33 cents an hour. I'd like it even better if my purchases helped my neighbors and helped build my neighborhood. And if that means higher prices, I guess I'll have to get by with less stuff.

So my new morning ritual is a little more ceremonial as I grind up a few coffee beans, smell the aroma and think about fellow farmers and fair prices.

Parking lot shootout

Masked bandit makes clean get away

April 5, 2004

It's been a tough year for next-to-new pickups in my neighborhood and a good year for body shop repairmen.

A few months ago, in our snowy season, I rammed my pickup into a snowdrift so hard and so far that, yes, I could see the other side.

But, it didn't matter. I was really stuck. Luckily, technology allows us to call our neighbor on the cell phone when we've done something that stupid.

My 23-year-old neighbor came with his nearly new, sticker-still-on-the-window pickup. He hooked his nylon rope up between the receiver hitch on the back of my pickup and the ball hitch on the back bumper of his.

He gave it a jerk. Nothing. Again. Nothing. He really started puttin' the throttle in the rugs and got a little movement. About the sixth time he yanked it hard, I looked in the rearview mirror and saw his entire rear bumper peel off the one end until it was in line with the tow rope.

It wasn't a good deal.

He had one of those real affordable insurance policies with a $1,000 deductible, so we were on our own in replacing his bumper. I figured it wasn't his fault that he came to help me out, so I threw in a few hundred dollars to get him a new rear bumper.

It was a pretty expensive pull, but at least my pickup didn't have to go to the body shop.

Until last week.

Armed conflict

I was sitting in my office late one night, when I saw something stirring around through my window.

I looked out, and there under the porch light was the biggest ring-tailed mask-faced kitty I'd ever seen with its head in the cat food dish. We were feeding the neighborhood raccoon on our front porch.

I had him caught red pawed. I loaded my 357 Magnum and got ready to throw open the door and give him a little western justice.

I came through the door and the coon fled. As he was scampering toward my pickup, I leveled my six-shooter and squeezed off a round before he escaped into the darkness.

I've never seen a raccoon move so fast. But after eating that high test 31 percent protein premium cat food, he was energized and ready to go.

I couldn't believe I missed him, but I hung up my hog leg and called it a night.

The next morning, I went outside to get in my pickup and found out I was missing a driver's-side window. I was more than a little disappointed. How could a pickup with such a tough receiver hitch have such a wimpy window?

I didn't believe I was such a bad shot that I hit my own pickup. I looked for an exit wound on the Dodge. Nothing. Not out the passenger window, not through the roof or the door or into the upholstery. It was a clean break, driver's side only.

The body shop man figured I must have hit a piece of gravel on the ground when I shot at the raccoon and the pebble flew up and hit the window. Try and do that twice.

I'm still not quite sure. I didn't notice the broken window after I shot and chased after the coon. I think he might have come back later in the night and done in my window for revenge.

I can just see the little bandit with his prehensile paws wrapped around a little crow bar as he walked by, munching a piece of cat food, and, CRACK!

If it was him, I hope we're even now. Those windows are expensive.

Fenceline learning

Beating the definition of insanity

May 31, 2004

Insanity, they say, is doing the same thing over and over again and expecting a different result.

I gave that some thought this week when I was out mending some fence and getting ready to turn cows out to pasture.

There're several places on the ranch where the winter snow drifts over the fence every year and breaks all the wires, leaving me with some spring fencing projects that you can set your clock, or at least your calendar, by.

So I'm out checking the fence and notice the fences flattened out by these hills and trees that catch the snow. Again. And I commence to splicing and stretching the wires. Again. And noticing all the prior year's spices. Again. And thinking to myself, again, maybe I won't have to do the same thing all over again next year.

It kind of made me wonder if I fit that definition of insanity.

I used to think fencing kept me sane. Some time alone out in the fresh air, sorting my thoughts and clearing my head. Pounding posts and digging holes to relieve any aggression. Stretching wire, taking the slack out, straightening the kinks. Splicing, mending, you know, feeling whole again.

Then I realize that I'm out there doing the same thing over and over again, expecting a different result.

I suppose the revelation should inspire me to start doing things differently. Instead of splicing those wires every year that break under the weight of the snow, I could install some kind of "fence zipper" that I could unzip in the fall before the snows blow and zip back up in the spring when the cows go out.

The next best option would be to put in some gates. Of course, a gate surrounded by trees, or on the side of a steep hill, with no trails leading to it or going away from it, might look a little odd. Kind of like the Winchester Mystery House in California with doors that open into walls and staircases that don't go anywhere. My neighbors would label me with their own definition of insane.

The idea of not doing the same thing over and over again brings a lot of examples to mind.

I suppose I shouldn't be patching old, bald tires over and over, expecting that they won't go flat again. I shouldn't be splicing 1940s-era barbed wire time after time and expecting it not to break with the next cow who sticks her head through and leans against it. I shouldn't be spraying leafy spurge the same way every year, thinking that it won't come back next year.

Some things I have changed. I figured out that I couldn't sell my calves or market my cull cows the same time year after year and expect a different market if it was the same time that everyone else was selling and marketing.

I got tired of calving cows out in North Dakota in March and expecting warm weather, or in April and expecting dry corrals. I'll try something new every year to try and get better conception rates on my first-calf heifers, knowing last year's methods will likely yield last year's results.

So maybe I will invent some kind of "fence zipper" to take care of my broken barbed wire problem. Or I could just alter my expectations.

I could alter my personality with built-in expectations for broken wires, flat tires and other failures. It might get me around that definition of insanity, allowing me to continue doing the same thing over and over again. I just won't expect a different result.

Nope, not insane, just hopeless. I think I'll go the other route and try some new things.

Steely resolve

Tell tale trailer hitches

Negative scrapes make for positive identification

Sept. 28, 1998

I was putting new license tabs on the plates of ol' Gray, the fearless Ford with more heart than horsepower, when I realized that there was getting to be less and less plate to tab onto these days.

The license plate on the front wasn't so bad, aside from the quarter inch build-up of bug guts. But years of solo "hit and hunt" hookups to my bumper hitch stock trailer had taken their toll on the rear plate.

It was downright difficult to find a piece of tin smooth enough to hold the adhesive on the renewal tab. You just can't glue that sticker down to the crumpled and crinkled parts of the plate and expect it to last a whole year.

Try, try again

You'd think after years of practice, my trailer hitching aim would be good enough to save the face of my plates. But, no, my success rate is still running about 1 in 10.

I have gotten better. I always hit the license plate and hardly ever hit the bumper. But close only counts in horseshoes and hand grenades, so I still spend a lot of time hunting, hitting, hopping out, eyeballing and try, trying again.

I've heard of people who put a mark on their tailgate and a flag on their hitch to mark the two spots that need to be lined up for one try success. That'd be the easy way, but it wouldn't be the cowboy way, as Ranger Doug of the Riders in the Sky would say.

That'd be like someone with a gooseneck trailer taking out the tailgate to reduce the chances of tailgate blight that seems to plague absent minded ranchers as they unhook and pull away from their trailers, tailgate up.

Positive identification

The nice thing about banged-up license plates and bent tailgates is that they provide some positive identification for ranch pickups in city parking lots. Not that there aren't plenty of other ways to identify 10- to 20-year-old vehicles with rusted out fenders, tree-bent antennae and bull-busted front grills.

But a cursory look at the back sides will quickly separate your ranch pickup from the less-abused rigs driven by bankers and urban businessmen.

First, check to see if the bumper has a ball hitch. In some cases, you might find two. Personally, I keep both a two and five-sixteenths for my trailer and a 2-inch right next to it for the trailers I borrow from my neighbors.

If it does have a ball hitch, check to see if the license plate is readable. If it is, that means it's been subject to nothing but super careful hookups to boat trailers and campers.

It's also a good idea to check the tailgate for dings and dents. Now if you find a pickup that looks remotely like yours, but it has a straight tailgate, a clean license plate and a hardly used ball hitch, check to see if the keys are in it.

If they are, I'd jump in and drive away, leaving my old jalopy for the banker. I'm sure they'd understand that it was an innocent mistake. And it'd be kind of fun to drive a nice pickup for a couple of days while the police are tracking you down.

To the finish

Last one haying is a flannel wearing freak

Sept. 14, 1998

Nobody likes to be last. Whether it's a foot race, a beauty contest or being picked for the softball team in grade school, we all kind of like to be somewhat close to the front of the pack.

It's the same with haying. Nobody wants to be the last one out on the meadow when the days start getting short and the enthusiasm starts running low.

Haying is kind of fun when you first start in June or July. The smell of the fresh-mown hay, the warm glow of the sun in a bright blue sky, the sight of the wildflowers on the knolls. That lasts about two days.

Then it gets be a grind. As the wire, tape and twine begins to wear, you find that the mower won't mow, the baler won't bale and the hay boss quits smelling the wildflowers.

It becomes a grudge match. "I'll cut this slough full of 3-year-old hay if it's the last thing I do," we vow as the moss and dead hay plug up the cutting bar every 10 feet or so.

Early finishers

Some ranchers don't get to experience the joy of haying on a crisp, fall day. With fields of tame hay and alfalfa, they wrap up their second cutting in August and call it a season.

If they live next to the road, they like to line up their recently retired haying machinery in the yard to remind the rest of us poor saps that they're finished and we're not.

If they really want to rub it in, they'll get an early start on moving their hay. They drive by in their hay-hauling trucks and tractors and wave at us laggers as we grease our mower on a cold, cloudy day.

The Taylor Ranch always seems to get in a little fall haying. Most of our hay is in native, subirrigated meadows and sloughs that aren't dry enough to even start haying until August. That generally means we're baling hay on into September without much of a thought.

Fall virtues

Fall haying does have its good points. You don't sweat as much since the sun is usually behind the clouds, and, although the bugs aren't gone, they are a little more sluggish and easier to swat.

The best thing about fall haying is that you don't have to put in those long, grueling days. The days are shorter and the dew stays longer in the morning and comes out earlier in the evening. You'll find yourself at home watching television a lot earlier than you did in July.

Hay quality in the fall may be the biggest negative gamble. Native meadows are still pretty green and produce decent hay, but if it freezes, that's another story. The debate over the feed quality of frozen hay was best explained to me by my father.

When I asked him if frozen hay was any good, he said, "It depends on whether you've got any. If you get all your hay up before the hard frost, you say, 'frozen hay ain't worth putting up,' but if you're late with your haying and you end up with a fair bit of frozen hay, you say, 'frozen hay's as good as the rest.'"

Just another one of those things on a ranch that depends on your perspective.

One piece at a time

Raising the standard of ranch machinery a little at a time

Nov. 2, 1998

This is sad news for my local parts dealers and it's likely to hit the American steel industry pretty hard, but I finally went ahead and upgraded the front end on my John Deere 4020.

I apologize for the economic tailspin that will likely occur among the spindle, knee and rim makers and marketers, but I couldn't continue to hold up their business with that old row crop front end on my loader tractor that did everything but row crops.

Pay as you go

When I bought that tractor, someone told me that I ought to be proactive and take the initiative to put a super heavy-duty John Deere 5020 front end under it.

I told the suggester that I was all for being proactive and I was plumb full of initiative, but how much would it cost me? About $1,000, he said.

I had no idea that being proactive would be so expensive. I took the low road of "pay as you go" tractor maintenance with no up-front investment.

It's now five years later and I have a collection of 4020 front-end failures stacked like cord wood in the corner of my shop. Three spindles, one knee, two rims and a few other assorted pieces and parts have been added to the ranch's horde of scrap iron. The replacement cost for that little pile? A little more than $1,000.

But this fall, the performance of my fatigued front end sunk below even my low expectations when the main casting cracked like a bad egg.

At first, I just shrugged it off and plugged in the welder. I preheated, I ground, I pinged, and I chipped as I carefully welded it with some $25-a-pound nickel welding rod. I was dang proud of the professional job I had done as I covered it for a strong, slow cool.

The weld lasted about five minutes. I finally caved in on my "pay as I go" pledge and went to the salvage yard for the much praised 5020 front end.

Piece by piece

I hated to spend the $1,000, but, with hard times upon us, we've gotta think about the quality of the auction sales we're going to have when we all go broke and quit.

You just about have to have a good loader tractor on the sale bill to bring buyers to your auction sale. For the sake of whoever's left to buy my equipment, the least I could do is have a well-maintained 4020 with a good, solid front end.

With a little help from the adapter kit provided by the salvage yard and a couple of neighbors, we got the new front end in place and bolted up. Hopefully, our hernias will mend quickly.

As I stepped back and looked at my new beefed-up tractor, I couldn't help but feel a little like Johnny Cash in his song, "One Piece at a Time," where he built a Cadillac with parts he snuck home from the factory in his lunch box.

I've already got my add-on jobber three-point hitch, and now I've got my add-on 5020 front end. Before long, I should have a pretty nice added on outfit – one piece at a time.

The next piece? Maybe a nice John Deere Sound-Guard cab off of a 4430 if I can force it to fit.

Momentum

May the force be with you

Nov. 30, 1998

Now that we've gotten our first 25 inches of snow, I find myself falling into some of my old snowbound habits.

My primary snow season habit is, of course, getting stuck as deep and as often as possible. Usually I can get out with the old "shift into drive, shift into reverse" rotation. A couple gallons of fuel and some severe abuse of the transmission will usually get me back on track.

Sometimes, though I need to pull out all the stops and get some real momentum going. That's when I really start to throw my weight around.

Rockin' on the ranch

I don't always notice the stupid subliminal things I do when I'm in a stressful situation, but the other day, I did notice one of my more fruitless subconscious efforts.

Rather than spend the time cleaning and piling the snow in the feedyard, I decided to do a little reckless free-wheeling and just drive through the drifts with a bale of hay in my raised grapple fork.

Before I knew what hit me, I was in a 3-foot snowdrift and quickly losing traction. The tractor started to lug and struggle to work its way out of the snow.

I had 90 horsepower of diesel, grease and rubber doing their best to get me out of a bad situation when my mind instructed my body to start rocking back and forth to give the outfit a little extra momentum.

I was giving it everything I had as I hung onto the steering wheel and threw my lanky rancher frame back and forth in rhythm with the struggling tractor. We finally got out of that drift and that's when I began to think of the physics of what I'd just caught myself doing.

My tractor and loader weigh about 11,000 pounds, not counting the pile of twine and the tools jammed into the corner of the cab.

I personally weigh about 170 pounds. However, when I'm decked out in my full winter armor of coveralls, overshoes, earlappers and gloves, I must tip the scales at about 220 pounds – a little more if I've got a pocket full of "extra bolts" from my last mechanical adventure.

Call me crazy, but I could of rocked till I dropped, and I doubt that a couple hundred pounds of me would have gotten 11,000 pounds of tractor out any sooner.

Automatic auto reaction

A couple days later, I was driving down a gravel road that seemed pretty clean. I figured the snow plow had been down it as I reached optimum Buick cruising speed.

About then, a snowbank appeared out of nowhere and I hit it doing snowbank-free speed. The bottom of the car caught on the drift, and although the car continued to head due east, the windshield and I alternated facing north, then south, then north, then south again.

I was cranking the wheel like my John Deere "A" with the speedy add-on roller knob. To complement my quick and fancy steering, I automatically threw my weight either right or left to help keep the car on the road.

Again, I'm not sure if a 170 pounds of cowboy did anything to right a few thousand pounds of car, but I don't suppose it hurt any.

Like the mouse said to the elephant after they got done crossing the bridge, "We sure shook the heck out of that, didn't we!"

Bargaining for bytes

Time to shop for a new micro chip to help track the cow chips

May 31, 1999

Sometimes replacement makes more sense than repair.

Like when a spindly old fence post breaks off. Rather than splice or splint it, we usually say the heck with it and pound in a steel replacement.

Or when the 1974 Ford Galaxy with the four bald tires loses its transmission, we'll go car shopping and pull the Galaxy into the auto graveyard rather than pour any repair money into it.

That's the line of thought I'm beginning to use with my recent computer breakdown. When the modem crashed, I tried another modem. When that didn't work, I realized my problem was a little bigger than I originally thought.

All this modem mechanizing was pretty high tech for a cowboy who used to think that modem was something you did to your hay fields in the summer.

The technical difficulties combined with the fact that the computer was ancient and obsolete – it's 3 years old – prompted me to hit the computer trail in search of a replacement.

Devaluation

I thought about offering my old machine as a trade-in to help cheapen the deal. With a little research, I learned that there wasn't such a thing as a trade-in in the computer trade. Most old computers are just graduated to the task of boat anchor or doorstop.

That didn't hurt my feelings much since very few of my machines cut it as a trade-in. I have a knack for milking every last ounce of utility from the things I own.

There's a line of old cars, a pasture full of old tractors and implements and a few cow skeletons to prove my point. I guess I'll just toss my computer out there, too.

I'm surprised that the depressed farm economy hasn't supported the price of used computers like it has the price of used tractors.

Since no one can afford new equipment, the price of used equipment has stayed pretty steady. My 1969 model 4020 is worth as much today as it was when I bought it six years and 4,000 hours ago. But I'm sure a few more years and a few thousand more hours will cure my appreciation of old assets.

I'm always more comfortable around things that I know will depreciate every day. I guess that's why I get along with computers.

Hardware haggling

One thing I do like about computers is that as they've gotten better and faster, they've gotten cheaper.

The best computer available today costs the same amount that my old kerosene-operated model cost eight years ago.

If we could make that work in the car business, a $32,000 pickup with all the newest advancements could be bought for the same money as a 1969 half-ton whose highest technology was triangular vent windows.

When I went to the computer store, I got a rundown of features that would rival the best car salesman out there who could rattle off about the tinted windows, cruise control and auto everything on each model.

His monologue on the megahertz, gigabytes and kilobytes per second ran off his tongue like a cutting horse man quoting you the bloodlines on his new best filly.

When he paused to take a breath, I saw my opportunity to run out of there and postpone the work of haggling over my next obsolete computer.

I heard there's another way to buy computers, though. You can get them through an online auction, like buying a cow at the sale barn.

Now, if I just had a computer to get online with so I could buy a computer on the online auction.

Hay squeezers

Traditional low-tech forage testers July 26, 1999

I put up my first 50 bales of haylage last week. Didn't even use the preserving wrap or plastic bags, just rolled 'em up, tied 'em and watched the water squeeze out and drip down the sides.

I generally like to make hay, not haylage, but the summer of 1999 hasn't been real long on sunshiney haymaking weather, so I just make what I can.

My baling last week didn't show the greatest of judgment, but I just couldn't stand another day of looking at that hay that had been down for a week.

The baling was tough. You could hear the tractor power down and groan as the baler sucked up the green, juicy grass. At one point, the PTO shaft on the baler just plain quit turning and the tractor began spinning around. Pretty hard on the cab.

I guess I shouldn't have ignored my pre-baling hay readiness tests.

To bale or not to bale

I've heard of hard-core hay guys with expensive electronic gadgets that produce a digital readout of hay's moisture content. They calibrate their machine, select some hay, peer at some digital numbers and gauge the keepability of their forage.

My background and methods are a little less sophisticated. No battery-powered hoodoos or statistically super-accurate calculations of moisture content within a tenth of a tenth. Nope, just two hands, a full set of teeth and a keen sense of touch, smell and taste.

Me and the hayers I hang out with test our forage by grabbing a handful, twisting it, squeezing it and, finally, chewing on it.

I was first exposed to those tactics when I was a 10-year-old scatter raker and working with my dad on "one more stack" in the wee hours of evening.

I remember he stepped down from the John Deere 60, grabbed some green looking hay and walked over to where I sat on my trusty Model B pulling the Rowse dump rake.

"We better make one more stack. This'll be good horse hay this winter," he said. "They'll chomp it right up. Yum, yum, yum," he told me as he started eating that hay like a horse at the manger.

At the time, I thought he was just trying to entertain a sleepy-eyed scatter raker and motivate a 10-year-old who just might stay on the tractor a while longer if it meant winter feed for his horse.

I now realize that he was just testing that hay as the evening dew came out, making sure that slightly green horse hay would keep in the stack and not turn moldy black.

Grasping grass

Taking his lead, I've been twisting and chomping ever since. I take a bunch of brome or bluestem, squeeze it and declare, "it's a little raggy, but I think it'll bale." Raggy is a rancher term used when juice squeezes out of the hay like water from a wet dish rag.

On the other end of the spectrum, I'll grab some sun-burnt yellow hay, toss a few of the sticks in my mouth, and if it shatters in my mouth like a dry soda cracker, I declare it just right. "Just right" means there's nothing you can do to get the moisture back anyway so you just as well think positive and see if you can still make a bale without turning it all to dust.

You just can't beat a little human objectivity when it comes to staying on schedule.

Remotely amusing

The ultimate in fingertip convenience

Aug. 16, 1999

The human thirst for convenience has reached a new high in lows.

Flipping through a car stereo catalog the other day, I was shocked to discover that the majority of the car radios came with remote controls! That's right, a remote for that radio located way off in the middle of the dash.

As the copy in the catalog read, "Add a credit card-style remote control for more convenience." How much more convenient can you get than an arm's reach away? Probably the most convenient part of the credit card-style remote, in the mind of the stereo sellers, was the credit card-style charge of an extra $24.95 for the option.

Techno upgrades

Car radios have come a long way, even in my short span of history.

My first major upgrade in the world of automobile audio was the addition of a genuine "FM Converter" from the J.C. Whitney catalog.

I was getting the family's yellow 1972 Chevrolet Impala ready for my 1986 prom date and I thought it'd be nice to have the FM band to increase the selection of radio stations at my remote-controlless fingertips.

The Impala had a pretty good AM radio with the standard push-button presets that could quickly take you to the news, static, the ag markets, static, the swap shop tradio show or more static.

I was pretty happy with the AM options of useful information, but I thought my date might enjoy some musical interludes. Thus, the FM converter, that, once wired in to the antenna and power of the AM unit, would be capable of blasting the latest in country, rock and easy listening sounds.

Music, of course, was an important element in the days of prom dates. Any voids not filled in with melodies would be dependent upon sparkling conversation, a tall order for young cowboys who weren't too sure of proper topics for discussion.

Prom time fell close to calving time, and I was unsure if I should discuss stories of calving woe with my date or just stick to small talk about the weather and the markets. The easiest option was to just reach over and tune in my newly mounted J.C. Whitney FM converter for some trendy tunes.

Remote reasoning

Who'd have thought that 13 short years later I could have gone to the prom with a radio that had AM, FM, cassette, compact disc and remote control.

I shouldn't discount the value of a remote control car radio, though. I did talk to a few fellas in the days following the prom who could have used such a convenience since they claimed to have spent a lot of time in the back seat with their dates on prom night.

In general, though, I think society could probably put up with having to reach the buttons and knobs clear in the middle of the console without resorting to a handheld remote. But folks do love their gadgets, and practicality doesn't often come into play.

Television remotes have become so commonplace that most of us shudder when we think of the days when we had to walk all the way to the TV to change the channel.

It reminds me of the lady I saw in the exercise room of a motel who was walking on a treadmill machine while watching the TV. When it came time to change the channel, she had her handy-dandy remote right at hand on the dash of the treadmill.

When you're busy walking for exercise, you'd sure hate to have to walk all the way over to a television to flip the channel.

Operation Meadow Storm

Building that bridge to the 21st century (hay supply) Aug. 23, 1999

Looks like we're going to close out the 20th century on a pretty soggy note.

I'm not sure how this century began for moisture, but we can head into the next one with a fully charged water table in my little piece of the world.

Unfortunately, I'll be heading into that same century with about half a hay crop thanks to the rains and the water it left over the majority of our lowland hay meadows.

Our hayland is what we usually call "sub-irrigated." This year, it'd be safe to call it "substantially flood irrigated."

I rode the horse across most of it last week. It gave me a real sinking feeling. Appropriate, since the horse was literally sinking up to his hocks in mud and water. I could just about imagine the depth I could achieve with the tractors and haying implements.

Creative panic

We've been waiting all summer for the meadow to dry up. Now that it's the end of August, I'm beginning to get a little concerned. We have about a fourth of the hay up that we need for the upcoming winter, so it's time to start getting creative on how to scratch up the other three-fourths that we need.

One of my first thoughts was to continually not hay and wait for the first hard freeze. With a good hard ice surface, we could run the sickle bars across the top and sheer off the grass left sticking through the ice.

Plus, the frozen water should make the meadow smoother than its ever been before. Like the smooth appearance of Jell-O that's actually loaded with rough chunks of pineapple, the water could turn a maze of 3-foot-deep, bone-jarring hogwallows into a slab of ice smooth enough for training Olympic speed skaters.

Hay quality might be a little marginal by the time it freezes over, but my desire to put up top-quality forages has gotten pretty marginal lately as well.

Military might

My other option is to quit messing around and start haying military-style. I'd even coin the remainder of my hay season Operation Meadow Storm.

In the movies, a little swamp or river wouldn't stop an advancing army. The commander would have his troops in the muck building bridges or he'd radio HQ and bring in some air transport.

There are a few high knobs on the meadow that could be hayed if we could just get to them.

Of course, I don't quite have the bridge building resources that you find in the military – oodles of troop labor and the financial backing of the federal budget. But I could take advantage of the one military tool available to common citizens – army surplus.

I haven't seen any inflatable bridges in the canvas tent and cookware section of the army surplus catalogs, but maybe I could go beyond the catalogs and locate a good surplus helicopter to aid in my island hay-hopping tactics of Operation Meadow Storm.

A good chopper could carry in the necessary tractors, mowers and rakes, and at midday, it could air drop vital lunch supplies. After a successful campaign, it would be great for the emergency evacuation of the hay bales before the attack of winter.

The benefits sound so good, I'd be willing to spend as much on a haying helicopter as I did on my ol' yeller baler.

I just wonder what kind of helicopter you can get for $3,000.

Beg and borrow

Help is only a farmstead away

Nov. 1, 1999

It never fails. Line up some work on a tight schedule and something is bound to break, bend or explode to keep you from getting the job done in the time you set aside.

If the job involves an outside contractor, like a semi-truck driver, the odds of things falling apart run even higher.

Line up a semi to haul some hay, and something is bound to go haywire.

Long haul

After our hay meadows turned to mud this summer, I began looking for some hay to buy. I found some about 35 miles away. However, I should have started looking for a hay hauler about a year ago to get locked in and scheduled for getting the forage from point "A" to point "B" before the points turn snowy, slippery and plumb miserable.

Truckers are a pretty sought-after group this fall, what with a fair bit of hay moving around the countryside and the onset of cattle hauling from ranch to market or feedyard.

When I got a phone call Friday night from a trucker who said he could haul a couple loads of hay for me on Saturday afternoon, I said, "count me in, I'll make it work."

"Making it work" meant finding a tractor to load the truck with and someone to run that tractor. We got the hay owner's tractor, but it was eight miles away and he was tied up with a dozen other pressing tasks.

I volunteered to drive the tractor over and load the bales. Good plan, but I should have known better than to get behind the wheel of someone else's loader tractor. It's an unwritten rule that anything you borrow usually breaks in two.

Borrowed luck

I started gathering bales while I waited for the truck to show up. That went pretty good for about a half an hour, then the hydraulic pump blew a seal and gave up the ghost.

Now, I had a situation – a truck was about to show up and was probably going to get $100 from me whether I sent him home with 40 bales or not. I wasn't completely soured on borrowed equipment, so I walked a half mile to a neighbor.

I found a farmwife and her son at home. I explained my situation and the son disappeared for awhile and then wheeled up to the door with a little International and a Dual loader. This was no time for me to be a hard-core John Deere man,

I gratefully climbed aboard the rig and went to meet my semi.

When the truck arrived, I began to load it very, very carefully. I didn't want to be responsible for breaking two other people's tractors in one day.

I actually got to be pretty handy with the old I.H. Since the tractor was similar to a lot of mine – more than 40 years old and well used – I felt right at home. My left leg soon got used to dislocating itself from its socket to fully depress the clutch and I soon perfected the move between third gear and reverse.

The Dual loader had a vertical reach of about 10 feet, which was fine, because the top row of bales only required 9 feet 11 1/2 inches.

I held my breath until I got the 40th bale perched atop the truck. I patted my new friend, ol' Red, on the hood and wheeled her back in the farmyard.

I think the next time a semi gets freed up for an afternoon, I'll say the heck with any big loader tractors. I'll just see if I can lease ol' Red for a few more hours.

Thar she blows

Casualties on the wind-driven prairie

Nov. 15, 1999

It's been pretty calm around the ranch lately, but the skin on my face is still drawn tight and blown back to my ears from the 70-mile-an-hour gusts we had a couple of weeks ago.

My face isn't the only thing trying to spring back into shape after the dry, horizontal hurricane we had for a couple of days. I'm still taking inventory on what's missing, tipped over or caught in a fence a half mile to the southeast.

Timbeeeerrrrr!

Most of the prairie is pretty devoid of trees, a fact most forest addicts note as they drive across the barren plains. Personally, I think we would have a few more trees in North Dakota if the dang wind would just lay off and leave us alone.

A couple days of a steady 40-mile-an-hour breeze with gusts twice as strong laid down quite a bit of the ranch's arboretum. I wasn't too bothered by the felling of the deadfalls in the pasture's poplar thickets. They're just the weeds of the tree family in our area.

But when the wind started picking on my cottonwoods, I got a little upset. The wind's worst work, though, was in a little spot we call "Elm Pocket." Elms are the king of the trees in North Dakota, and a nice stand of the old statesmen made their home in an old, healed-up sand blowout in one of our pastures.

Growing up, I always considered Elm Pocket to be one of the prettiest places on the ranch. Lush green grass in the middle and ringed by tall, shady elms and a ridge of sand on the perimeter, I thought it would be a good place for my future homestead.

Luckily, I never built my claim shack there. Dutch Elm disease moved in and killed most of my stately old shade trees. Then a couple of weeks ago, that wind tore them down and left them in a jumbled pile of sticks and splinters.

Steely downfall

The wind knew no mercy. It didn't even spare one of the prairies' most beloved symbols, the antique threshing machine. Or, as cowboy poet Rodney Nelson calls them, our "dragons of the prairie."

The threshing machine on our side of town didn't even have a hill to rest on. It just sat near a corner of our gravel road.

There used to be a farmstead on that corner with some trees and old buildings, but they got bulldozed and burned to reclaim a couple acres of land capable of raising a few more bales of hay or some more $2.80 wheat. The old steel thresher couldn't be burned, so it survived and sat on the corner as the old farm's sole survivor.

It was a good landmark for people coming to the ranch for the first time. "Go six miles south of the old threshing machine," we'd tell them. We didn't have a yellow road sign saying "corner here," so we put some reflective tape on the side of the threshing machine to warn nighttime travelers of the upcoming hard right turn.

On Nov. 1, however, our faithful friend got shot down by an evil wind.

The sight of her laying there with her iron wheels in the air was a sad one. So sad that I might even go up there and see if I can tip her back up. And, just in case, I might brace her up a bit for the next big wind.

No worn-out bargains

Year-end tractor shopping proves fruitless

Jan. 3, 2000

Between improved cattle prices, "Cowboy Logic" book sales and the fact that I spend more time working off the ranch than I do on the ranch, something really, really odd has happened.

Yes, it looks like I'll be contributing to the income tax coffers this year. It's going to be tough to live that down, and I'd like to start by apologizing to everybody for my modest financial success this year.

Prairie folks have a tough time dealing with prosperity, and I'm no different. But, after years of tax refunds, negative taxable income and "no tax due," it's probably about time that I kick in a little.

However, now I'm in a real pickle. With agricultural allowances for "expensing" a certain amount of depreciable assets and lowering taxable income, I'm pondering a couple of year-end purchases.

The decision now is whether to borrow money from the bank to pay income tax or borrow money from the bank to, say, buy a tractor and pay income tax, but a little less of it.

Borrowing is still a key point because I made the foolish mistake of using this year's extra income to pay off past debts, leaving me cash poor, a situation I've grown comfortably used to.

Cruising the lots

So I've been spending the last couple of weeks looking through the ads and driving the long green, red and blue lines of the tractor dealerships.

Like a coyote too poor or too lazy to kill the healthy or the newborn, I circle the herds of tractors looking for the old, the decrepit or the nearly dead. Both the coyote and I are hungry for the easy, and inexpensive, kill.

We'd like to swoop in on a fat, young ewe, but we just lack the energy, and the cash, so we wait and we look for something older, more diseased and tougher to chew.

It's been a pretty disappointing experience. I've driven enough lots to safely say that there are not a lot of old, affordable "cull tractors" sitting around with price tags that are within reach of the coyote rancher/shopper.

There are, however, more late model, new and exorbitantly expensive tractors out there than you can shake a stick at. The lots are full of these worthless pieces of modern engineering.

For every $8,000 tractor you might locate, there were 80 of those dang $80,000 units with power this, super that, and, most importantly, mega financing options. I wasn't even in the $8,000 market. I was leaning more toward something in that $5,000 range, but I could of just as well been on the hunt for Frosty the Snowman in the devil's back yard.

It looks like time might be running out for me to find my half wore-out, but fully depreciated, dream machine with 80 percent tread and dual hydraulics, a three-point hitch, and a four-digit price tag.

I guess it really doesn't matter anyway. If time truly does roll back to the year 1900 at midnight on New Year's Eve, I won't need a tractor anyway. Income tax management will be the least of our worries if we can't even a plug a tractor in to get it started on a cold morning.

I better spend my remaining hours oiling up the horse harness and getting the ponies ready to pull the hay rack and bobsled for the chores on New Year's Day!

Irregular maintenance

Every 10 years or 150,000 miles

June 5, 2000

I had Ol' Gray, the half-ton hauler with more heart than horsepower, in the big city of Bismarck last week.

I decided to celebrate her trip to the big city with a bath and a trip to the doctor. Like old bachelor ranchers going to the clinic for a checkup, I thought it would be best for Ol' Gray to get the outermost layers of grime scoured off before we went in to the shop for an examination.

I bought her two brand-new tanks of gas, front and rear, to get a $1 discount on a car wash. The two tanks of gas, however, run me about $100.

We entered the wash. I could see on the faces of the attendants that they were surprised anyone would want to wash a pickup with so little paint left on it.

They power blasted the remaining paint off the fenders and buffed the rust on the cab. Ol' Gray was idling in neutral and going through the paces of wash, scrub, wax and rinse. Then it was just in neutral, and the idling was a memory.

The guys who were hired to do the hand drying, got the bonus job of hand pushing Ol' Gray out of the wash and out of the way.

But before long, I got the distributor dried off and the wet engine was ready to motor me across the street for an oil change.

Lubing up

Ol' Gray just had fresh oil 10,000 miles ago, but I felt like shootin' the moon on some premium auto care.

I usually change my own oil, but I believe in letting some new eyes look things over once in a while. Plus, the quick change artists do things I never do, like grease the zerks, vacuum the floorboards and top off the windshield washer fluid.

So I sat in the waiting room, drinking coffee and reading the paper while the crew performed their 10 minutes of maintenance magic.

It reminded me of a doctor's office. Several people sitting in cushioned chairs, a nice selection of magazines and certificates framed on the wall that detailed the qualifications of the staff.

And, just like a doctor's office, someone would come in to counsel the family members on the disheartening test results of the patient in the next room. I watched as the other people in the waiting room got detailed on the things ailing their cars.

Then it was my turn. "Mr. Taylor, I'm afraid we've got some bad news." He was carrying a list as long as my arm of the things needing immediate attention to keep Ol' Gray from slipping into the grave.

He was carrying something black and charred looking that resembled an air filter. He talked about dirty oil in the transmission and differentials, burnt-out tail lamps, ragged windshield wipers and a little filter the size of my finger that hadn't seen human hands since 1986.

Most of the items on the list were supposed to be performed every 15,000 miles. I must have misread the maintenance schedule because I'd been waiting until the odometer read 150,000 miles to get them done.

"Is there any hope?" I asked. "Do you think she's gonna make it?" They weren't sure, but they thought that if I gave them my credit card they could pull her through.

So I passed them the plastic. It was the least I could do to make her last years the best possible. Besides, patients and pickups hate to waste a trip to town and a fresh bath.

Eye of the beholder

Prairie trash, working prairie memories

Aug. 14, 2000

Like sophisticated art appreciation, not everyone "gets it" when it comes to old tin structures out on the prairie.

Personally, I like to keep a few relics and pieces of our homestead heritage scattered across the pastures.

Our heifer pasture has an old car body in it that's been grown over with poplar trees since it was parked there more than 70 years ago. The car was a Willys Knight, and it served as a sheepherding camp for an old homesteader.

I remember when Dad asked me if I wanted to go see the body of Willys Knight in that thicket of trees. My eyes got wide as I imagined us finding the skull and skeleton of some unlucky rancher. I was half relieved, half disappointed when we walked up to the old steel shell manufactured by the Willys car company.

Another quarter of our land has a whole array of neat stuff from the family that built their homestead on that piece of infertile soil. An old cookstove, the remnants of a clapboard shack, the bones of a Model T Ford and a fifth wheel trailer, remind me of that homestead's history.

Another corner of the pasture serves as the final resting spot for an overshot hay stacker, and the far end sports a 10-foot-wide blue and white mobile home that served as the gathering point for a group of teenaged boys growing up in the not-so-distant past.

Pastures are meant to grow grass, but a few pieces of tin and steel tell us that they also grow their fair share of memories.

Clean it up

The most majestic tin, though, is the classic four-legged windmill straddled atop a thirsty well cylinder.

The Aermotors of Chicago brought clean water, and life, to many a prairie pasture. They separated ranchers into those who were and were not afraid of heights as they climbed their way to the top with a crescent wrench and a jug of oil to feed its gears. And they gave cows a place to hang out on a hot July day.

Last winter, windmills gave the North Dakota State Land Department a reason to write to my family about "abandoned water well sealing and trash cleanup on school trust land."

The two school quarters we've rented and grazed for years were given an inspection that revealed "abandoned" water wells and windmills. They even sent us a couple of nice color photographs that may or "may not show all of the trash on the tract."

I know the wording was of the form letter type and wasn't meant to hurt my feelings, but I was a little taken aback by anyone referring to my favorite pieces of pasture decor as trash.

I just recently called the fella who'd signed the letter and assured him that the one windmill and well was not abandoned, but merely resting until the next drought dried up the water hole that the cows were drinking from.

The other windmill was more retired than abandoned, but if I had to, I could get it moved off. He thought that I should at least pick up the fans that had fallen to the ground for fear that a cow might cut herself up.

I assured him that our cows were tin savvy, having been born in a "Sanford & Son" junk yard calving pasture, but, all the same, I would get those fans picked up.

I reckon when his requests are satisfied, the state's rented pasture will look a little tidier. But I'm glad we own the rest of the land that we graze on because I like the silent stories told by the tin that less appreciative people consider trash.

Luck of the draw

Everybody thinks they can be a winner

Aug. 28, 2000

I'm a signer upper. Give me a pen, a slip of paper, a cardboard box and a chance at anything worth more than $2, and I'm signin' up.

A couple of weeks ago at the Dairy Queen, I was lured in again by the elusive jar full of paper slips with the picture of a Corvette pasted across the front. I gave away my vitals – name, address, phone number – for a chance at a chance at the hot rod.

I had a good feeling about my odds as I walked out of the DQ with my M&M Blizzard. Sure enough, I had a message on my machine a few days later telling me I was qualified for the great Corvette giveaway.

They told me to tune in to KBTO for the details and to plan on being in Bottineau, N.D., on Aug. 19 because – here came the catch – you had to be present to win.

I tuned in and I drove up.

Short go

I was feeling pretty special about getting drawn for another chance to be drawn. It turned out that there were about 1,500 special people just like myself.

Well, not quite just like myself. When I got to Bottineau, I stood in a long, long line behind a biker decked out in Harley Davidson leather, an elderly lady with a four-footed cane and a businessman in a white shirt and pleated pants.

Our common thread was a hopeless faith in our ability to win the big prize. The big prize was parked in the street beside us. The white Corvette wasn't new by any means. It was what the radio people called a "classic."

Classic meant it was nearly 20 years old. It was a 1981, and it had probably seen 100,000 classic miles. I thought the tread on the tires looked a little thin, but one doesn't look a gift horse in the mouth.

I wasn't about to mouth this gift horse anyway because I was pretty sure this one's teeth were worn to a nub. Besides, I was going to win this pony free and clear. Who cared about the details.

After standing in line for an hour, I got to reregister for the chance at the chance. Another slip of paper in another big rolling basket. A 1 in 15 chance at being one of the 101 people drawn to maybe get the Corvette.

The tension was thick as they called out the names, one at a time. I stood with as unlucky a group as you could imagine – a county agent, a brand inspector and a couple of ranchers. We were all thinking of what we could trade the $7,000 classic Corvette for – a used up hay baler, a new field pickup, maybe a blue roan ranch gelding. But our karma was bad, and none of us had to file up for a chance at our dreams.

Needless to say, I didn't win the 19-year-old car with the slight sputtering noise in the motor. But a small North Dakota town did get me to drive up for a Saturday afternoon to do some shopping. It was a clever way to boost the local economy.

The example sat well with me. That's why I'm going to pitch the idea to my hometown commercial club. Heck, I'd even donate the classic 1974 Ford Galaxie to bring in my fellow shopping signer-uppers.

Progressive regression

New tractor bargains on the ranch

May 21, 2001

Right in the midst of a fuel crisis, I went and doubled the amount of green diesel horsepower here on the ranch. Yes, I now have not just one, but two 4020 John Deere's to lead our operation into the 21st century.

I stayed with my machinery-shopping theory of "sticking with something you already know how to change the oil on" when I went to a neighbor's machinery auction a few weeks ago.

Sure, there was an orange and tan tractor there that went for a reasonable price. Not so reasonable that I was willing to retrain myself on how to fix and maintain all the things that I've already learned how to fix and maintain on the green one, though.

And the green one I ended up buying was a real bargain compared to what I'd seen advertised on the machine lots. Of course, this one had some extenuating features that helped cheapen it up a bit.

Start 'er up

I knew the bidding would be a little less competitive when the owner stepped into the cab of the 4020 and when the auctioneer said, "start 'er up," he turned the switch and nothing happened.

I smiled just like I do when a good bull comes into the sales ring, charges the crowd, puts the ring man on the run and blows snot at the breed association rep. Even a high-performing bull's going to bring a few hundred less with that attitude.

Of course, buying the bulls that clear the ring and bidding on the tractors that don't start can get you a corral full of man-eatin' calves and a pasture full of dead iron. But at least you didn't have to pay full price for them.

When that 4020 played dead after hitting the switch, I wondered what the comeback would be for the seller and auctioneer. Quick as a lick, the seller whipped out his plier and jumped an arc to the starter the old-fashioned way. The auctioneer never missed a beat and declared, "Let's sell 'er, and the plier goes with the it!"

Now I knew that whatever I might end up paying, I'd have that $6 bonus starting plier to help justify the cost.

Even with the plier, the day was frosty enough to make the ol' diesel not want to fire off. It was back to the toolbox for a can of ether. This tractor was starting to suit me more and more every minute. Plus, the more it suited me, the less it suited some of the less-courageous bidders who weren't real comfortable with pliers and starting fluid.

Sold!

It wasn't long before I got that victorious-but-sick-to-the-stomach feeling that I was the last one bidding. The auctioneer begged for someone to get me off the hook, but that green piece of steel was mine. Pliers, ether and enough fuel to get it at least a mile down the road.

Actually, the price seemed pretty good. I couldn't quite figure it out. Then I did the math. My new tractor was 37 years old. Older than my oldest field pickup, and older than the oldest horse that ever died on the ranch. No wonder bidders started dropping out.

I used to think Dad's 1952 model A John Deere was old when I was mowing hay with it back in 1982. Heck, that was a mere 30 years old. Like father like son.

I'd have never guessed back then that our speed of technological advance could gain even more backwards momentum.

Man and machine

Admiring the sights of the season

July 30, 2001

When it comes to driving around the Great Plains, I like August.

No, it's not the sight of a deep blue thunderstorm or the image of golden grain ripening in the sun that pleases my eye, it's the sight of man and machine at work in the fields.

Granted, Mother Nature is pulling some spectacular stunts when it pours rain and lightening from the sky or when she puts together the right mix of sun, soil and moisture to make things grow, but have you ever watched a farmer in the hay field try to coax out a square bale that's properly compressed and tied? That's a remarkable feat.

The untrained tourist will say there's not much to look at when they're driving across the prairie on their summer vacation. They must be blind to all the activity in the fields they're speeding past.

Speaking of tourists, a friend of mine sent me an e-mail titled, "Rules when visiting North Dakota." It had some punchy little tips for the urbane visitor like, "You bring Coke into my house, it better be brown, wet, and served over ice." A few of the rules helped explain our culture like, "We all started hunting and fishing when we were nine years old. Yeah, we saw Bambi. We got over it."

The one I really liked though, was, "So you have a sixty-thousand dollar car. We're real impressed. We have quarter of a million dollar combines that we use two weeks a year."

Just like the BMW or the Jaguar car in the city, the combine is a symbol of wealth in farm country. Wealth is an interesting concept. The Native

Americans measured their wealth in horses, the Spanish ranchers of Mexico measured their wealth in cattle, and, for some reason, the European immigrant farmers of the Midwest decided to measure their wealth in large collections of green- and red-painted steel.

August is one of those times of the year when they can show off those collections. For those of us who'll never own a pile of steel and rubber worth that much money, it's fun to admire them from the road.

Real admiration

As impressive as the high-tech machinery is, my real admiration goes to the guys along the road who're still slugging out the haying and the harvesting with machinery stuck somewhere between "overvalued collectibles" and "overpriced modern."

They may not be the symbol of modern wealth and success, but they dang sure have the corner on personal determination as they tweak their junk to get the job done.

A local implement dealer recently demo'd a new mowing machine in my neighborhood. A self-propelled, disc-cutting, windrowing beauty, it was as high in price as it was horsepower. A mere $85,000.

Sure the seat was comfortable, but I had to remind the salesman that I was currently cutting hay with a sickle bar mower that still had wooden parts! How do you convince a man to drop $85,000 on a machine when he still goes to town to buy hickory pitman sticks for his Kosch mower?

So if you're behind me while I'm driving down the road this month, keep an eye on my brake lights to make sure you don't rear end me. I may just drive by the $200,000 combines, but I'll be slowing way down to admire and wave at the guy baling hay with a 930 Case and a Vermeer 605 C.

Every 42 years

Remembering that new smell

Jan. 14, 2002

I've always been proud of my stubborn rancher aversion to newly painted steel and cutting-edge automotive technology, so what I'm about to say is really difficult.

I bought a new pickup.

I know. I know. A lot of faithful readers are going to be sorely disappointed in my falling off the wagon. I've fully fallen off of the junk wagon that gave me hit-home stories about ol' Brownie, the wonder Chrysler, and ol' Gray, the half-ton with more heart than horsepower. But we'll always have those fond memories of junkers gone by.

I might have bought a new pickup, but at least I didn't pay cash for it. So

I still have a little rancher pride in the deal.

The car manufacturers were singing my song when they announced zero percent interest on their vehicles before the end of the year. Ranchers have never minded borrowing money, and if you can borrow it for nothing, all the better.

So as long as a guy could get zero financing, I went for the three-quarter ton. I'd had enough fights with the half ton pulling an overloaded trailer with sides bulging and mud flaps dragging.

And I went for the diesel. No more five-mile to the gallon trips to the gas station. Just as well get the extended cab, too. That way, when I start throwing stuff behind the seat, there'll actually be a place to throw it and I can throw more of it.

It's a pretty nice rig. But it ought to be for what it cost. Talk about sticker shock! It's strange to be driving a vehicle that cost twice as much as the house you live in. At least it's not real money, just those 36 not-so-easy installments.

I'm pretty sure this outfit will outlive the payments, though. Seven years or 100,000 miles on warranty should get me beyond the payment period.

In all honesty, it was about time that the Taylor Ranch had another new pickup.

Way back when

I asked Dad when we last had a new pickup on the place. He's 80 years old and he rattled off the dates like he'd just bought them yesterday.

"I had new GMCs in 1947 and 1953 and new Fords in 1957 and 1960," he said. My 2002 Dodge was the first new pickup on the place in 42 years and the first Dodge, too. Things have changed.

Dad also remembered selling steers for 28 cents a pound when he bought that 1960 black Ford three-quarter ton. The pickup cost $3,000, and he remembered vividly that the spare tire was extra. I think we always remember the times when the car dealer sticks it to us for some frilly add-on like a spare tire.

We always like to compare the inflation of the things we buy compared to the things we sell, so I did the math. Steers are now about three times what they were in 1960, and that new pickup was better than 10 times as much. Interesting statistics, but nobody at the car dealership or cattle auction really cares. We just like to talk about it with other ranchers at the coffee shop to amuse ourselves.

The other interesting piece of trivia was that Dad's last pickup was bought a year after he got married and just before his first son was born.

It was solid proof of a statement that the salesman made while we were dealing on my new pickup. He said if you're going to buy a new pickup, you better get it now before you get married and have kids. You'll never get one after that.

I thought it was just part of the sales pitch, but I think he spoke the truth.

Cruisin' in a classic

Old cars and newfound fun

June 17, 2002

I used to think that driving a brand-new vehicle was the key to over-the-road happiness.

I started out driving late-model rental cars to get that new car feeling, then I had the use of a company-provided lease car that was just off the assembly line, and, finally, zero percent financing broke me down and I bought a new pickup of my own last winter.

All those new vehicles have been fun to drive. I like the fact that they start when you turn the key, there's lots of new gadgets on the dashboard to fiddle with, and people don't point at you and laugh when you drive by.

But the best drive I've had in long time was last week, and it was not even close to being in a new vehicle.

I was looking for a vehicle to drive in the parade at a local museum's summer festival. The parade is long on neat old stuff – steam engines, tractors, fire engines and cars.

A friend of mine came through with a family heirloom, a 1948 Dodge fluid drive four-door coupe. She was black and shiny and ready to roll. He said she was mine to use.

His great-grandfather had bought the car brand new back in '48, and everything was original except for the new exterior paint. The wood grain interior, the seats, the floor carpets, everything was still showroom fresh. It had been well cared for.

His great-granddad was 96 years old when he bought the rig. That's what I call an optimist. When I'm 96, I'm going to do the same thing. I think it'll help keep me young and on the move.

After some instructions on operating the fluid-enhanced "three on the tree" transmission, some details on adding brake fluid, running the vacuum windshield wipers and putting extra lead in the gasoline, I was ready to make the 50-mile drive to the museum grounds.

I got behind that big ol' steering wheel, put 6 volts of cranking power to the motor, and I was off.

I hit the sweet spot in the car's machinery when I hit 50 miles an hour, so I kept her pegged right there. It cruised like a Cadillac at that speed. I got passed by plenty of people, but when you're driving a classic roadster, the more people you can see and wave to the better.

I turned on the AM radio, and once the tubes warmed up, I was enjoying some crackling oldies. I opened up the ram vent that pops up on the hood and enjoyed comfort that was close to air conditioning.

The parade was great fun, and, as I expected, it was chock full of "neat old stuff."

I left the car there for my friend's father to retrieve the next day. When I got home, I began to worry about leaving the old girl out in the weather. I called my friend and he said not to give it a second thought.

A little rain would wash the dust off nicely and it takes a pretty big hail stone to put a dent in something built with 1948 steel. It'd have to be the size of a boulder to crease that tank.

So I went to bed, and, sure enough, we got more than 2 inches of much-needed, surely-sent-from-heaven, rain. Yes, the car was just fine.

But now I know how to break a drought. If you're in need of some precipitation, let me know. Maybe I can get you set up with a certain 1948 Dodge to leave in your yard for a night or two.

Back in time

Fall from car grace

Jan. 27, 2003

It's only been a few weeks since I left the comforts of a job in corporate America, and I'm already feeling more comfortable.

Shortly after my resignation, the company decided to call in the company vehicle that I was provided to help peddle cow drugs and horse meds across North Dakota. For four years, I was outfitted with a brand-new SUV that the company leased and traded in each year.

A new vehicle each year brought reliability, fully functioning gadgets, clean floorboards and that great new car smell.

But with that gone, I've stepped back behind the wheel of Ol' Yeller, our 1984 Mercury Grand Marquis land yacht.

Sometimes it starts, sometimes it doesn't. The important gadgets like the windshield wipers and headlights usually work. The floorboards have seen years of accumulation, the simulated wood grain dash has a crack or two, and the car definitely has some smells, but nothing that I'd call "great" or reminiscent of "new car."

Ol' Yeller is comfortable though. It will comfortably seat eight or nine, and once you get her on the open road and lock onto the horizon, she practically drives herself. And it keeps a pretty comfortable climate inside as long as you crank up the heat and plug the gap in the driver's side window with a big blue bandana.

Transportation transport

Although I really like Ol' Yeller, it was tempting to continue driving the 2002 Jeep Liberty. I guess that's why they sent a man to take it off my hands and reduce the temptation.

I was gone to the state Capitol when I checked my home phone messages at 5 p.m. one day and discovered a string of messages from some guy who said he was at the gas station in Towner, N.D., to pick up the Jeep.

I guess the company who knew me so intimately for four years failed to tell this fella that there's 17 miles of gravel road between my home and that gas station. He jumped off the bus early in the day, started calling my empty house and must have drank a lot of coffee and ate a lot of aging rotisserie hot dogs while he waited.

Better yet, the bus company lost his luggage somewhere between his home in Arizona and Towner, N.D. He got off the bus with no coat, no gloves, no cap and probably no idea how uncomfortable that would be in North Dakota in January.

With no motel in Towner and no way to get a hold of me, he bought a jacket at the gas station and began hitchhiking 22 miles to the town down the road with a motel. Luckily, my hired man met him on the road and took him to the Taylor Ranch to retrieve the stray SUV.

Last we saw, he was heading south with the heater on full blast and studying the road map intent on reaching Arizona.

Back on track

I'll miss that new-car smell, but it's good to be back behind the wheel of a car with some character. Ol' Yeller is the best boat I've been at the helm of since Ol' Brownie, the wonder Chrysler.

I take a lot of pride in passing people on the highway with a car that's twice as long as anything else on the road.

And when I pull up to the gas pump, there's no doubt about my commitment to increasing the country's economic activity.

Honest deals

Tractor shopping a test of character

Feb. 24, 2003

I'm not sure what set me off to look for a different loader tractor this winter, but along about December, I went down the road in search of a new hunk of steel to park on the ranch.

I'm not a big believer in having a lot of equipment laying around the place depreciating, but, unfortunately, a ranch needs a few implements to get the cows fed.

I could get by with a team of horses and a pitchfork like my dad did when he was my age, but back then, he had a third as many cows, fewer bills and nowhere near the trappings that we consider absolutely necessary in today's technological consumer age.

Progress marched forward in the cow-feeding biz and brought ranchers little tractors with bird cage Farmhands, bigger tractors with front-end loaders, canvas heat houses, then cabs and finally, soundproof cabs with heaters and radios.

I'd gotten as far as having a 33-year-old tractor with a cab and a front-end loader. The cab is more of a frame and roof since the windows started cracking and falling out. I figured if I was going to upgrade I could just as well look for a 20-year-old tractor with a cab that still had all its windows and maybe even a heater!

Classified information

I know guys who never buy anything but love to look through classified ads and make phone calls. Me, I hardly ever buy anything, but I hate the process of poring through the papers, dog earring the pages, circling the ads and tracking down the seller with the telephone.

I started my tractor shopping and went through all the motions. I slowed down every time I drove by an implement dealership and even jumped out and test drove a tractor a couple of times.

It was always a disappointment to find a tractor that fit your price range and then pull into the lot and find this faded, dented, smooth-tired tractor with more than enough hours on the clock to warrant an overhaul. It's enough to make a man ponder raising his price range.

Finally, I spotted a little four-line classified ad in the back of an ag magazine that also happens to run my column. I called the owner, got the specs on the outfit and made the drive out to Oslo, Minn., to take a look.

Sales tactics

I pulled into the farmyard and wondered if I'd find another beat-up, wore-out tractor that fit my price range. I was pretty pleased with what I found under the lights of the shop. We ran it awhile, drove it, poked it, prodded it and looked for leaks and cracks. It was passing inspection.

The best part though was when I went to the house to introduce myself, the couple recognized me from my column, invited me to stay for supper and even offered me a place to stay if I didn't want to make the four-hour drive home.

"Good people" is how I would describe them. Somewhere in the warm afterglow of the hotdish, lefse and dinner conversation, I decided to seal the deal and signed a check for $17,500 and left it, along with the tractor, to these people I'd only met a couple hours earlier.

That would probably make a lot of people nervous, but honest people have a way of calming those nerves. I did get the tractor delivered, and the owner even covered the trucker's cost until I could reimburse him.

A little trust goes a long way in doing business. And a home-cooked meal for the travel-weary shopper doesn't hurt, either.

Sliding stop

Big wheels didn't keep on turnin'

March 24, 2003

Some folks think the invention of the wheel was quite an advance, that the advent of those rounded edges was a huge step forward for mankind.

I beg to differ. Wheels have put my life on a downhill roll for some time now.

Flat rounds

Currently, I'm fighting a rear flat on my Mercury cruiser. Wheels are nice when they're round, but a real pain when they get out of round.

It's still winter, so I could be driving a snowmobile. Ever see a flat tire on a sled? Just flat tracks and flat skis, and that's just how they ought to be.

Luckily, for me and the Merc, air is cheap. I can still pull her up to the gas station, put on 40 pounds of tire pressure and make it a couple of days before people start rolling down their window, pointing at my tire and advising me of its "unroundedness."

I'll keep doing that until I walk out one morning and find the Mercury sitting squarely on the rim. I'll act surprised and wonder how it went so flat so quickly.

I'll grudgingly jack her up, loosen the wheel bolts and rummage around the trunk for the spare. With a little luck, the spare will even have some air in it.

Runaway

I've been surprised by flat tires before. One of my first full-fledged flat tire adventures came when I was 12 years old and cracking out as a newly trained hay mower.

I was driving an A John Deere with a 9-foot sickle mower and I was intent on doing my job. I looked at the mower to monitor the fall of the hay. I looked at the right rear tire and adjusted my steering to keep things in line.

Mower, right tire, mower, right tire. I was as proud as a 12-year-old could be with my new occupation. Finally, I broke my trance and looked up to see our hired man on the other mower waving at me.

I stopped the tractor. As I did, I noticed that my intently studied right tire was fine, but my left tire was gone! I was driving along on the rim. About 50 feet behind me, by the last corner of the field lay the tire.

When I turned that last corner, the tire that must have been flat for some time popped off clean as a whistle. At least I saved everyone the work of removing the tire to repair it.

Last weekend, I was feeding with my "new" tractor, my pride and joy, my 4440 John Deere.

I was driving through a gate after rolling out a bale for my first- and second-calf heifers. Kalunk! I went from driving on two back wheels to driving on one.

Now, losing a 38-inch tire and wheel is a pretty severe adjustment. I lost the whole works, left side tire and wheel, and the tractor tipped sideways until it rested on the axle.

I made the very short jump down from the cab to survey the situation. Apparently, the casting that held the wheel on the axle had come loose and fell out. My feelings went from shock to disgust.

Things were bad and I was mad, but the ultimate insult? I didn't even have a tire close by to kick!

Cab conversion

Open air unconditioning

Aug. 25, 2003

Ever since I was old enough to run a cutting torch and drive old cars, I've toyed with the idea of creating my own convertible.

With the help of a little oxygen and acetylene, I figured I could whittle down the top on the 1972 Chevy Impala and have her looking as sleek as a factory issue Mustang ragtop.

I could see myself swinging into the parking lot at Towner High School with the wind blowing through the hair beneath my cowboy hat. My buddies would rush up to admire the smooth edges left by the torch tip on the steel uprights that once framed the Impala's rooftop.

But the dream never came true. By rights, it was Mom and Dad's car, and they weren't ready to take the top off of anything that had a functioning heater in North Dakota.

Topless tractors

I grew up without a convertible car, but we did have a fleet of old tractors and not a single cab amongst them. So, as it goes, I yearned for a topless car while I longed for a tractor with a cab.

Finally, John Deere's 1969 model 4020 and cab depreciated enough for me to buy our first enclosed tractor in 1993. It didn't have a heater, and the old air cooler on top of the cab was merely ornamental, but I was indoors.

Now, after 10 years of bouncing across cab-jarring frozen cow pies and hayfield hogwallows, the cab had more sway in it than a Hawaiian hula dancer. The cab would move a good 10 inches fore to rear every time I shifted gears or stepped on the brakes.

The welded welds were breaking faster than I could reweld, steel uprights were tipping like felled timber, and glass was cracking and falling out as we drove it down the road.

It was time to fulfill my convertible dream.

Light the torch

I backed her into the shop and I wheeled my cutting torch into place. Yes, cabs can be removed completely, but I figured I'd just cut off the top half. That way I could keep the loader controls where they were mounted halfway up the front of the cab. And it'd give us the extra floor space to keep our water jug, a toolbox and an assortment of left handed gloves.

I began by removing the remaining glass before torching the four corners. I was pulling the seal from one when it made a jump for the floor. I made a spectacular catch of the airborne window, when it hit me, "Glass is sharp!" Too late, it'd already sliced into a quarter inch of the meat on my thumb.

The hired man pulled into the yard, walked into the shop, then tracked the blood trail from the shop to the house to find me nursing my wound with a bandage, a cup of coffee and a fresh piece of pear pie.

We went back to the shop and finished the job. I cut off the corners, started a couple of small fires in and around the cab and sliced the doors in half. For a moment, the cab had Dutch doors and I felt pretty Dutch during this whole low-cost conversion.

We drove out from under the cut-off cab and wow! The 4020 looked as fit and trim as an old farmer who'd just completed Weight Watchers!

My hired man got the pleasure of taking the trimmed-up 4020 for her maiden voyage. I really would have liked the pleasure of driving that converted convertible with the wind blowing through my hair in the 100-degree sun, but I had to run the baler.

Incidentally, it was hooked to a tractor that still had a cab and air conditioning that worked. I guess I'll wait for a more temperate day to experience my dream convertible.

Going backwards

Ranching with a rearview mirror

Oct. 6, 2003

I've come to realize that a lot of farming and ranching is about driving. Driving around and around the fields, driving down the road to market, driving back and forth moving equipment.

Secondly, I've come to realize the skill that really separates us farming and ranching drivers from society's run-of-the-mill drivers is not how well we go forward, but, rather, how well we go backward.

Your average, everyday driver has nothing to worry about when they shift into reverse but the tail end of their car. Their tail end might stick out a little farther than others if they drive a big SUV or a vintage gas guzzler, but, generally, it's a pretty stress-free deal to wheel out of a parking spot.

The farmer driver is usually hooked up to something really expensive and really wide. It calls for delicate maneuvering. The rancher driver is usually hooked up to something narrower and less expensive, but able to jackknife in an instant. Still, it requires good handling.

Storage steering

I thought about the importance of good backing when I was maneuvering my hay baler into a corner of the shop for winter storage.

Our shop isn't real big, so space is at a premium. Still, I figure the baler, although 24 years old with a book value of about $1,292, is deserving of some protection from the belt-withering, bearing-rusting elements.

It needs about 96 square feet. I try to convince it to fit into a space about 89 square.

This year, I discovered the perfect corner to park the baler. It'd be protected, yet out of the way, allowing me to keep two loader tractors indoors – the one that should start and the one that might start.

It took me about 48 tries from numerous angles and a number of jumps from the tractor cab to survey the situation and scratch my balding pate, but I got it right where I wanted it.

Today, you would look at that baler and swear that we built the shop around it. Not an inch of wasted space around its perimeter. I just hope we don't have to tear a wall out to extricate it come next haying season.

On target

Another great recent feat of reversal was backing our 30-foot-long bale trailer into the shop so I could do some torch work on it without having the wind take my sparks to the nearest neighbor's place three miles east.

There's only about 31 feet of space in front of the shop to start from, so you have to cut it in from an angle. And the mover has a free-pivoting fifth wheel-style hitch, so it's like shooting a three ball combination in billiards. I had to unhook a time or two, but I got it in.

Good backing skills were honed on our place by backing up 9-foot sickle bar mowers through hay meadow hogwallows 4 feet deep. It's a jackknifing obstacle course.

We learned even more by backing up our bumper hitch horse trailer to a chute that not only runs at an uphill angle but its surrounded by fences that run at slightly different angles. The facilities were designed for a pickup and stock rack, but now we use them to load pot-bellied cattle trailers pulled by big, long conventional semi-tractors. Truck drivers just love us.

Yup, I don't mean to brag, but I think I'm a pretty decent backer-upper.

As a matter of fact, my loan officer once told me that I was going backwards more than anyone else he knew. It was the nicest thing he ever said to me.

Disposable society

Hard to toss for folks who like to fix

June 14, 2004

I admit that I'm not the neighborhood's best example for fixing things up or maintaining flawlessly the tools that keep a ranch going. But I do like to milk every last breath of life out of everything on the place from tractors to pickups and even the lowly things like garden hoses and extension cords.

The big things continue to cost so much that I really don't have any option but to fix up the old and prop them up for another year of hard labor.

The little things, however, have gotten to where it's cheaper to buy them new again than repair the old.

Hoses and cords

Like garden hoses. When we're watering thirsty cattle across miles of big country, we use a lot of high-tech equipment like green garden hoses.

Now I don't always need a new 50-footer to get water from a pump into a tank. When the ends start to leak, the frugal repairman in me wants to just cut the hose a little shorter and put on a new end.

Of course, it's gotten to where you can buy a whole new hose for the cost of two ends and a splice.

That bothers me. I could have 15 or 20 feet of perfectly good hose and I'm supposed to toss that in the garbage and go buy a whole new one just for the ends.

It's the same – or worse – with electric extension cords.

For some reason, we go through a few extension cords. Some get lost, some short out, some get a little flat on the ends after being driven over a hundred times. Last winter, one of our cords was pretty much devoured by a herd of bored calves attracted to the bright blue chew toy I'd inadvertently left hanging in their corral.

I like to fix my frayed and damaged cords. I use my roll of black electrical tape and wrap with gusto. But when I go to put on some new ends, plug or plug-in, my wallet gets the shock.

There's no comparison between the low cost of a new extension cord and the high cost of putting new ends on an old cord. It's even worse if you figure your time is worth anything at all. It doesn't make any sense.

Life or landfill

It doesn't end there, of course. I have a humidifier needing a replacement filter that costs as much as the humidifier did. No one repairs televisions or radios or videocassette recorders or most any other electronic gadget. It doesn't pencil out.

Out to the landfill with the old, into our disposable households with the new.

I'm going to keep fixing my old garden hoses and extension cords, though, even if it doesn't pay. It's not that we're seeing any landfill crowding here on the ranch. I just like the personal satisfaction of fixing something more than the empty satisfaction of throwing it in the garbage.

I guess I've already got the screwdriver and utility knife, so why not use them to salvage the slightly used and easily discarded.

And, with a little extra effort, I can fix them up better than when they were new.

The motto on my workbench? Built to last…a little while.

Retro rags

Old clothes clean up with character

July 26, 2004

I'm not the most conscientious recycler in the world, but I don't go to town to buy a box of shop towels to wipe my greasy paws during the oily season on the ranch.

No, we like to provide our own eco-friendly grease rags. Recycled from the clothes right off our back.

Rather than throw away those holy socks, threadbare T-shirts or old underwear, we put them in the rag box and give them one more chance to contribute their absorbent clothiness out in the shop.

I can see the allure of a nice, tidy box of store-bought shop towels in the easy-to-dispense package, but where's the character and originality in that?

Second use

When I find myself up to my elbows in grease, I reach in our rag box and pull out that day's surprise.

Sometimes, I pull out a rag and find myself reminiscing nostalgically about the piece of cotton I'm about to turn dirty black.

"Ahh, look, it's my Nitty Gritty Dirt Band T-shirt. Wow, that was a great concert," I say as I wipe my hands across their catchy 1987 concert tour logo. Another tee takes me back to a Minnesota Twins baseball game or a family vacation to some tourist town. I'd kind of like to slip them back on, even though they're a size too small and shrunk to muscle tee tightness.

They're not just rags, they're memories. And you can't get that in a pale blue sheet of wood pulp on a roll.

I try to slit my old socks up the side with my jackknife to increase their total square inches available for cleanup. Sweat socks are the best when it's rag time. Those slippery little dress socks won't mop up nothing. Of course, fellas who wear a lot of dress socks don't usually need a lot of shop rags.

The old underwear that find their way into the rag box have their good points and not-so-good points. They are cotton briefs, so they are pretty soft and absorbent. They do have that elastic waistband, which, trimmed out correctly, is almost as handy as a rubber tarp strap around the shop.

The downside is that they are your old underwear, and, although you might not find it weird or disgusting to grab a pair of your once-white briefs to clean your hands, it's probably best not to hand a pair to your hired man. Yup, your underwear, your rags. Anything else would just be wrong.

The right stuff

I feel fortunate to live in a time when natural fibers are in fashion. Cotton clothes can go on to be pretty good rags. I pity those farmers and ranchers back in the 1970s trying to wipe up anything with those polyester and synthetic blends.

And it's probably just as well that I can't afford a lot of silk. Not a lot of use there, either, beyond their wearable days.

Deciding on when the wearable days are over can be a bone of contention. My wife would like me to retire some of my clothes to the rag box a little earlier than I do.

As a matter of fact, I found one of my favorite shirts out in the shop's rag box just the other day. You can read a newspaper through the well-worn fabric and the shoulders are a little snug, but I changed shirts right there in the shop to spend one more day with that old friend. And if I needed a rag later in the day, all I had to do was pop the snaps and put it to use.

That's what we call a versatile wardrobe.

Free air?

The high cost of a cool breeze

Aug. 9, 2004

One of the lessons I remember from my college studies of economics had to do with the concept of elasticity.

It wasn't related to rubber bands or other stretchy items, but it did deal with how people would react if the price of something took a real bounce up.

If the price of something went up considerably and people continued to demand the same quantity, we would say the demand for that product was pretty inelastic. In my mind, it was the things people needed no matter the price. It's the kind of stuff ripe for greed and price gouging.

If you were bleeding to death, your demand for a doctor and a few pints of blood would be pretty inelastic.

Today, it seems like folks demand about as much $2 a gallon gasoline as they did $1.40 gasoline. That's relatively inelastic and a little scary.

And after last week, I added another item to my list of inelastic innovations – tractor air conditioning repairs on a hot day. When it comes to fixing the air in your tractor, it seems like money's no object.

Cool, man, cool

I don't have a lot of experience with tractors equipped with air conditioning. Most of my entire haying career has been made in the open air, under the sun and in the breeze.

But now I have a tractor cab with a knob that says "cooler," and it's left me with a wallet that says "emptier."

I put $100 in the outfit before the haying season started. That lasted about a day, just before it started getting really hot.

I called the repair shop for some ideas on remedies. They recommended some new pipes and hoses to stem the loss of refrigerant. He gave me a $400 estimate, which usually means $600 by the time you get the bill. True to my inelastic economic theory on air conditioning, all I could say was, "when can you do it?"

They could get it in the shop the next day, so I went out to bale some dry sweet clover in the hot sun before sending it off.

Tractor cabs made for air conditioning are pretty miserable without air. The windows open just wide enough to let all the dust and hay and chaff in, and that's about it.

I baled up that dry clover and finished every bale with the wind at my back. Every powdery particulate possible blew into the tractor cab. When I stepped out of the cab, I looked like Pig Pen from the Peanuts cartoon.

The air conditioning repairman could've doubled his price right then and I wouldn't have batted a red, puffy, irritated eye.

What next

With the help of a minor mortgage, I have my air conditioning back on track. Now it looks like my alternator is on the way out. Flip the switch for the air conditioning and bury the ammeter needle in the red zone.

If I want to put any twine on with the electric tie arm or know anything about the bales with the electric monitor, I have to shut off the air and open the windows again. Like we say around this outfit, if it ain't one breakdown, it's two or three others that are just as expensive and frustrating.

I haven't priced the alternator yet, but in terms of its machine repair elasticity, I'll probably do my usual shrug and say, "well, I guess we gotta have it."

Either that, or I could crack the windows and finish baling the hay with a pair of aviator's goggles and a respirator and look forward to fall.

Metrication

Hayfield no longer a standard operation

Aug. 20, 2004

I guess I've been avoiding it long enough. I finally had to buy a few metric wrenches for the ranch tool bucket.

It all started innocently enough. I upgraded my hay baler. I went from my 25-year-old model to one that was brand spanking new. My new baler was assembled in Iowa. I had no idea that the generally careful Iowegians had suddenly converted to the metric system.

I was setting the wheels down on the baler hay pickup when I discovered that my fifteen sixteenths wrench was a tad too big. My seven eighths inch box end was a bit too small.

I asked myself, why would they put a twenty-nine-thirty-seconds inch bolt on a baler? That's a tough wrench to try and find. They didn't have one at my local gas station. I didn't even ask if they had a fifty-seven and fifty-nine-sixty-fourths inch double box end.

Then it hit me. What I needed was a 23 millimeter! My baler had been metricated! Of all the dirty low down tricks disguised under an innocent looking coat of green paint.

The only metric wrench I had on the place was a 15 millimeter bought to change oil on the only metric car I ever owned.

Other than that, all I had was a metric crescent wrench, a metric vise grip pliers and a variety of metric pipe wrenches.

I wasn't anxious to immediately round the edges of the bolts on my new baler, so I broke down and got the cheapest set of metric wrenches I could find. The salesman said they were guaranteed to work at least once before breaking or bending.

With all these new tools, I'm going to need a bigger bucket.

High time

I suppose it's about time that I join the rest of the world on this metric thing. Invented in 1670, it looks like the system's here to stay.

According to what I read, it's only me, Liberia and Myanmar who have yet to officially get on board with the metric system. OK, me and most of the United States.

I'm even an international writer. I still make my Canadian editors convert my miles to kilometers, my pounds to kilograms. I'm sure they'd appreciate getting my columns pre-metricized and ready to print.

I guess I'll start by getting used to my internationally acceptable baler made in Iowa.

I want to take good care of it, so I hope I can find some metric grease. Luckily my grease cartridges come in both 14 ounce and .397 kilograms. Thank goodness for dual labeling.

I used to lube the grease zerks in sets of eight strokes, but to be fully metric I'll give 'em a series of 10 strokes or decimals thereof.

In rough ground, I'll try not to pull it faster than 4.8 kilometers per hour. And to reduce the strain on the belts, I'll limit the size of the bales to 182.88 centimeters or less.

I'll complete my new metric haying operation by adapting the metric time system. Yes, in metric time, there are 100 metric seconds in a metric minute, and 10 metric days in a week.

The way my haying's been going this year, I need at least 10 days in my week to get the job done before freeze up.

Tough breaks

It could have happened to anyone

Sept. 6, 2004

One of the good things about ranching is being able to work with your spouse. One of the bad things about ranching is being able to work with your spouse.

My wife grew up on a farm with a little more modern equipment than what I've got on the ranch.

This summer, I've been training her in on our old equipment and a few new haying tasks she never saw on the farm.

Some days go better than others.

She started out the season by inadvertently leaving a switch on for our old red tractor and draining the batteries. I gave it a jump start and told her, "Don't worry, it could've happened to anybody."

Once the tractor was running, things went better. She did get stuck once with the wheel rake next to a slough. I said, "That's OK, it could've happened to anybody. I've already been stuck twice."

Once in a while a lever breaks or a bolt falls out or a hydraulic hose blows or something else disintegrates. She kind of takes it to heart, but I tell her, "That's been on the way out for quite awhile. It could've happened to anybody."

She's still not quite used to everything being on the verge of a meltdown. I told her it's taken me years to resign myself to that fact.

Monkey business

I've introduced my wife to some new implements. I make the customary training round with her and turn her loose to learn the rest.

I got her started on a 36-foot dump rake, an implement that only ranchers in central North Dakota and the Nebraska Sandhills can really appreciate.

Running that rake in our axle deep hogwallows was a little frustrating for my bride.

She was really getting mad when she said, "I don't know why I can't run that thing better, it always works for you." I was about to console her with how I'd been running that rake since I was 9 years old, and that it takes some practice to learn how to steer straight while you're looking backwards and working the hydraulics to make the windrows.

But then she said, "Really, a monkey could do that job." So, rather than go on about the complexities of a task I'd been perfecting for 25 years, I just walked away, knuckles dragging on the ground and went to eat a banana.

Snap of steel

I think today was probably her most outstanding bad day in the hayfield. Everything she touched went to heck. I kept telling her, "That's OK, it could've happened to anybody." And it was the truth. Some things are just ready to break, and it's just bad luck to have your hands on the controls when they go.

The last straw came when the wheel rake she was pulling broke plumb in two. The 4-inch steel pipe tongue for the outfit snapped like a twig and it came down in a heap. She was on the verge of tears.

It was bad engineering, it should've had a third wheel to support the tongue, and everyone I know with a rake like that has had them break in exactly the same spot.

I wanted to explain that to her, but I'd already told her a half dozen times today that "it could've happened to anybody." I had to try a new line, so I said, "Wow, I didn't think anyone could break that!"

I don't know who I'll get to help me in the hayfield tomorrow.

Money, markets and mayhem

Bears on the street

They get a little more attention than bears in the country

Sept. 7, 1998

Bells are ringing, there's panic in the street. Didn't you hear the news? The Dow Jones industrial average dropped 512 points last Monday. It could be the new "Black Monday" forever remembered in the financial world.

Well, maybe it'll be remembered as more of a "Gray Monday." The market gained half its loss back on Tuesday, but the loss to the U.S. stock market still amounted to some $2 trillion.

On the Monday evening news, I heard the anchorman say that the stock market had stepped back in time all the way to 1997. When the Dow dropped and closed at 7,539.07, that was a level last seen in November 1997.

Imagine that! People have invested money in something that is now only worth what it was 10 months ago.

Give me a break

The news says this sends danger signals to the millions of Americans who dabble in stocks or have their retirement savings locked into 401(k) plans.

We're beyond the danger signals in agriculture and the millions of Americans who do more than dabble in the business of farming and ranching think a 401(k) is one of those new foreign-made tractors with the drawbars that were whittled out with a blowtorch.

I was really entertained by the serious tone of the newsman when he said, "a level last seen in November 1997." With a little help from the USDA charts on the Internet, I checked the levels last seen in agriculture in November 1997.

The weighted average price for 550-pound steer calves was 90 cents way back in the dark ages of November 1997. Today, they're 75 cents. It would sure be nice if our market could "slip" back to those November levels.

The Des Moines price on slaughter hogs was 45 cents. Today, they're 28 cents.

I know my friends in the grain farming business would like the market to slide all the way back to those November prices when the Dow was a dismal 7,500 points.

The Minneapolis price on 14 percent protein dark northern spring wheat was $4.15, today's $3.24; choice milling durum was $6.90, today's $3.95; feed barley was $1.70, today's $1; corn was $2.60, today's $1.64; oats was $1.74, today's $1.18.

But you won't hear much about the goings-on in agriculture on the national news programs. They've got bigger things to worry about like the drop in Microsoft stock. I just hope Bill Gates can find enough pennies in his account to buy some of the lowest-priced, most abundant food in the world.

Diversified portfolios

There would be a way to get more people interested in what's happening down on the farm. Clearly, folks are too dependent on the technology stocks, "blue chips," etc. They really ought to set aside 20 or 30 percent of their portfolio for investment in the "brown chips."

Put a couple hundred cattle on feed, plant a quarter of wheat, maybe farrow out a few sows. Then they, like the rest of us in America's outback, would be plumb tickled to see the markets "slip" to those November 1997 levels.

Inventory reduction

Ranching in the wireless age

Sept. 21, 1998

In a bold move to reduce the overhead costs on the old ranch, I've implemented a new method of inventory management.

It's similar to what folks in the business world call JIT, "just in time," inventory control. That's the system where distributors order and ship items as they're requested rather than maintaining warehouses full of expensive stuff.

I call my version the DBN, "don't buy nothing," system. It keeps my shelves bare at all times and could also be called NHAWYNI, a word that looks like it comes from a native language but really is an acronym for "never have anything when you need it."

The DBN system has its advantages, costwise, but it's really not very handy when it comes to sudden breakdowns and spur-of-the-moment building projects.

When Dad was running the ranch, he was an inventory man. If he happened to be in the local farm supply store, he'd buy a few pounds of bolts or a box of nails even if he didn't have an immediate use for them! Of course, that was back when it didn't take an entire calf to pay for a sack of supplies.

Provided you could find where he put those bolts and nails, they were there when you needed them.

Going wireless

A long time ago, Dad bought a jumbo roll of heavy, smooth wire. That roll of wire, more than anything else – hard work, ambition, high-interest loans, government sympathy, scientific advances – can take credit for holding this ranch together.

You can see pieces of that wire strewn from one end of the place to the other. Most every gate, corral and piece of machinery is held together by that common thread of steely sinew.

As a lad, I remember looking at that gigantic roll and thinking it as unending as the prairie skyline. Like a bottomless cup of coffee at the cafe, I figured it would surely last forever.

But all things eventually do have an end, and that roll of wire saw its end about a year ago. Since then, the ranch has been, like today's digital world, "wireless."

Now wireless might be a great thing in the world of satellite communications, but in the world of ranching, it's a wreck.

Poor substitutes

Wire is one of those things you need "right now," not "just in time" a day or two later. So if you don't have the flexible, smooth stuff, you grab whatever's handy.

A lot of times, I try to substitute a little barbed wire. It's really not too user friendly if you're gloveless and squeamish at the sight of blood.

Other times, I try to make do with some high-tensile electric fencing wire. Twisting that stuff is like wrestling an alligator, and just when you make the final twist, it usually breaks.

Black friction tape will work, but it's hard to undo every time you want to open the gate you just taped shut. The same with the knots in plastic twine.

That leaves me with just one other option. And although it goes against my DBN management, I may have to inventory another jumbo roll of smooth wire because it's considerably more convenient than standing there and holding everything together with my own two hands.

Why fight it?

Workin' for a way of life is no way of life

Oct. 5, 1998

Most business people do what they do to make a profit. Most farmers and ranchers do what they do because they like it. It's a way of life, a tradition, a good place to raise a family, an opportunity to be your own boss. And those good things are fundamentally bad problems for agriculture.

If your primary motivations are something other than profit, you'll keep on doing what you're doing, regardless of profit. You'll take another job to subsidize your lifestyle, you'll eat up your equity and work yourself right into the ground to maintain that great way of life.

When we say things like, "Oh well, I guess I'm not really in this business for the money," it's a self-fulfilling prophecy. There won't be any money in a business where people won't quit when it gets unprofitable.

When we are forced to quit, it's especially painful because you know that this usually is the absolute last resort. We hold out until we're flat busted and our banker makes the decision for us.

But until then, we'll love our lifestyles so much that we'll clamor for more land to make up our losses in volume. Our perpetual land rush raises rental rates and land prices for everybody in the neighborhood and we all get squeezed a little harder.

A lot of us talk about the future of agriculture and whether the family farm will give way to large, corporate operations. I say, let 'em have it. Love 'em or hate 'em, you can say one thing about the multinational food companies we've sold our commodities to for generations – they are profit-driven. They won't run a ranch just because they like the lifestyle. They'll expect it to make some money, and if it doesn't, they'll either quit or change. That could be a lesson.

If the multinational food companies do take over agriculture, I would assume that they still would need someone with experience to take care of our old homestead. This is where I'd step in to negotiate the kind of compensation package I never could get when I was my own boss.

I'd go for the standard middle-management level salary from $50,000 to $80,000 a year. Then I'd shoot for the benefit package that always used to be out of reach – good health insurance, three weeks of paid vacation, a retirement pension, stock shares and a solid-gold 401(k) plan.

Now that would be a quality of life. No more worrying about losing the farm – it's already lost. We could just concentrate on spending our money and enjoying the free weekends and vacation time with the family. And I could look forward to a comfortable poverty-free retirement.

Of course, the danger would be that I wouldn't lose my old yearning for being a ranch owner. I could save up my wages and my employee stock shares to buy the old homestead back in a few years.

Then I would fall in love with the sunsets again and start selling my commodity to my corporate neighbors for below the cost of production because, you know, we're not in this business for the money anyway.

Y2K, Y worry?

Looking forward to a clean slate millennium

Jan. 4, 1999

I hope everyone enjoyed ringing in the 1999 new year. Because, to hear some tell it, it'll be the last new year we celebrate of the civilized world as we know it.

Yes, some high-priced, solution-wielding computer consultants say, the world will be brought to its knees when the clocks of our digit-deficient machines roll from "99" to "00."

It's called the "Y2K" dilemma, and it's all based on the fact that some miserly computer programmers got a little stingy with their machine's memory and shortened years from four digits to two. Now, computers might read "00" to be 1900 instead of the year 2000.

The lights will go dark, banks will crumble, and mass anarchy will likely ensue. These Y2K doomsdayers go to disaster movies just to cheer themselves up.

On the ranch

I can understand the woes of the computer programmers on the Y2K problem. I've made a similar mistake of high magnitude right here on the Taylor Ranch.

You see, I like to tag and freeze brand my cows and replacement heifers with numbers that clue me in on the year of their birth. For example, cow No. 121 was born in '91, cow No. 454 was born in '94, and No. 728 was born in, you guessed it, '97.

I'm even worse than the two-digit computer geniuses, I went with a single digit to signify the year!

Like the fellas saving computer memory, I devised my system to save space on the ear tags and hide on the cow's left hip. Have you ever tried writing a number like 1991-21 on a 3-inch-wide plastic eartag with an ink-blotting tag marker? And think about the amount of liquid nitrogen it would take to make that big of a freeze brand. I just had to call that cow No. 121.

So now, when I've got heifers entering the herd from the calf crop of 2001, I won't know those cows from the ones born in 1991. And considering the poor job I've been doing of culling the elderly herd matrons, I might even confuse them with some born in 1981!

I truly understand the shame and guilt that is now being felt by our computer programmers who thought they were doing the right thing in the 1960s and 1970s.

Y2K positives

Although there's plenty of chances for doom and disaster with delinquent computers, embedded chips and the machines and systems that depend upon them, I do see some silver linings on this dark Y2K cloud.

I've been really hustling to try to make payments on the ranch loans before the annual Jan. 1 deadline. Actually, I've been hustling to contact the bankers and let them know that their money is still on the hoof and that they'll likely have to wait till February to get my money, but, all the same, I've been really hustling.

However, next December, I plan to take it easy. When the bank's computers hit the millennium, they'll roll back to the year 1900 and I'll be celebrating a truly happy new year as my debts magically disappear. It's sure a good thing that I haven't made enough money to put in savings accounts that might disappear as well. Whew!

As for the solution to my Y2K cow numbering dilemma – I'll just quit numbering them. There's really no sense in keeping such close track of cattle that I'll finally own free and clear anyway!

Planning for success

Waiting for the stars to align and the dollars to flow

March 1, 1999

It's that time of year again when we cross our fingers, cross our hearts and step forward with shaky knees, sweaty palms and a worry furrowed brow.

Ranchers are finishing up the marketing of last year's calf crop and getting ready for the next one. Grain farmers are figuring out what crops they want to plant this spring and what seed they want to book.

We're all mailing in our tax returns, or at least we should be, since the IRS has decided that a bunch of bookwork-hating farmers and ranchers should mail in their returns before March 1, while all the paper-loving business types and W2 fill-in-the-blank wage earners can wait until April 15.

If you have a spouse that works, at least you can look forward to a refund. Remember, wage-earning spouses, you have your agricultural life partner to thank for getting that money back from Uncle Sam. Kind of makes you glad you married a farmer, doesn't it?

And right behind the tax filing comes the joy of making out next year's farm plan and cash flow projections for the banker. So dust off the crystal ball and bring out the dice cup.

Cowboy confidence

Although I've closed the books on last year's tax return, I have yet to close the chapter on last year's calf crop marketing. Not one to learn from my mistakes, I sent the steers to a commercial feedlot for finishing again. One more roll of the dice.

I'm sure that the stars are finally going to align and allow me to make at least $100 a head on these feeders. I've had quite a few banquet speaking jobs this winter, so like Baxter Black says, "I feed a few cattle…but I'm an entertainer, so I can afford to!"

Of course, I'm not near the entertainer that Baxter is, so I did have to take an advance and set up feed financing to get the gain on my steers. Plus, I'll be selling some heifers to create a little quick cash, which will help me put my light calves on grass to become big, fat profitable yearlings.

I'm sure that there's going to be a point in this cattle business where we'll all get rewarded for owning as many as we can as long as we can. It'll be that magic moment where the calves get bigger while the price gets higher, and we'll all be rich, rich, rich!

Of course, that's what I thought was going to happen last year, and the year before, and the year before. But I remain optimistic. Like the monkey said when he got his tail in the lawn mower, "it won't be long now."

My attitude is a lot like that of a fella my Dad told me about. The fella had been racking up quite a winter heating bill with the local coal purveyor. The coal man was ready for his money.

The fella smartly informed the coal man that he was running a trap line and that he'd pay his bill as soon as he sold his coyote pelts. Satisfied with the thoughts of him settling up soon, they parted company. A couple weeks passed and the fella still hadn't paid his bill.

The coal man confronted the trapper again and asked him, "Just when are you going to sell those coyote pelts?"

"Well, shoot," the fella said, "I gotta catch 'em first!"

Secrets to profitability

Even better than buy low, sell high

April 12, 1999

You're never too old to learn valuable lessons from your mother. Even though I'm the one in my family with the college degree in agricultural economics, my wise 66-year-old gray-haired mother is still able to teach me ag econ lessons that I never learned at the university.

Her latest ag econ lesson comes in the area of "successful livestock feeding operations" or "how to turn a profit in the bum lamb business."

If you follow my column, you know that I retired from the sheep ranching business this winter. I sold 'em all (at least all the ones that didn't commit suicide on the way to the sale barn), and I vowed that I wouldn't miss those less-than-intelligent creatures.

The Taylor Ranch was sheep-free, and I was enjoying ranch life surrounded by nothing but rather personable and semi-intelligent cattle and horses. That good life only lasted a few weeks.

Kitchen company

You can imagine my surprise, and displeasure, when I returned to the ranch from a few days on the road and found a bum lamb in a cardboard box in my mother's kitchen. We were back in the sheep business.

She had gotten the lamb from her cousin who ranches north of Towner. Already knowing the answer, I asked her what she had to pay for her new livestock project. "Oh, nothing, of course," she said. Ag econ lesson No. 1 in livestock feeding – search for low-cost, or free, feeder animals.

Next to the cardboard lamb house I spotted a brand-new bag of lamb milk replacer. I asked her where she got that at. "Oh, I picked that up at the elevator," she said.

Again, already knowing the answer, I asked her what it cost. "Oh, nothing," she said. "I charged it to you!" Ag econ lesson No. 2 in livestock feeding – search for low-cost, or free, feed for your low-cost, or free, feeder animals.

Payback time

I'd say my mother is in a good position to turn a profit in the bum lamb business. Her combination of free stock and free inputs should prove to be a winner.

I admired her ability to find the free feeder animal, and I didn't even complain too much about her charging that bag of milk replacer to me. I think she learned that trick from some high school kids she once knew who had always filled their cars from her and Dad's bulk gasoline tank, or, as we called it, "the best little gas station on the prairie."

Likewise, a few bales of hay and a few buckets of feed from the parents' stash ended up in a few of the horses and cows I had as a lad. It's only fair compensation that I now return the favor with a little milk replacer, I guess.

Although things look good for my mother to turn a profit, I warned her that even no-cost agriculture has the potential to lose money.

But she told me that she wasn't in it for the money anyway. She said she got the lamb so that her 4-year-old grandson would have a little animal buddy when he came out to visit Grandma and Grandpa at the ranch.

And if you've ever seen a lamb's tail wiggle and a little boy giggle as he feeds a bottle to Grandma's pet lamb, you know that some livestock feeding ventures don't need to turn a profit, and I guess that would be ag econ lesson No. 3 in my mother's livestock feeding short course.

Countdown

Counting hay and counting days

April 19, 1999

It's that time of year again when I thank my teachers for letting me in on the secrets of counting.

They started me out at an early age with the 1 to 10 routine, but once they realized that I wanted to be a rancher when I got big, they worked hard to get me upgraded and counting from 1 to 100 or 500 or even 1,000.

Without their careful tutoring, I'd be at a real loss now when I'm counting and monitoring the "rate of burn" of my hay pile and cross-referencing that to the countdown when the pastures become more of a feed source and less of a holding pen.

The teachers must have known that I would have a real need for counting skills as a rancher out counting calves in the pasture, counting cows as they were sorted through the gate and counting the bills as they pile up in the mailbox.

Counting keeps everyone honest as we count the fenceposts while we're loading them, the salt blocks as we stack them and the cattle as they jump into the belly of the semi-trailer.

Counting is one of those activities that still require good ol' human mental concentration. I haven't yet run across any computerized or robotic mechanisms that can do the counting as economically and efficiently as a cowboy out wagging his index finger and mumbling numbers to himself.

Roughly accurate

Cowboy counting may not produce the most exact numbers, but they're close enough for the guys I hang around with. When a big knot of cows push the sorting gate wide open and make a run for it, we usually just add 10 and call it good.

When we approach a big pile of round bales, we count one semi-representative row and multiply it by the number of rows in the pile and subtract, rather than add, 10.

By overestimating the number of cows and underestimating the number of hay bales, we can usually keep ourselves free of feed shortages. Plus, the extra cows make the balance sheet look better for the banker.

Got hay?

The spring countdown of the calendar and count of the cows and bales has most ranchers making their annual resolution to cull more cows and make more hay in the year to come.

Balancing the cow inventory with the hay inventory reminds me of the story (and supposedly it's a true one) that I heard about a bachelor rancher who was getting the sales pitch on a single gal that someone had spotted for him.

The matchmaker extolled the finer features of the gal and went so far as to detail the nice dowry that came along with the deal. "She's got 50 good cows, a couple quarters of farmland, a pickup that runs and a house that she owns free and clear," he said.

The bachelor took in all the information, but wasn't fooled by the slick-talking matchmaker. He liked the idea of snaring a wife with 50 cows, but he also knew how long it was between fall grass and spring grass.

He wasn't about to let loneliness and the chance at love blind him to the economics of taking a wife with 50 extra mouths to feed, so as serious as could be, he had to ask, "but does she have any hay?!?"

Real neighborly

New ways to keep up the neighborhood

May 10, 1999

Freeze branding the new heifer recruits for the Taylor Ranch cow herd went smoother than usual this spring. Thanks to a good squeeze chute and headgate, the heifer branding went off without a hitch.

Of course, the new chute and headgate weren't there on account of my pocketbook. A kind-hearted, benevolent representative of the equipment manufacturer let my neighbor "demo" the unit, in hope of a future sale.

When one person in our neighborhood demos something, the whole community gets in on the act. Before my neighbor so much as whispered the news to the rest of us, we were already in his yard with our pickup beds cleaned out, ready to haul.

I was second on the list to use this fine contraption. It proved to be a real labor-saver. I was a little short of freeze branding help that afternoon, what with everyone calving hard and a couple of my younger neighbors getting their cars waxed up for the prom. I needed some machinery that would trim my crew from four to two.

The new rig proved to be a dream. You could trust the headgate to hold tight and the drop gate behind kept them moving forward. The demo deal was working. I felt myself needing one of these fine wonders of welded ingenuity.

I snapped out of the demo trance when I was informed of the price. The cost of that piece of equipment that saved feeding two extra ranch hands was a whopping $2,300! For that amount of money, I could have talked my one neighbor into not checking the cows and the other neighbor into ditching his prom date and helping me work heifers in my wooden chute with the tricky headgate and the iron pipe backstop.

Boosting the neighborhood

I don't want to anger the manufacturers of all the equipment that makes ranching less dependent on humans, but spreading the money to neighbors that is currently spent on contraptions that replace neighbors could be a valid tactic for rural revitalization.

Instead of buying that $800 calf cradle, pay the neighbor kids a little extra for their help at branding time. Instead of spending $100,000 on an elite lineup of tractors and haying equipment, give five neighbors $20,000 each to help them stay in the neighborhood and help you make hay with a less-than-elite line of equipment.

The entire neighborhood could go to a seminar on animal behavior, "flight zones" and the how-to's of herding for what it would cost to construct a set of corrals that funnels cattle like widgets on an assembly line.

As long as we're diverting a part of our budget to the neighbors to keep them around and keep our communities viable, we could even go a step further.

Instead of running your neighbor up another $50 an acre on that land that's up for sale or jamming them another $5 on the cash rent price, let's dedicate that extra money to keeping us all on the land. Forcing your neighbors to go broke with sky-high rent will leave you in a pretty lonely position when the dust settles.

It's like the story about the little rancher and his cousin, the big rancher. The big rancher was driving around the little rancher's country, complimenting him on all the nice neighbors he had in his community.

"Well, hell," he said. "You'd have some nice neighbors, too, if you hadn't bought every piece of land between your place and town!"

Wearin' the brand

The world of revenue-generating promotion

July 12, 1999

It's high time that I get in sync with the world of Calvin Klein and Tommy Hilfiger.

Not that I personally wear anything from ol' CK or Tommy, but I have to admire their ability to reap a profit on shameless perpetual self-promotion.

You see, I'm one of those guys who used to think that anytime I wore something promotional, like a baseball cap advertising cattle pour-on or a jacket that plugs a company's cattle feed, I had better have gotten those pieces of clothing for free.

It's a system that has worked well for a lot of farmers and ranchers with small clothing budgets. Heck, if it weren't for seed companies and equipment manufacturers, some farmers I know would be walking around practically naked.

We consider it a fair trade – free promotion for free clothes and trinkets.

Times have changed

These days, though, people pay good money for the opportunity to promote a company's brand.

Case in point. I was feeling a little under the weather the other day so I did what most people, even a few sick cowboys, do. I put on some sweats and a T-shirt and dedicated myself to some lazy healing.

My sweat pants were emblazoned with "North Dakota State University." My T-shirt said "Eddie Bauer, Established 1920, Seattle, U.S.A., Fine Quality." I finished off the ensemble with a "King Ropes, Sheridan, Wyo." baseball cap and a pair of socks sporting the Nike swoosh.

I sat down, drinking coffee from my Cenex Convenience Store travel mug and realized that I was worse than a walking billboard. I was a walking billboard who had paid out a substantial amount of cash for the right to advertise for everybody else.

It's not that those clothes weren't worth the money that I laid out for them. Socks, sweats, T-shirts, caps and coffee cups do have a real value.

What's surprising is that people can put their logo on them and not feel compelled to give them away. And, in the case of Tommy and CK, they actually feel compelled to get a substantial premium to the normal price.

Cowboy logic line

Well, move over Tom and Cal. It's time to make room for a rancher with some real practical knowledge in the arena of branding. I doubt that Hilfiger or Klein or even Ralph Lauren have put a hot iron on as many calves as I have, and it's time I take that experience with "the brand" to the marketplace.

With a little infusion of capital, I could introduce a complete line of Cowboy Logic clothes – faded denim shirts, ripped jeans, sweat stained hats – all the cool used cowboy stuff that brings the big bucks. I'd tie it all together with the usual line of T-shirts, caps and coffee mugs that promote the entire line. The whole campaign might even stimulate some auxiliary book sales.

The T-shirts could have a Cowboy Logic logo on the front and a little gem of cowboy wisdom on the back. Like "vegetarians don't live longer, they just look old," or "the bigger the hat, the smaller the ranch."

And if this proves as lucrative for me as it has for Mr. Hilfiger, I'll have to get me a smaller hat because I might finally have enough money to run a big ranch.

Buyer or seller

A whole new perspective

Sept. 27, 1999

Everybody's looking for a deal these days. I know I do when I'm working the buying side of the coin.

But when I'm selling, it's a whole different story. Then I'm kind of hoping people will open up their wallets and dig right in.

This year, flooded hay meadows have made me a buyer of hay. And although I'd like to help out the fellow ranchers and farmers who are selling hay, I gotta do my best to get it "bought right."

My bargaining strategies aren't much different than most people's. Ask 'em how much they want, counter with a much lower offer, dicker back and forth a little and settle for half the difference.

The crucial elements of this game are what the seller should ask for and what the buyer should counter with. From there, you know you're going to meet in the middle. That way, everybody feels like they did OK in the deal – a little give and a little take.

Still, the seller needs to ask a figure somewhat resembling market price, and the buyer has to offer a price that doesn't totally offend the seller and send him down the road in search of a different purchaser.

I'm kind of surprised that hay sellers will even ask a price for their hay. Because they're farmers too, and usually we just take whatever price we're offered. Asking a price for any of our commodities is a whole new concept for most of us.

Margin magic

The last few years, I've been in the precarious position of being both the buyer and the seller of my own calves in the fall.

I know other producers who've been both, but not on their own calves. They've sold their own calves for the best price possible, and bought back some poor fella's lighter calves at the sales ring to feed or graze for the lowest dollar they can.

It's a fine line to balance when you tell the cattle buyer how high calves ought to be out of one corner of your mouth, while the other corner of your mouth starts telling that same order buyer to find you some light steers and keep 'em cheap.

In my last three years of finishing part of my calf crop in a commercial feedyard, I've had to wear hats of both greed and generosity. The only way I could really get the haggling done was to stand in front of a mirror.

Last year, I tried to get my calves bought for 72 cents, but the guy in the mirror told me to take a flying leap. He wouldn't put them on the truck for any less than 85. Me and myself insulted each other's offers, dickered a bit and ended up settling for 79 cents.

After the cattle were fed out and sold this summer, I made a little profit by buying my calves from myself. I can hardly wait to start haggling on this fall's calf crop before I send them to the feedlot.

The rancher in me is a little nervous, though, because he knows that the easiest way for the cattle feeder in the mirror to make a profit is to simply price 'em in cheaper. Just in case, I better ask for a dollar to get that 95-cent counter offer.

Heavy construction

Profit potential in the pipeline project

Oct. 11, 1999

You have to admire folks who can get a big job done. Like the folks in my neighborhood who are part of a crew laying 2,300 miles of natural gas pipeline from British Columbia, Canada, to the Chicago area.

It's impressive. I'm still trying to build 200 feet of corral that I've been "meaning to get around to" for the last five years.

The pipeliners dug a 6- to 8-foot deep trench in the same kind of land that I couldn't get a baler across without sinking in up to the axles. And, as far as I know, if they got stuck, they got everything pulled back out.

Of course, the Alliance Pipeline budget packs a little more wallop than the operating note for the Taylor Ranch. The pipeline plans on spending $3 billion to complete their project.

The labor situation is a little stronger for them, too. At peak, they'll have 6,500 workers on the payroll, which is slightly more than the one overemployed rancher and the hired hand who are on the job site at the Taylor Ranch.

Prime pasture

The pipeline project has been a real economic boost to the area – for business owners, local laborers, even ranchers. Of course, I missed the boom on all fronts. I don't own any local restaurants or camper sites, I don't have any skill in operating heavy equipment or driving a semi-truck, and the pipeline didn't cross so much as a corner of our land.

Projects like the pipeline have always been pretty good to the folks whose land they cross. It's almost always more lucrative for a pipeline, a coal mine or an oil company to "disturb" land than it is for a farmer or rancher to grow food or grass on it.

Unfortunately, for many of us, the healthy easement checks never came. I'm not giving up yet, though. I think the pipeline still holds a lot of economic potential for progressive beef producers.

Protein pipeline

The 42-inch pipe is designed to move 1.325 billion cubic feet of natural gas per day from the gas-producing areas of northeastern British Columbia and northwestern Alberta to the people producing areas of Chicago, the midwestern U.S. and eastern Canada.

The pipeline is putting Towner, N.D., on the map, by locating one of its 14 mainline compressor stations in the area. We're listed right there between Alameda, Saskatchewan, and Wimbledon, N.D., two other large industrial metropolises.

Considering the $3 billion, the 6,500 workers, and the six publicly traded American and Canadian companies who are investing in the system, I have just one conclusion – there must be a little profit in getting gas from point "A" to point "B."

My other thought was that getting any kind of commodity from a production area to a consumption area might offer similar high returns. Before Towner became one of the pipeline's 14 "compressor capitals," it was North Dakota's self-proclaimed "cattle capital," and a new, straight avenue heading straight for the big city might come in handy.

I assume that a mainline compressor station has access to the underground pipe, and this could be the answer local cattlemen have been looking for to access large, lucrative, urban markets for their beef.

We could switch our breeding programs to some of the new miniature beef breeds, put the little critters inside the 42-inch pipe, turn on the gas and – Whammo! – it's a whole new kind of cattle drive.

It could well be the fastest way to get fresh, home grown beef to the marketplace, and, if the cowboys loading the pipeline happen to be smoking on the job, the beef could even arrive precooked.

Catching the crest

A new year, a new market

Jan. 24, 2000

New habits are easy to break, and I'm convinced that in today's fast-paced world all habits should be new habits. It'll be our key to flexibility.

The past three years, my new habit was to finish my steers in a commercial feedlot. I didn't really want to break this new habit. I enjoyed seeing my calves get to 1,200 pounds, learn about their carcass traits and even make a little extra profit on occasion.

But when the feeder cattle market began its recent rise, I had to rethink my new habit.

Being a 21st-century cowboy, I cracked open my laptop computer to learn what I ought to do with my 1999 calf crop. I booted up the spreadsheet and plugged in some numbers to see how high the calves would have to be before I'd let someone else have the fun of feeding them out.

The computer gave me my breaking point. Then I fired up the Internet and went online to see what the market was doing that week, that day, that hour.

I checked the futures, I checked the presents, I considered the pasts. I got the averages of all the cattle sold on the satellites and at the sale barns, and not just the sale toppers that everyone brags about at the coffee shop.

It looked like the market was willing to pay me more than I was willing to pay myself to own them any longer.

Park the pails

The decision to sell was made easier by getting in touch with my lazy side. Fewer calves at home means fewer chores. Fewer calves equals fewer pails.

The deal was struck to rid me of the entire calf crop, minus a handful of replacement heifers that I kind of needed to keep to ensure some future calf crops. Chore time for my hired hand and I was looking a lot sweeter.

The only thing sweeter was the price the cattle brought, especially compared to the last several years. The only problem is now I can't complain about the market and keep a straight face.

Maybe I'll break up some pastures and put in a little wheat so I can have a low market to grumble about. The cattle market is just too good for complaint. But I won't apologize for it, and if it goes even higher, I'll just grin and bear it.

One thing I missed when I was feeding cattle in a commercial feedyard was the opportunity to get into the local Rancher's Scale Association to weigh the cattle for sale. There's always a good crew to visit with there. The office at the scale is fertile ground for telling stories and skirt the issue of the cattle market, and when I weighed calves this year, it was no different.

A few people at the scale had already sold their calves, a few were still holding on. Everybody was curious about what everyone else got for a price, but most folks won't come out and ask what you got.

If someone does ask, you'll hear nebulous phrases like, "Oh, I got a little more than last year" or "I got enough to keep the fella at the brick building on Main Street happy."

Funny thing about most tight-lipped ranchers is they'll probably tell you they're all for mandatory price reporting for beef packers. Just don't make 'em tell their neighbors what they got for their calves.

Hard cash

Bucks that jingle, jangle, jingle

April 10, 2000

Merle Haggard may have wished a "buck were still silver," but I think he'd approve of our new buck made of copper, brass and manganese.

What's important is that it has a little heft to it. They're not as weighty as the Liberty or Eisenhower silver dollars, but compared to paper bills, you can sure tell when you have a couple of the new Sacagawea "golden" dollars jingling in your jean pocket.

Silver dollars, and golden ones, too, are the kind that John Wayne would flip to the barkeep for a bottle of rotgut at the local saloon. They're the ones the Lone Ranger would toss in the air and shoot the middles out of with his pistol.

Ever try and flip a dollar bill? You'd be lucky to get it to fly a foot, much less across the saloon or 20 feet in the air. You could wad it up in a ball and give it a toss, but a crumpled-up wad of paper is just plumb short on drama.

Dakota heroine

There're lots of reasons why I like the new brassy bucks. What North Dakotan wouldn't want to circulate a dollar with a picture of our own Sacagawea on it?

This is a woman with real ties to North Dakota. George Washington, as good a guy as he was, never spent any time camping by Washburn, N.D.

But Sacagawea, there's a gal who could understand how we feel when we watch the sunset on the wide-open prairie. She didn't lead troops in the Revolution, but she sure helped a bunch of white guys get across the continent.

So, nothing against George, but when I need some bucks, I'm heading for the Sacagawea coins.

I've always liked coin money. I sometimes go to Canada just to get my hands on some "loonies" and "toonies," the $1 and $2 coins of the northland.

I give the Canadians a lot of credit for creative cash. No stuffy old monuments, they put wildlife on their money – caribou, beavers, loons and polar bears. And they aren't stuck on greenbacks; a little pink and blue helps keep each denomination distinct.

"I don't know how you boys from the States keep your money straight," a Canadian friend told me once. "It's not so bad," I told him and grinned. "Especially since it takes a lot less of ours, we get credit for a whole dollar instead of just 65 cents you know."

But I'd bet the Canadians would have never made a 25-cent twin like the Susan B. Anthony and tried to pawn it off as a dollar.

Thankfully, it looks like Sacagawea is leading us in the right direction of different looking dollar coins.

Use 'em

I've already gone though a couple rolls of golden dollars. I get the same reaction from everyone I've given them to. "Wow, that's the first one I've seen." Then they stick it in their pocket and say they're going to save it.

It's OK to save a coin or two, but the mint estimates that there's already $7.7 billion in coinage sitting unused in homes today.

So do what comes natural, spend 'em!

Be warned, though, the brass/copper/manganese coins will tarnish. Personally, I think it adds character to our young Native American guide. Like any person of the prairie, a little tarnish is a badge of honor. Like a rancher's scarred hands, wind-burned cheeks or frostbitten nose.

And I bet a pop machine will still take a tarnished dollar coin. Try that with a limp, crumpled-up dollar bill, though, and you better be packin' a steam iron and some starch.

Fries with that?

Building the order everywhere you go

June 19, 2000

There're places where you expect to get harassed for the extra sale and places where you don't.

Going through the fast-food drive-through, I expect the pre-programmed high school kid to hit me up for the side order of spuds.

"Would you like fries with that?" they mumble through the garbled loud speaker that gives everyone a voice quality similar to that of Charlie Brown's teacher. "Waa woo wike wy's weh wat?"

I usually cave in and get the fries. "Super size it?" they press, thinking they're on a sales roll. And, for a mere 20 cents, I usually go for a few more crinkly cuts and the 55-gallon drum of pop.

"How about a big cookie?" By then, they've driven me over the edge of sanity. "OK, OK! Just leave me alone and let me out of here! Here's my money, just take it all and give me some food!"

No refuge

I expect some pressure when I'm getting fast food, but it's starting to look like a guy isn't safe anywhere these days.

Like at the post office. I just want to mail a dang letter. "Would you like insurance with that?" No! It's just a letter, I'm prepared for you to lose one every once in awhile. "Would you like Priority Mail? It's just 5 cents more." OK, OK, super size it. That seems like a decent deal.

"Any stamps for you today?" No! And I don't want a big cookie either!

Then I go to the bank to deposit a couple of checks. "Would you like to look at our certificate rates and take out a CD?" No, I like earning 2 percent interest, alright?

Off to the everything-under-the-sun store to get a couple of widgets. "Would you like to pay for that with your everything-under-the-sun store credit card?" No, I don't have one. "We can sign you up right now and give you 10 percent off today's purchases." I suppose, I've only got 14 other credit cards. You never know when you might need one more device for drop-of-a-hat debt on demand.

Go to buy a new power drill and they're peddling the extended warranty. "Only $14 to extend the warranty another three years." No, I say, I think I can wreck this sucker in 12 months or less.

Everyone's goal is to increase single-ticket revenue. Management likes it if the average ticket goes from $38 to $41. That's how you build gross sales and net profits.

On farm add ons

I think I'll take a tip from the kids selling the drive-through burgers when it comes time to sell the critters that make the burgers this fall.

When the cattle buyer offers to buy the heavy top end of the steers, I'll ask, "Would you like some runts with that?" If he's in tune with today's marketing, he'll gladly accept the lighter bottom end, too.

If I don't get the calves sold and I decide to send them to a feedyard for finishing, I can use the same tactics on the packer buyer. He might take a look at them when they weigh 1,100 pounds, and I'll tell him he can "super size" the load for $50 a head more. If my cattle feeder's any kind of a corn salesman, I'm sure he'll put another three weeks of feed and 75 pounds on to meet the super size requirements.

And no matter what kind of friend or customer is leaving the yard, I'd have to ask, "Do you need any wild barn cats to go with that today?"

e-haa, little e-dogies

Gittin' along on the super cow-way

Feb. 26, 2001

Times have changed since Dad loaded his steers on 36-foot railcars headed to South St. Paul, Minn.

Back then, buyers would gather up at the stockyards to see what the cowboys sent to town to trade for some cash. Dad sold a quite a few that way for 8 to 12 cents a pound back in the 1940s. Of course, back then you could get a beer for a dime and a room for $5 at the Hook 'Em Cow hotel and saloon in St. Paul.

Slowly but surely, the cattle, and their hook 'em hotel cowboys, began staying closer and closer to home. St. Paul was a fair bit closer than the earlier markets in Chicago. West Fargo got you a little closer than St. Paul. Then barns and buying stations filtered out to Mandan and Minot and Dickinson and Devils Lake.

As if 25 or 50 miles was too far to go to market, now we can sell the critters right from the comfort of our computers, cyber-linked to cattle feeders across the Midwest and Great Plains.

Sold!

I'm not afraid to try something new, so I tried a little Internet calf marketing this winter.

I put our calves on Cattlesale.com's website to learn firsthand about this new e-marketing outlet. Now everyone in the world could see my calves, and if they were registered and had some cash destined for cattle, they could buy the critters.

It was a pretty honest deal. Show 'em what you got, lay out your terms, figure your price, and see if the market will let you have that price.

We weighed the calves at the rancher-owned scale in Towner and sent the steers a packin' to Iowa, and the heifers hitched a ride to Nebraska.

Even our old scale shack in Towner has gone high tech. No more weigh bars to manipulate and balance (or not balance, depending on whether you're buying or selling the steaming stuff on the floor). No sir, now it's a certified digital readout at the Ranchers Scale Association, a fully fledged e-scale.

A little more e-xact than Dad's first calf sale as a lad. He sold his FFA project steer to the local butcher for 5 cents a pound and it weighed 800 pounds. When I asked where they weighed it, he said, they didn't. They just guessed it at 800.

There ain't a cattleman and a buyer out there who can agree on a guess these days. At least not without taking matters outside.

e-cowboys

As my calves headed down the road, I realized it is a small e-world after all, as the Disney folks would say in today's e-lingo.

Yes, e-lingo. New words are popping up all over the printed places with a little "e" in the lead position. It started out innocently with e-mail and e-tickets. Then everything became part of e-commerce, you know, the e-tailers out there doing e-business. They did so much e-business they had to e-cruit some new e-ployees, fattening everyone's e-wallets.

It's e-crazy but I think it might be time to adopt some e-language for today's cattle e-ranching.

We'll trade in our yee-ha's for some e-ha's and gather up our e-dogies from our homes on the e-range. As suspected, any good e-rancher will have to take advantage of e-banking.

And if this cattle market hangs in where it's at, maybe we'll be online depositing more than we're online borrowing.

Wouldn't that be an e-lief?

Rich rancher, poor rancher

Howdy assets, adios liabilities

Sept. 10, 2001

I've been trying to solve the ultimate riddle – how to become a rich rancher.

I always thought the concept of a rich rancher was something akin to the Easter Bunny, Santa Claus and the Tooth Fairy. Nice ideas, but tug on the beard and it usually proves itself imaginary.

There are a few so-called rich ranchers out there. But scratch through the surface and you'll usually discover a rich oil baron who ranches, or a rich lawyer who ranches or a rich banker who ranches. Unfortunately, I've never met a rich columnist who ranches.

So the challenge remains to really get rich in the cow business.

To help solve the riddle, I turned to the bookstore. Of course, there weren't any existing books by nonexistent rich ranchers, but I did find one by a rich investor and business owner. It was even a No. 1 New York Times bestseller. I decided to add to the author's wealth and invest the $15.95.

Dueling dads

"Rich Dad Poor Dad," is about Robert Kiyosaki's upbringing by two fathers. His real father was educated, hard working and struggled financially. Sounds like a rancher with an ag degree, but he was actually a school teacher.

His friend's father, who took Robert under his wing, never finished the eighth grade but became one of the richest men in Hawaii.

Rich Dad taught Robert some lessons that I thought sounded pretty simple. You know, like, "rich people acquire assets, poor people acquire liabilities." And the difference between the two is that "assets put money in your pocket, and liabilities take money out of your pocket."

Armed with some new knowledge on imitating the rich, I decided to start classifying my holdings.

Most ranchers have cows. This year, cows are an asset. Five years from now, they'll probably be a liability. Clear as mud.

Most ranchers have land for their cows to roam on. If a person's willing to sell land and the pasture is suitable for condominiums, I guess it's an asset. If you had to take out a big loan and outbid a land-hogging neighbor and an out-of-state hunter to buy your pasture, it'll probably be a liability for a long time.

Most machinery will be a liability, too. Rust, repairs and depreciation doesn't make it much of an asset. But some tractors, like the 4020 John Deere, will hold their value and I'm not sure how you'd classify them.

Steel fence posts and portable corral panels are definitely an asset. I've seen enough of these sell at auction sales to know that they will increase in value as they age and bend.

A couple other thoughts from the book were that the rich don't pay taxes, they have their own business, they don't work for wages, and they make money work for them.

I think I can pull all these lessons together and take a stab at being a rich rancher instead of a poor rancher. Ranchers already own their own business, they don't usually pay taxes (because we don't make any net income six out of 10 years), and they do own a few assets.

So I think we're closer to the secrets of wealth than we realize. We just gotta quit acquiring those liabilities.

And as soon as I pay the credit card that I charged that book on, I'm gonna go cold turkey on acquiring liabilities.

Marketing 101

Cattlemen salesmen

March 25, 2002

You know you're in trouble when you refer to your annual marketing effort with something like, "Yup, we finally got rid of them."

I don't think I've ever walked into a really nice, high-end store and had the salesman say, "Would you like to buy our stuff? We're tired of walking around these things and we really need to get rid of them."

Very few of the sales people in those stores have ever told me, "The bottom's about to fall out of the market for this stuff. I was hoping to dump it on you this week to cut my losses."

And even fewer would tell me, "Our high-quality brand name stuff is better than the bins of crap at the discount store, but we'll take whatever price you're willing to pay over there."

But that's kind of how I market my cattle.

Selling skills

Every year for the past three, I've been a guest lecturer for the ag sales class at North Dakota State University.

It's pretty refreshing to be around a bunch of young people on a college campus. I can see why professors enjoy their jobs. Being surrounded by all that youth and enthusiasm keeps them going.

Not many people like to admit to being a salesman, but I've proudly sold a lot of things – animal pharmaceuticals, stock shares, books on cowboy logic, stories, speeches, raffle tickets and FFA fund-raising fruit. Nobody in this world has a job – those who build, those who entertain, those collecting a taxpayer's paycheck – until somebody sells something.

So I gladly go to NDSU to talk to students about the sales process.

We talk about how to approach customers, how to position a product's features and benefits, how to lead them to a decision to buy that product. We talk about handling objections, working with different personality types and serving the marketplace with respect, integrity and good old-fashioned niceness.

And I try to practice what I preach, except, it seems, when I'm selling cattle.

Dumping time

I usually market the calves based on careful research. Like "this is when we always sell them." Or I might sell them when we get short of feed, or when we just get tired of feeding them. Or when I think we've finally reached the bottom of the market.

And selling cattle isn't like selling anything else. We don't spend a lot of time positioning those cattle with the customer. Usually, we try and get someone else between us and our customer and keep everything a secret.

We spend a lot of money on genetics, feeding programs and health programs, and we try to treat and handle them right, but we're too modest to make a big deal of it when we're selling them. Our main feature is that they're for sale, and it's main benefit is that you can buy them for whatever you think they're worth.

We handle objections – like rat tails, unpopular hide colors and frozen ears – by letting them lower the price.

And we don't have to worry about dealing with a bunch of different personality types. There's just one personality, including ours, and that's greedy.

Despite my greed, I was able to hit a really nice dip in the market. Now it's gone down even more. Maybe next year with a little better timing I can hit the very bottom.

Or, maybe next year, I can use some of the sales skills I taught the students. But, for this year, at least we got rid of them!

Let us profit

Lettuce leads the way

April 8, 2002

The West wasn't won on salad. At least that's what my buddies in the beef business like to say.

We like to think the West was won on meat and potatoes. Ever since it was won, though, we've acquired a little taste for some salad greens beforehand. The refinements of civilization.

But even the finer things can get so finely priced that we go back to our former ways. Right now, the hamburger is costing a third of what the lettuce does per pound. Looks like we'll have to go back to baked beans to keep our burgers company.

Salad supply side

I don't always pay real close attention to grocery prices, but even I noticed that the lettuce heads were getting a little precious.

I got confirmation of my suspicions in the USA Today newspaper. Lettuce had gone from a buck a head to more than $3 a head. The writer called it classic supply and demand.

Forget the cattle cycle, lettuce was riding up the graph of green bars on the "y" axis.

I was glad to hear that it wasn't just a rally of retail prices benefiting a few greedy brokers. No sir, even the lettuce farmers were getting in on the green.

At least the ones who had a little lettuce to sell.

It sounded good. The farm price for lettuce had gone from $15 a hundredweight a year ago to a whopping $86.50 a hundred this March.

Then I realized it was a lot like every other run in agricultural prices. The market was up because no one had anything to sell. Classic supply and demand.

Oats for $2 a bushel. None to be found. Wheat through the roof, but it was a drought year. Calves for $1.10 a pound, at least the ones that didn't die in the blizzards. And lettuce for $86 a hundred, but yours all froze in the surprise cold snap.

It's like the old "Hee Haw" joke about the guy who lost $30,000 because hogs went up and he didn't have any.

Baggin' demand

I guess the lettuce run wasn't all supply driven. The salad sackers had been doing a little work building demand with consumer convenience. Just two words...bag lettuce.

Specially designed for those who can't stand sweating over a hot cutting board chopping a head of lettuce. Just open the bag and pour out the green goodness.

Complementing the boost in demand caused by human laziness was some unseasonably warm weather in the East. More summery salads being sold and fewer bowls of wintry soups. Sorry, beef barley.

It looks like lettuce prices will be working their way back down, though. Even with heightened demand, farmers in California are working to bring in the harvest and boost the available supplies. More lettuce, less money.

Seems like the only thing that can go up in price without a real decrease in supply is gas in the summer. Looks like the gas pumps are getting a jump start on their Memorial Day pricing.

Farmers have watched the gas and fuel market long enough to decide that there's an opportunity in that gouging. Keep an eye out for those ethanol blends and the new soy biodiesel. We could just as well be supporting the corn and bean growers while we're driving down the road.

Just make sure and grab a big double hamburger as you leave the pumps. Heck, I'd even recommend a leaf of lettuce on that sandwich as you drive away burning biofuels.

Farmers and ranchers need to stick together to boost their prices. Maybe we can get all of our prices so high that USA Today makes our success a regular feature in the Money section.

Income support

Cranking out cowboy crafts

April 22, 2002

I never thought of myself as a victim of Third World child labor, but I may have been.

The outback of greater North Dakota may not be Third World, but I don't know if it's quite the industrialized First World. It must land somewhere in between. And maybe I wasn't into full-fledged child labor, but I did braid nylon string for hours on end to make my first off-ranch bucks as a mere 15-year-old.

I guess it was different from the pre-teen children weaving rugs or sewing soccer balls in the dark, dank corners of Asia to earn 5 cents an hour to help buy bread for their family. I was braiding nylon parachute cord into bridles and reins so I could buy myself a new Remington rifle.

I did get my rifle, and I got strong hands, too. Some local businesses and neighboring ranches got to help out a young craftsman entrepreneur, and some horses got nice, functional tack out of the deal.

Spending cash

I was reminded of my nylon cord braiding youth a few weeks ago when I was visiting a friend.

He's a rancher. So, of course, he does a lot of other things to help keep the checkbook balanced. His most important task is to make sure his wife doesn't oversleep, so he gets up early to make sure she isn't late for her job in town.

Plus, he's got a nice collection of part-time ranch supportive careers – brand inspecting cattle, crop insurance adjusting, shoeing horses, breaking colts. I'm surprised he doesn't drive school bus or have a mail route yet.

Those tasks should keep him cash flowing, but he's also a team roper. So, the income stream needs to flow even fuller to fund the road trips, rodeos and jackpots.

One of his team roping buddies was in the same cash-strapped predicament. He bought a septic tank service. He's his own boss, but he still has to do a lot of sucking up. Yes, team ropers will do just about anything to fund their habit.

My friend wasn't ready to go that far for his entry fees. Seemed like a crappy job to him. But it did start him thinking about turning other's waste into economic security.

Roper's rubbish

Looking around, he noticed he had a lot of old nylon lariats that weren't good enough to use, but weren't bad enough to throw away. He also noticed people selling some cutesy bowls at western craft shows made from old coiled-up, melted-together ropes.

The light went on in his mind as he envisioned turning ragged ropes into riches. He made his first one. Coiling it up and fusing the nylon strands was like wrestling an alligator with one hand. There had to be an easier way.

Being a ranch engineer/inventor, he began to think. In no time at all, he'd modified an old exercise bike with a couple of welded on gears, rods and a plate to bring his venture into the industrial age.

The rope-winding process sped up considerably, but there were environmental considerations. Melting that nylon rope together with his soldering iron created some nasty fumes. He was forced to move his factory into a ventilated area.

He crammed his exercise bike rope-wind-o-matic into his 4-foot-square bathroom and turned on the overhead fan as he melted and fused.

He felt pretty ingenious as he peddled away in his little bathroom, sniffing nylon fumes and turning 30 feet of stiff rope into darling little bowls.

He was kind of worried, though, that being outdoors snaking a hose down a septic tank might have been a better gig! It's amazing the money that can be earned with bathrooms and team ropers. You just have to pick which end you prefer – heads or heels.

Easy money

Bums make it big on ranch

May 20, 2002

To be successful in the ranching business, you really have to control your expenses. Under that model, there's not a more successful rancher around than my mother.

Her best racket in the low-cost ranching business has been her sheep enterprise. No, she doesn't have a flock of prize ewes that she herds year round on lush pastures. She takes in bum lambs from her cousin's ranch, grows 'em, sells 'em and goes on holiday until the next round comes in.

The key to her quick turns and large profits is twofold. First, her cousin gives her the lambs for free. Second, she goes to the grain elevator and charges the milk replacer to my account.

Somewhere between the free feeders and the free feed, she captures a right tidy profit. Heck, I even paid for the lamb nipples to put on the bottles. And, if memory serves me right, I bought and emptied the Coors bottles she uses to feed them.

She could write a book on profitable sheep ranching. It looks like she could do a series, too. She could follow up " Making it big in bum lambs" with "How to convert calves into quick cash."

Orphan calves

Last year, Mom put her money-making theories to work in the cattle business.

I'm almost always long on cows and short on calves during the calving season, but last year was an odd one and I ended up long on calves and short on cows.

Actually, I had enough cows, but a couple of the old gummers who were working way past their retirement age just didn't have enough milk. My young cows who'd lost their calves were already pulling duty for a couple of spare twins that we'd had. It looked like my only option for these milk-poor orphans was the barnyard care of my sweet old gray-haired mother.

"I'll take care of the little guys if you give them to me," she offered with the shrewdness of a Wall Street financier. What could I do? I couldn't let them starve out in the pasture with their shrivel-uddered, milkless mothers. I gave in and gave her the two-head herd.

Needless to say, I noticed an increase in my monthly bill at the local elevator. The line item on the bill said "feed," but I knew every time that I saw "feed" for $28 on the bill, it meant milk replacer for the calves I'd given away.

Like most bottle calves, they never grew up to match the rest of the herd, so we kept them, and kept them. Mom eventually switched them off of the expensive milk replacer and on to so some expensive pelleted feed. Nothing but the finest for Mom's babies and my charge account.

Finally, this week they went on the trailer and I took them to the sale barn. I threw the freight in for free. I guessed that she wouldn't want to pay any trucking for her free calves who'd grown big on their free feed.

Sometimes freight can be the deal breaker when it comes to profit or loss in the livestock business. We've all heard of the ranchers shipping cattle and sheep to South St. Paul in the 1930s and getting a bill instead of check since the critters didn't cover the cost of their trip.

Mom's going to come out all right on her deal, though – much better than I will. I haven't seen her calf check yet, but I'm sure it'll cover her expenses.

Enron Ranch

Creative accounting could turn things around

July 1, 2002

You can't throw a rock these days without hitting a crooked company, a shady accountant or an unscrupulous inside trader.

Enron and Arthur Andersen. Martha Stewart and ImClone. Now, WorldCom goes to the top of heap, and dozens of others from Tyco to Adelphia are all under the microscope of regulators and shareholders.

It makes you wonder if there's an honest business left out there.

Honest failings

Look no further than the family farm. Cooking the books and propping up profits aren't too common in our accounting methods. When we're losing money and going down the tubes, we step right up and take it like a man.

I think we've gotten so used to operating in the red that it's never crossed our mind we ought to be doing something else. We didn't realize that the rest of the free capitalist world admires a profitable bottom line. Sometimes we even boast of our misfortune.

Luckily, we don't have to worry about shoring up stock prices and bolstering shareholder confidence. Most farms and ranches only have one or two shareholders, and they're also the executive officers, and the board, and the accountants and the janitors. It's hard to know who's going to fool who and hide what from where when you're in every department.

At least we don't have the additional expense of a paper shredder.

Inside info

Martha Stewart is being investigated for possibly selling 4,000 shares of ImClone stock based on inside information about an FDA drug rejection. It's not a good thing.

Now the shares in her own company have plunged 45 percent since the inside trading investigation began. It's not a good thing, either. Funny she didn't unload some of her own stock when the investigation started. She had to be one of the first to know that little gem of inside information.

It might be the same reason I don't sell calves when someone tells me the market's heading south. I'm a stubborn Pollyanna.

I've had cattle buyers, bankers, economists and neighbors bend over backwards to try to give me some inside information on the cattle market. They've warned me time and time again about falling cattle prices, and I've ignored them and held out for higher prices every time. I'd make a poor inside trader.

Most cattle ranchers are longer on optimism than they are on recognizing smart inside information. I guess that makes us honest by default.

WorldCom's world

WorldCom has admitted to mishandling $3.9 billion in expenses by calling current expenses long-term investments. It let them show a $1.4 billion profit in 2001 instead of a big, fat loss.

Accountants say it's the oldest trick in the book, but apparently, it's an effective one if you don't get caught.

When I get tired of losing money on the ranch, this might be the way to give me a Schedule F that I can brag about.

The feed I bought for the cows could be a long-term depreciable expense. If you don't feed that 2-year-old heifer she sure won't be around as a 10-year-old brood cow. The chemical I use to spray the leafy spurge and the fuel and repairs for the sprayer must also be an asset instead of an expense.

I call my vaccination program an investment, but I've been expensing it. I figure when I rent land I'd like to buy someday that must be some kind of investment in my relationship with the landlord.

Before you know it, I'd have a ranch showing pure profit. But as good as it would look, we'd still be broke. And I guess that's just what's coming to light on the national scene.

Solid investments

A rising rate of return on the ranch

April 19, 2004

I'm not the kind of guy who's ever had a lot of extra money to invest. I've dabbled in some mutual funds, bought a few shares of stock and stuck some money into business ventures that have yet to pay a dividend.

I've stepped out on a limb and put my extra cash into savings accounts earning a whole half of a percent in interest and occasionally kicked it up a notch and gotten into a certificate of deposit yielding a whopping percent and a half.

But, for the most part, I've plowed every dollar back into the ranch. Tractors and machinery guaranteed to steadily lose value, cows that grow old, horses that go lame and most anything else with a rapid rate of depreciation.

Last fall, however, I made a few winning investments and didn't even plan it.

Increasing inventory

I've often heard that successful businessmen really control their inventory. Just keep one on the shelf and order it as you need it.

I didn't plan on having much extra inventory last fall, but I did, and that stuff is the best investment I ever made.

I meant to replace a 12-foot gate in the corrals last fall. It's still sitting there, but now it's worth 20 percent more than when I bought it.

I didn't get around the pasture fences like I meant to last year. So I carried over about 100 steel fenceposts. I bought them for $2, now they're selling for $3.10. A tidy little 55 percent return on that investment. My extra roll of barbed wire is pegging a yield of 33 percent, going from $30 to $40.

I had 100 gallons of gasoline left in the ranch bulk tank that I bought a few months and 30 cents a gallon ago. And I got in on another 500 gallons just recently that, thank my lucky stars, has gone up 7 cents a gallon since I bought it.

I had a small stack of plywood put together for a little building project. It's been there awhile. I think I bought it for $10 a sheet. Lumberyard says its $22 today. I've never doubled my money on anything before. It's got me feeling like Donald Trump!

They tell me the plywood's on the increase because of all the sheathing materials going to rebuild Iraq.

The OPEC countries are turning down the spigot on the oil supplies and they're in the driver's seat when it comes to the cost of me driving.

China's buying every scrap of metal they can get their hands on. Their economy is booming, their appetite is huge and my steel posts, wire and wire are skyrocketing.

It's bad enough that China's getting all our manufacturing jobs, now I can't even fix a little fence or rebuild some corrals without breaking the bank. In Iraq, my taxes are being used to bid up the price of my plywood and chip board here at home. And the oil supply is plumb out of my hands.

I guess I should just be thankful for the inventory I've got in the yard and the 20 to 100 percent return I'm seeing on those investments. Of course, to realize the return, I need to sell that inventory.

Trouble is, I need all those supplies and then some. I guess all I can do is keep on buying and have the investor's satisfaction of knowing that the price will probably go even higher.

Travels with a Taylor

What's in a name?

A lot if you're a fugitive

Dec. 7, 1998

I've always been proud of my middle name. That's why I keep my byline and write my signature as "Ryan M. Taylor," instead of just "Ryan Taylor."

Most people guess my middle initial to stand for "Michael," like the fella on that one soap opera. It's a good guess, and it's probably a good middle name for a lot of guys named Ryan, but it's not mine.

My "M" is for "Marshall." Not a name you hear everyday. It's my father's name, although most people know him as "Bud." And it was his uncle's name before him. His middle name, by the way, was "Nye." Definitely not one you hear much any more.

Great Uncle Marshall was killed in 1921 at the tender age of 20. Butted in the chest by a steer while working cattle, he died of the injuries a couple of days later. An interesting young man for his day, he was a homesteading cowboy, a school teacher and a pretty good piano player.

I think of him quite a bit, realizing that I've already lived eight years of my life that he never got to experience in his. It sure makes you appreciate the days you're given.

So I write the "M" behind my name to remind me of the stock of men that I descend from. I write it out of respect for my father, my single greatest hero, and I write it to honor my great-uncle, who I suspect to be my guardian angel as I work around the ranch.

Mistaken identity

But there were reasons other than pride and nostalgia that really made me appreciate my middle name last week.

Driving home from the Canadian Western Agribition in Regina, Saskatchewan, I was pulled over for going a few too many "klicks" per hour. The Royal Canadian Mountie checked my driver's license, told me to "just slow it down a bit, eh?", so I said "thanks, eh", and went on my way, eh.

Down the road a ways, he was behind me again and riding my tail like a horse trailer. I set the cruise at exactly 100 kilometers per hour and let him follow me.

A half-hour later, when I turned to go south, he pulled me over again. Both officers got out and one said, "Would you come back to the car?" I follow orders pretty well when they're given by two men with sidearms, so off I went.

I got to sit behind the cage in their back seat, and they asked me what my middle name was. "Marshall," I said. They told me that they pulled me over because they'd gotten a "hit" on my name when they ran it through.

"We think there might be a warrant out for your arrest," they said. "Are you aware of any?"

"Absolutely not," I said in my firmest what-the-hell-are-you-talking-about voice. But, newly informed of my middle name (which was on my license), they said it was a mistake and that I was free to go.

So, if you've got a baby boy to name, don't give him a common middle name. It could land him in a cold, Canadian clink, wondering why he had to have a middle name like Michael or William or James.

For extra positive identification, you may even want to consider something as old-fashioned as Nye.

Do it yourself

Cowboy car maintenance

April 5, 1999

I'm generally a do-it-yourselfer when it comes to minor car work. Not because I enjoy it; I actually hate it.

Cattle ranchers are blood and dust kind of guys, not grease and grime kind of guys. No, I do my own car maintenance because I'm conservative, or frugal or just plain ol' cheap.

In college, I remember the kids with the cashy parents taking their cars to the auto shop for even the smallest of repairs. Me, I'd drive one side of my trusty AMC Concord, the Conk, up on the curb, crawl underneath along the street gutter and change the starter with my Vise-Grips and my medium-sized crescent wrench.

Other students would cuss the parking lot vandals who broke off their radio antenna and run to the auto store for a factory-made replacement.

When the Conk lost her antenna, I just made do with a small u-bolt and a piece of rusty barbed wire. The sharp, pointed barbs not only pulled in the distant FM stations, they were also a great deterrent to any punk walking along and snapping off antennas for late-night entertainment.

If you wanted to mess with my car, you'd best be packin' a fencing plier and some leather gloves.

The barbed-wire antenna was handy for critical roadside repairs, too. If your muffler started dragging, you could always borrow a little wire from your antenna, put up with poor reception for awhile and make it home without leaving a trail of exhaust scraps.

Professional service

Considering my proud history in shoddy car maintenance, it was a sad day when I swallowed my pride and let one of those big-city 7½-minute drain-and-lube outfits change the oil in my trusty Buick a couple of weeks ago.

I have had others change my oil on occasion, but it was in a local shop where they respected my wallet and knew I wanted to get my vehicle out for less than $20 ransom.

That big-city crew had no such respect for my budget. Sure, the oil, filter and lube was only $24.95, but they had to go snooping around with their so-called free 21-point checkup.

There're a few things we'd like to go over with you, they told me with their checklist and clipboard in hand.

I straightened up, clenched my teeth and told them to go ahead and give me my beating for automotive neglects.

Well, they said, your air filter is packing 5 pounds of prairie blow sand, your fuel injection is really more of a drip system, you've got enough steel filings in your transmission fluid to throw a compass off of magnetic north, and your serpentine belt has more crack in it than a New York City housing project on cocaine street.

They said something about those things needing to be replaced every 10,000 or 25,000 miles. With 80,000 miles on the odometer and a short memory, I couldn't say with certainty if they'd ever been replaced, much less replaced regularly.

I handed them my credit card and told them to give me half of what they thought I needed. It turned out to be the most expensive $24.95 oil change I'd ever seen.

It was an expensive lesson in car maintenance and one that should teach me something in other areas of life, too. I'm sure not looking forward to my next trip to the dentist or the doctor now!

Mission mosquito

The only good skeeter's a dead skeeter

June 14, 1999

If you're an insect rights activist, don't read any further. If you deplore the savage mass killings of millions of mosquitoes, you'd best go rent some insect-friendly movie like "A Bug's Life" or "Antz" and leave this week's Cowboy Logic to the cruel and unusual.

Readers already know that I spare no love for wood ticks. I'm intent on bathing every one I can in my portable unleaded gasoline chamber. But it's not just wood ticks that bring out my creative sinister side.

Driving down the highway at dusk the other night, I come across a good way to reduce our booming population of mosquitoes. As a matter of fact, you might say the idea (and the skeeters) just kind of hit me. Or hit my windshield to be more exact.

Mass blasting

In the past, I've been fairly satisfied with the single-shot approach to mosquito eradication. Enticing the hungry skeeter with my high-quality Norwegian and English blood, I would let him tap in, pull a pint or two, and then I'd squash him flat while he was full, sluggish and slow.

Progress was slow with the ol' single-shot. Personal satisfaction ran high, but the insect body count never got too significant.

What I discovered on the highway with my windshield is more akin to a fully automatic machine gun than a single-shot cap gun. In the right conditions, like driving next to a shallow slough, some might call the approach downright nuclear.

My new approach in skeeter eradication is to drive around, at the right times, and in the right areas, hitting every one of the miserable little bloodsuckers I can. It's a bit of a kamikaze approach, except that I, the pilot, get to live through the mission.

You might have noticed me driving down the highway. I'm the guy swerving back and forth to increase the killing power of my lethal windshield. I cover so much of the highway that I once racked up 100 miles on a 50-mile trip.

Kamikaze comaraderie

You might also notice me making frequent stops at the gas stations to squeegee the bug guts off the glass and take a tally of my eradication efforts. Sometimes it's tough to get a good body count, but just like counting cows for your banker, a close estimate will do.

At night, I'll be extending the squeegee treatment to my headlights as well. The skeeters have figured out that if they completely blacken my head lamps, they can force me off the road, saving scores of their cousins and hatch mates.

But gut-blackened head lamps don't keep me off the road for long. Strategically located gas stations allow me to hit the road again with a clean windshield, brighter bright lights and a renewed vengeance against my six-legged nemesis. And just in case I have to go skeeter hunting through an isolated area that's short on squeegee pit stops, I'll top off my windshield washer fluid reservoir to help me clear the glass in between gas stations.

At the gas stations, I also get a chance to boost my morale and fraternize with my bug fighting comrades. Sharing squeegees and dipping into the sudsy concoction of guts-be-gone, we swap stories from the front lines.

"How many'd you get tonight?" I'll ask. "About 1,654, but I'm sure I crippled a few that glanced off the glass and went in the ditch to die," they say.

"Way to go! High five!" I'll tell them. And with a little luck, we'll smack number 1,655 between our hands in the high five.

A mosquito mercenary's work is never done.

Traffic congestion

Wide open in Dakota Territory

Feb. 7, 2000

Traffic is a tough concept to grasp for most folks on the plains. Like hurricanes and cockroach infestations, it's something we've heard of but never really experienced.

Granted, there's that day we were in Fargo and couldn't change lanes when we wanted to. And there's that trip we took to Bismarck when we had to actually sit at a traffic light with cars on all sides of us, but, for the most part, we've lived relatively traffic-free.

Sometimes a life free of traffic is a joy. Other times, it's kind of nerve wracking.

Sidekick comforts

Like a stagecoach driver with his trusty sidekick riding shotgun, modern drivers like to know there's someone else out roaming the range with them.

We don't need a lot of comfort. Just the sight of another car every few miles or so will do. If it's a clear blue day, a car every five or 10 miles will suffice. If it's a howling white blizzard, we'd prefer to never lose sight of at least one car directly in front of us.

I got to thinking about this comfort level when I was taking a little-known dirt road from Golva, N.D., to Marmath, N.D. It was about 30 miles long, began with a road sign that said "drive at your own risk" and went through some really pretty country.

I'm used to remote places, but this stretch of road was a little too remote. Driving by myself, in the winter, without anyone knowing where I was at, it had me feeling a little lonely.

I looked down at my cell phone. With barely one bar on the signal screen, it was about as useful as a knife in a gunfight.

I don't usually get nervous, but I was feeling a little apprehensive. It might have had something to do with the fact that there weren't any ranches visible from the road. There weren't even any cows in sight.

Finally, I saw some cows, and where there's cows there's ranchers. Sure enough, around the bend was a ranch and a pickup coming down the road. The only human I'd seen on that trail. It was quite a relief.

Higher highways

Of course, that was a dirt road and they're supposed to be remote. Paved roads are the busy byways.

Like the paved highways from Lemmon, S.D., to Newell, S.D. After speaking in Lemmon last week, I struck out for Newell. It was about 9:30 p.m., so I expected traffic to be kind of meager.

I drove the entire 139 miles, and I saw a whole two other vehicles. Man, the traffic was just nuts that night.

I held the wheel, gave them plenty of room to get by me, and I wondered what people from New York would have thought of that stretch of road.

I didn't mind the lack of traffic so much. I didn't feel entirely lonely since there were lots of yard lights and signs of human habitation along the road. There were even some towns.

What did bother me was that I didn't get a Coke for the road before I left Lemmon. I didn't sweat it, though. There was sure to be a pop machine between Lemmon and Newell. Nope.

Nothing in Shadehill, Usta, Maurine or Mud Butte. Or Newell either. I was in Sturgis before I got something wet to wash down the pound of sunflower seeds I'd eaten on the trip.

And I guess that's why people move to the urban spills of the big cities – cold Coke and companionship out on the road.

County confusion

Finding what's where

Feb. 14, 2000

In some areas, people don't come from towns, they come from counties.

My friends in Iowa don't say they're from Larrabee or Sioux Center, they're from Cherokee County or Sioux County. If you're not familiar with the layout of the counties, it can be a little confusing.

I'm not sure how widespread the county calling craze is, but it seems pretty prevalent in cattle feeding country. Quite a few feedyards take their name from the county they're in – Decator County Feedyard, Knox County Feeders, Grant County Feedyard.

Some county feeders will even send their cattle to slaughter with county packers. They don't go to IBP in Garden City, they go to IBP in Finney County, Kan.

The whole county cattle feeding thing struck me on a couple of runs south I made for speaking jobs with the Lincoln County Cattlemen's and the Dawson County Cattlemen's Associations in Nebraska.

If you think I spoke in Lincoln, Neb., for the Lincoln County Cattlemen's, you've made a sensible guess, but you're wrong.

But that isn't much different from North Dakota geography.

County cross-ups

People have always had a tough time pinpointing where I live.

Once in awhile, people confuse my name with my location. They think I'm from Taylor, N.D., and that my name is Towner. I wonder if my dad had the same problem. They might have figured him to be from either Marshall, N.D., or Taylor, N.D.

Some guessers will put me further northeast in the state's layout, figuring that Towner, N.D., is in Towner County, but that would be too simple. Towner's in McHenry County. However, McHenry, N.D., isn't.

McHenry, N.D., is close to Steele County, but Steele, N.D., is not in that county. Towner County is next to Cavalier County, but, of course, Cavalier, N.D., isn't in Cavalier County.

Mercer, N.D., isn't in Mercer County, but Golden Valley is because it wouldn't want to be in Golden Valley County. Hettinger County isn't too far from there, but don't expect to find Hettinger, N.D., in that county. It's in Adams County.

Some North Dakota towns did happen to luck out and land in their namesake. Grand Forks, Bowman, Bottineau, Rolette and Pembina all ended up in the right place. And, believe it or not, Dunn Center, is in Dunn County, but it's not smack dab in the middle of it.

South Dakota and Montana must have had a larger selection of politically influential people to name places after because their towns and counties don't hardly clash at all.

Despite the confusion, North Dakotans with years of practice can generally keep the cities and counties straight. It was probably a real hassle when the place names were fairly new at the turn of the century.

The fact that our cities are few and far between probably helps us remember locations. I think it was the sign outside of Palisade, Neb., that proclaimed, "nicest little town for miles around." An honest assumption, since it was the only town for miles around. It was bound to be the nicest in a field of one.

What really disheartened me, though, was the writing on the bottom of a billboard coming into Ainsworth, Neb. It greeted me with, "Welcome to the middle of nowhere, Ainsworth, Neb."

When folks ask me where I'm from, I usually answer, "pretty much the middle of nowhere." The people I've told that to have probably been driving all over Ainsworth to try and find me.

I'll have to start telling them, "500 miles straight north of the middle of nowhere."

Altitude adjustment

Lookin' down on the world

Sept. 25, 2000

Living on the prairie, I've always enjoyed a good, long view of my surroundings.

Climbing atop a windmill or peering from the pinnacle of Maggie's Hill, I was always impressed with the miles of scenery that I could ponder.

I guess that's why I always feel a little claustrophobic when I'm in tree country or when I'm driving through mountain valleys. I just can't see far enough to satisfy the depth of field I've grown accustomed to.

So when I knew I was going to Rapid City, S.D., for some meetings last week, I planned on getting a new perspective on things in the Black Hills from the top of Harney Peak.

Up there

The Black Hills are really more than hills, just like the Turtle Mountains of North Dakota are really less than mountains. Perhaps geographers accidentally swapped the two terms while mapping the plains.

Harney Peak lays claim to the highest peak between the Rockies and the Pyrenees Mountains of Europe.

At 7,242 feet, you can see into Nebraska, Wyoming and Montana from the South Dakota mountain. It's easy to see why one of its early climbers, Valentine McGillicuddy, had his ashes placed at its peak. McGillicuddy's remains are marked by a plaque with his Lakota name, Wasicu Wakan, "holy white man." If I had a name like Valentine McGillicuddy, I'd have Wasicu Wakan put on my plaque too.

The Oglala Sioux considered Harney Peak the center of the world, which was crushing to me because I always thought that Towner, N.D., was. But if the medicine man, Black Elk, thought it was good for vision quests and spiritual rejuvenation, I figured I should give it a go.

Alpine staples

Before heading up the mountain, I went uptown and got geared up. I couldn't find a trendy outdoor boutique to shop for coordinated polar fleece and ergonomic hiking staffs, so I just went to Pamida to see what I could find to help me in the wilderness.

I knew the climb would be strenuous, so I picked up the staple foods, beef jerky and chocolate.I also figured I might need something a little more hiker-like in the fuel category, so I rummaged around for some of that crunchy stuff like they eat in California. I found a couple of bags of nuts and twigs in the foraging aisle.

They had some pieces in the bag that looked like range cubes fresh out of the extruder. I kind of wondered what was in those pellets, but, like sausage and hot dogs, I decided I was better off not knowing.

With supplies assembled, I picked up my climbing partner and headed for base camp. There were two routes to the top. In essence, one sign read "the easy way," and the other read "the cowboy way." We, of course, chose the latter.

It was a real butt buster. Most people ascend the easy way and come down the cowboy way to avoid the steep climb. But Tommi Jo and I were both ranch raised and used to misery. Climbing 2,142 feet in $2^1/_2$ hours wasn't much worse than climbing around, up and over the workin' alley for a couple hours while vaccinating calves.

We made it to the top where the old Civilian Conservation Corps had built a fire lookout tower in 1939. We ate our nuts, twigs, jerky and chocolate and decided that if we came up the short, steep way, we could just as well go down the long, coasting trail. That way we could have both a difficult and lengthy journey.

Now I suppose I'll have to hit the top peaks in the Rockies and the Pyrenees. But I better get some more nuts, twigs and mystery pellets.

At a loss

If you want it, keep it close by

Jan. 15, 2001

I don't make a lot of trips on an airplane, but when I do, I usually have pretty good luck with my luggage.

I give the folks at the counter my bags, and when I get where I'm going, they give 'em back to me.

I usually don't travel with anything too necessary. Just some clean clothes and a toothbrush. And just in case they don't arrive, I've done a lot of training on the ranch to get used to week-old clothes and a piece of chewing gum to keep the molars clean.

When I got into Denver last week to take in some meetings, I took the usual comfort in seeing my overstuffed green bag come down the chute and land in the carousel at the baggage claim area.

Whew! I had clean clothes and a toothbrush. What I didn't have, however, was the snowboard that I packed to help me get down the slopes of the Colorado Rockies in style. Business trip packing takes more than suits and ties, you know.

Boardless

I peered at the oversized bag carousel for 45 minutes before I gave in and asked the baggage person (bag lady?) where my snowboard disappeared.

She made a couple of phone calls, typed a few things in her computer and told me I didn't have a snowboard any more, but I might in a day or two.

She said they'd get on task and try to deliver it sometime soon. Her last words were, "We'll pay for a snowboard rental, but don't go buying anything." So much for my plans of upgrading to a snowboard worth twice as much, compliments of United Airlines.

I never found out how a bag that was 6 feet long and a foot wide could get lost on a direct flight from Bismarck to Denver, but I reckon it took some doing. You'd think those baggage handlers had their training on the Taylor Ranch.

It's been a tough fall in the lost and unfound department on the ranch. We never did find a couple of pipe wrenches that the hired man laid somewhere the day before the first fall snow. And then a couple of light log chains got gobbled up by the snow snakes this winter.

I suppose the same thing happened at the Denver International Airport. Someone dropped my bag or maybe it fell off the bag wagon and there it was – gone.

The nice thing about dropping things on a busy airfield is that someone's bound to find it. There're enough vehicles, planes and people traversing that concrete that someone's sure to spot a 6-foot-long bag laying on the ground.

Sure enough, someone spotted the bag and it got delivered to the hotel where I was camped out. I still ended up on the mountain with a rented board, but at least my gear was in hand for the trip home.

I was actually pretty impressed that the airline got the lost board and bag returned so quickly. I don't plan on seeing my pipe wrenches and log chains until April or May, if then.

Maybe I should get that United crew to come out and help on the ranch and lose my tools for me. At least we'd have them found in a day or two, and if they didn't, I'd at least have a paid rental to tide me over until spring.

The Big Apple

A small-town guy takes a bite

March 12, 2001

New York, New York. Like Disneyland or the bearded lady at the state fair, it's something everybody should see. Heck, the idea for Disneyland or the bearded lady herself may have even come from New York.

You can see, hear, smell, taste and experience just about everything the world has to offer right there in the Big Apple. Funny though, no matter how much individuality the melting pot of Manhattan boasts, you'll still turn heads if you walk down Broadway with a cowboy hat on.

Cowboy in Carnegie

Last fall, my brother told me he was going to be performing at New York's Carnegie Hall with the San Francisco Symphony & Choir. I immediately knew this would be my best excuse to go see the big city and all it had to offer.

My brother's always been an accomplished musician. He can play most any instrument and sing like a bird. Of course, his talents weren't always appreciated on the ranch.

He used to practice his singing while out on the meadow cutting hay with the John Deere "A" and a 9-foot sickle bar mower. One time, Dad flagged him in off the field to find out what the noise was. When Justin told him he was singing, he said, "Good, I thought there was a bearing going out on the mower!" Probably not the greatest compliment received by a future Carnegie Hall performer.

Not many south Towner hay mowers make it to New York to perform with a Grammy Award-winning symphony, so I decided to fly out east and take in the performance.

The hall was grand, the symphony was excellent, and the evening was memorable, to say the least.

Tourist stuff

From Carnegie Hall, I did the usual things one needs to do in New York. I saw a Broadway musical, "Annie, Get Your Gun," with Reba McEntire playing Annie Oakley.

I rode the elevator to the top of the World Trade Center and the Empire State Building. I rode the subway, checked out Central Park and Greenwich Village and made a stop at the Museum of Natural History.

I walked down Broadway and stared at the lights. I ate some spectacular food and paid some spectacular prices for everything from hotels to shows to food and drinks. It's a pretty cashy city.

I rode the ferry out to the Statue of Liberty and Ellis Island. That was a pretty meaningful stop. My grandfather, Syvert Dokken, was just there 91 years ago. He bid goodbye (forever) to his family in Norway, got aboard the soon-to-be-famous ship Lusitania and set out across the pond for the promise of America.

Now, less than a century later, his grandsons live in a world where people can fly thousands of miles just to see a symphony. He has a grandson he never met singing in America's greatest hall. Another grandson is able to balance a ranch, an off-ranch career, and a writing habit because of computers, cell phones, e-mail and modern automobiles.

It's been a hell of a century, and despite its faults and shortcomings, America has offered tremendous opportunities. And that's what Syvert was looking for when his ship pulled in to New York harbor.

New York still plays host to people looking for opportunity. Every other person on the street talked a language I didn't understand. Funny, though, coming from North Dakota where people generally look and talk and act "like Americans," I felt most like an American in that mixed-up place they call Manhattan.

Hat trick

Headgear grabs the attention

March 26, 2001

According to the Eagles, city girls can open doors with just a smile. According to me, a cowboy hat in New York City can get people to open their mouth, drop their jaw or even greet you in a city short on casual greetings.

My recent trip to the Big Apple gave me ample opportunity to study people's reaction to my headgear. A guy walking around in a turban or a Dr. Seuss Cat-in-the-Hat lid gets fewer looks and double takes than someone in a simple wide-brimmed Stetson.

Walking around Manhattan with a cowboy hat on got me the usual geographic accusations of, "Are you from Texas?" If I had a dollar for every time someone asked me that, I could buy a west Texas mansion and rightfully answer their question with a "yes."

The other common comment from people who don't say hello to hardly anyone was, "Hey, cowboy!"

I'm always at a loss for an answer to that salutation. Their greeting related directly to my attire. So do I pick out a feature of their wardrobe to greet them by? Something like "Hey, blue suit woman" or "Hey, black jacket guy!" Or do I try to guess their occupation by their appearance and say, "Hey, office drone" or "Hey, street vendor!"?

I usually just return their astute observation of who I am with a "Hi" or even a "Howdy" if I really want to make their day.

Cowboy privilege

New York City had lots of daytime attractions to check out, but a trip to the big city wouldn't be complete without seeing a little of the nightlife as well.

A hometown buddy of mine was working a construction job in Connecticut this winter to support his cow habit, so he came down to Manhattan while I was there to traipse around the city with me. If you thought one guy in a cowboy hat could attract attention in that city, you should've seen the looks we got with two guys in hats.

We had both seen the movie, "Coyote Ugly." We went to the show thinking it was a documentary on livestock predation by unattractive wild canines, but it turned out to be a pretty fun movie about a rowdy bar in New York City.

Since we were now in New York, we decided to see if this saloon really existed. It did, but "Coyote Ugly" was just its stage name. The real bar went by the name of "Hogs & Heifers." Seemed like the perfect place for a couple of cowboys to spend a Saturday night.

We jumped out of our yellow cab in front of Hogs & Heifers, and were greeted with a long line of people waiting to get into this quaint little pub. We went to the back of the line to wait our turn.

We weren't there two minutes when the lady at the door walked right up to us at the back of the line and said, "You two, come with me." She took us right to the head of line and we were in like Flynn.

It was rock star treatment. We were "the chosen." And it was all because of our hats. They needed a couple of North Dakota cowboys to add to the special ambience of Hogs & Heifers.

Our hats also got us noticed later that night by some panhandlers, a pimp, and a couple of hookers. "Hey, cowboy," was their best shot at an original opener.

Of course, once they found out we were real cowboys (meaning we actually owned cows), they left us alone. Hat or no hat, there's something about a cowboy's empty wallet that really turns those folks off.

Story time

Tall tales on the hi-line

May 7, 2001

Have you heard any good stories lately? Well I've just heard a bunch of them, and even told a few myself. I spent last week in and around Cut Bank, Mont., for the Montana Storyteller's Roundup, and I've decided that even a single evening with a group of good storytellers is worth more than a month's worth of more modern "entertainment."

Storytelling is getting to be a lost art in the world of video games, dvd players and cyber entertainment. But set a bunch of kids (both big and little) in front of a good storyteller and the human voice can still hold the attention as well as, or better than, the world's most advanced microchip.

I was there to do rope spinning with a bit of cowboy philosophy. I joined people who could sing and play guitar, perform Native American sign language, tell stories from the hollers of Tennessee and dress up like mountain men, miners or old time drovers to relate history in story form.

It was a great group to ride the trail with.

On the trail

And we did ride the trail. The organizers of the event worked hard to share the talents of the group with as many people as possible in Glacier County.

I jumped in the car with my bag of ropes and was carted off to elementary schools on the Blackfeet Indian Reservation, a couple of Hutterite colonies, some high schools and an auditorium in Cut Bank where people, young and old, from far wide, came for some good, old-fashioned entertainment.

It was a big event for a town like Cut Bank, population 2,000, to tackle. Like most small town events it was accomplished with a lot of hard work by a few very dedicated people.

The community was gracious in their support. The Glacier Gateway Inn, official motel of the Storyteller's Roundup and home of Chilly Willy, the 27-foot-tall talking penguin, even made the performers a home-cooked supper of turkey and all the fixings.

Local Hutterite colonies had their homemade bread included in our gift baskets, and the young ladies of the Seville Colony sang some beautiful multi-part harmony for us after we finished our performance for them.

By the end of the week, my cup runneth over with the culture of the Blackfeet Indians, the German-speaking Hutterites, the Texas drovers who ranched the Montana range, the Irish hard rock miners of Butte and the other people who continue to sing and write poems about life under the Big Sky.

Choo choo chugga

One of my favorite parts of traveling the hi-line of Montana is the opportunity to hop on the Amtrak in Rugby, N.D., and let someone else do the driving to points west like Malta and Havre and Cut Bank.

When it comes to low-stress travel, it's hard to beat the train. Sit back, watch the prairies roll by, take a snooze, do some reading and meet some interesting folks.

Every once in a while a person wonders if he's missing out on something by making his life out on the remote plains. On the train, I had the pleasure of dining with people from Cleveland, New York, Seattle and San Antonio who thought maybe they were the ones missing out by not making their home on the range.

So the story I took home from the Storytelling Roundup is that with a little appreciation for the people, places and simple things around us we can all decide to "live happily ever after."

Packing light

The trials of travel

Aug. 13, 2001

I've never considered myself much of a clothes horse, but I have put together a bit of a wardrobe over the years.

It's enough of a collection that when I pack those duds for a four- or five-day trip, the suitcase they go into fails to cut it as a carry-on bag. So the airlines tell me to check the bag, board the plane and leave the luggage to them.

The scary part is you never know how long you'll be leaving that luggage to them.

Bag check

Last week, I was off to Kansas City for a few days worth of meetings. I packed a suit and tie, some real clothes and enough socks and underwear to make the week. I was ready to take on the big city.

Of course, my flight out of North Dakota got delayed, and it doesn't take much of a delay to eat up the one hour that was in the schedule to make my connection in Minneapolis.

Being an optimist, though, I walked to the gate where my plane for Kansas City was probably revving its engines, backing out and hitting the runway. I strolled up to the gate at 1:35 p.m., and, by the grace of Northwest, my 1:30 p.m. was still sitting there!

I gave the gal at the gate a wink and a smile and asked if she could still get me on that plane. She said, "Hurry up, let's go," unlocked the door, motored the jetway back up to the door and knocked on the little window of the big plane.

I took my seat and was glad to have made the flight, but I knew my luggage was a goner. I served my time at the baggage claim in Kansas City and made the obligatory lost luggage report. Eight hours later, I was back in business, toothbrush and all.

A few days later, I packed those bags back up, crossed my fingers and turned 'em over to the airline for the return trip.

Two in a row

Once again, I got on a delayed flight, except this time, I got to my 1:15 p.m. connecting flight at 1:10 p.m. I was pretty sure my bags were going to stay in Minneapolis a lot longer than I was.

The plane took off, but 30 minutes later, the pilot came on and said we were turning around and going back to Minneapolis. How nice, I thought. They must be going back to get my luggage!

Actually, they had a heat indicator light that came on and he decided to go back and get it checked out. It seemed a little cautious, but when you're 26,000 feet in the air, it probably pays to be a little cautious.

I've overheated a lot of tractors and drove 'em until they boiled over to get a little more hay baled, but making hay's more critical than getting a plane load of people to Minot, N.D. Especially at the risk of their lives and one pretty expensive airplane.

We got on another plane an hour and a half later and we each got a coupon for $100 off our next trip. A day later, I got my clothes back and another coupon for $25. I guess if you have your choice between an emergency landing and lost luggage, go for the emergency landing. It's worth more.

So now I've got $125 to work with the next time I fly the friendly skies. But I think next time I'll pack a little lighter and keep my luggage close at hand.

Where ya from?

The great "Dakota" debate

Aug. 27, 2001

It's getting tougher for me to give a straight answer when people ask me where I'm from.

It's not as easy as saying, "I'm from North Dakota," anymore. Not since the debate began about changing the state's name to, simply, Dakota.

The debate has been great fodder for columnists, news anchors and television talk show hosts. A lot of ink and newsprint have been devoted to the subject. Even Dave Barry took a run at understanding the idea in his syndicated column.

Barry, and most everyone else who's analyzed the idea of taking away the North and just leaving Dakota, have focused on the belief that we can change the weather by changing the name.

No one really thinks that South Dakota is free of snow and cold just because the word South precedes Dakota.

If they did, it could get as ugly as the picture painted by Dave Barry where, "Millions of tourists, lured by the word 'South,' flock to South Dakota every winter, often wearing nothing but skimpy bathing suits. Within hours, most of them die and become covered with snow, not to be found until spring, when they cause a major headache for South Dakota's farmers by clogging up the cultivating machines."

I don't think creating a winter-free, warm image was the whole reasoning behind the name change idea that came from a meeting called the New Economy Initiative sponsored by the Greater North Dakota (or, Dakota) Association back in June.

It was one of many ideas that the group proposed, but the other ideas on such mundane things as creating jobs, stemming outmigration and building wealth never got the media buzz that the name change did.

Since the proposal, outside experts thought if we really wanted to change the name we should go with something like Baja Manitoba to get a real southern feel. Or Nike Dakota to get the most commercial bang for the buck and maybe even lighten the load on property taxes with a little corporate underwriting.

No, I don't think the real intent of the proposal was to make North Dakota seem warmer, to attract national attention or even to signify our willingness to change and make a fresh start in the new economy.

I don't think it had anything to do with marketing. I think it all came down to abbreviation.

Sans syllables

As busy as everyone is these days, I don't think we have a lot of time to waste on extra syllables in our quick and punchy sentences. We've traded lengthy letters for to-the-point e-mails, swapped meaningful one-on-one conversations for voice mails that make it under the two-minute whistle.

I think it's crucial that we drop the word North for the sheer time savings afforded by having one less word to describe where we're from.

Dakota itself is a shortened translation of the Sioux word, WoDakotah, which means "harmony." We dropped the "Wo", added the "North", and we're right back where we started.

Yup, from now on, official or not, I am from Dakota – short, sweet and to the point.

I just hope I don't have to waste a lot of time telling people where this state with the new, shortened name is. I don't think I can afford the extra minutes in today's new economy.

Viva Las Vegas

In the holiday spirit

Dec. 31, 2001

I'm not much of gambler, at least not casino style anyway, so I had to wait for a good non-gambling excuse to go to Las Vegas. The National Finals Rodeo and the chance to meet up with a couple of friends was just the catalyst I needed.

There's a lot more pride in saying, "I'm going to Vegas for the National Finals Rodeo," than there is in saying, "I'm going to Vegas to spend mindless hours in front of a slot machine spending my retirement savings and going to big production burlesque shows."

I always heard how cheap and easy it was to fly to Las Vegas. The theory was that the casinos wanted you to get there as cheaply as possible so you had more money to gamble with. Whoever I was listening to must have been lying.

I was attending a cattle meeting in Casper, Wyo., and I wanted to get from Casper to Las Vegas. It was not cheap and it was not easy.

The best direct flights were already full, so I flew from Casper, Wyo., to Salt Lake City, Utah, to Los Angeles, to Las Vegas. Some extra lead time for checking in and a few lengthy layovers kept me occupied from 5 a.m. to 4 p.m.

But I was there man. Sin City! Um, I mean, respected home of the Professional Rodeo Cowboy Association's National Finals Rodeo.

I met one of my buddies at the airport, and we got ourselves checked in at the neon-bathed Stardust Hotel on Las Vegas Boulevard.

Supper timing

We then ran headlong into another Las Vegas misconception – you can get prime rib anywhere you turn for $5 a plate. My buddy and I must have taken a wrong turn because we sat down to a prime rib that, albeit extremely good, cost us $30 a pop.

But the prime rib turned out to be a bargain after all that night. Because had we not eaten at that particular restaurant at that particular time and been walking back on its particular stretch of the Strip, we would have missed out on the best luck we had in Las Vegas.

We were walking back like two typical North Dakota bumpkins when a fella in an SUV pulled up alongside of us and asked if we were going to the rodeo that night. We figured the guy was some scam artist, spotted our cowboy hats and picked the most obvious opening line.

"No we aren't," we answered since we had just planned on catching the next night's performance, and the fella came back with, "Would you like to go? I've got two tickets." We said, "well sure," but we had been in that city long enough to know that this kind of kindness came at a price. "How much?" we asked.

That's when he shocked us with, "Nothing, you can just have them. I don't want these tickets to go to waste, and I can't use them." It didn't take us long to say thanks, catch a cab and plunk ourselves down in the lower-level, mid-arena seating that would have cost us $100 or $150 from anyone else in that town.

So, yes, Virginia, there is a Santa Claus, and he was driving an SUV on the Strip in Las Vegas on Dec. 14. The holiday season does definitely get people in the giving mood.

Of course, the casino managers, pawn shop brokers and card dealers still had a ways to go to find that spirit.

Surrounded

Inescapable information

Jan. 28, 2002

I never knew how busy we had gotten until I went into the bathroom at a restaurant and saw newspapers posted above the urinals.

Granted, we're living in the "information age," but it seemed like this was taking it a little too far. Do we really need to be using every little bit of idle time in our day?

Will newspapers above the urinals really broaden our base of knowledge, improve our productivity and substantially increase the gross national product? Maybe, but I think the improvement would be minimal.

I give the restaurant an "A" for effort and ingenuity in pasting their papers on the wall, but overall, I'm giving the practice a thumbs down.

First, you can't focus your full attention on the newspaper. Reading wasn't the No. 1 focal point of the trip to the can, and the best it can do on the list of things to do is a close runner-up.

Second, there isn't enough time spent standing there to get a good enough grasp of the information to be of any real use. Maybe this is where speed-reading talents could come in handy.

And third, there're enough decisions to be made in life and in the bathroom. I don't need any more. It used to be as simple as choosing between the tall urinal or the short one, next to the wall or in the middle.

You still have to decide tall or short, wall or center – plus, now, you have to make a decision on front page, regional, sports, entertainment or classifieds. Trips to the bathroom were supposed to give you physical relief, not create more mental anguish.

After leaving the restaurant and their reading restroom, I decided to do something a little less stressful like fuel up the vehicle.

High-octane news

I drove up to the gas station, jumped out, unscrewed my gas cap and made a grab for the unleaded with ethanol. I flipped the lever, and before I could even start feeling good about helping out the corn farmers, I started hearing voices.

Being a little unstable anyway, I didn't think anything of these little voices in my head. But I noticed the voices sounded a lot like newscasters and the topic was the war in Afghanistan.

I turned around toward the pump and, sure enough, there was a little 8-inch screen with a talking head projected on it. And they were filling me in on the day's events around the world.

The information age had me painted in a corner. I was looking forward to just standing next to the gas pump with my hands in my pockets, shoulders shrugged against the cold, contemplating the steam from my breath.

These days, I guess there's no contemplation allowed. I had to spend my three minutes of fueling time watching the dang news.

So I learned three minutes worth of current events, shut off the pump (and the television) and paid for the gas.

Back behind the wheel, I decided it was time to get selfish and do some reflection and contemplation. I turned off the radio, stepped on the accelerator and headed down the road.

I looked forward to a media-free trip, at least until the next bathroom stop.

Seattle sea time

Land loving cowboy heads west

May 6, 2002

I haven't been to every state in the union, but after last week, I can go to my list and put a check mark next to Washington state.

I flew into Seattle, Wash., to kick around in the rain for the weekend. I think I saw Mount Rainier. At least it was supposed to be there somewhere in the clouds.

I did see the Port of Seattle, the freighters, the tugboats, the containers being loaded off the docks. They were all new sights and sounds for a landlocked cowboy from North Dakota.

I even did a little seafaring myself. It was an even bigger deal than my pontoon ride on the Missouri River. On Puget Sound, I lined up my rental car with a couple dozen other autos and actually drove on to a boat. My first ferry ride was a good one. We didn't sink and I didn't get seasick.

I saw a couple people on the ferry with binoculars, but I didn't give it much thought until I disembarked and had someone tell me about A-73, the orphan orca.

Whale tale

A-73 was an orphan killer whale from the A-Pod, hence the prefix. Her mother died when she was just a yearling, and she struck out on her own and wound up in Puget Sound.

She's been hanging around the Fauntleroy-Vashon ferry route ever since.

None of the binocular toters seemed to spot A-73 while we were on the ferry, though. I know how they felt trying to find a shy critter like A-73. I once had a calf named T-3 hunker down in the brush and evade me for hours. Angus and orcas can both blend in with the scenery.

Back on shore, I got to see plenty of other big fish at the Seattle fish market. They did more than peddle halibut there – they entertained. They could work the crowd, sling the salmon and have fun while they did it.

The fellas at the fish market are even out telling corporate America how to have fun in the workplace. It's good to see some apron wearing fish slingers out making consultant's wages and teaching tie-wearing executives how to lighten up.

I ought to invite those fish slingers out when we work our calves. If they think "flying fish" are fun, they'd have a blast "throwing calves." I hope they bring some of their customers with them. Folks who'll pay $20 a pound for smoked salmon shouldn't blink an eye when I open up my freezer and sell some beef for the same money.

Getting home

Seattle was a great city to visit, and the sun even came out before I boarded the jet for Billings, Mont.

From Billings, I had to board what I affectionately call the "flying culvert," a 19 passenger prop plane. The flight went great, but getting on it took three security checks.

First, I won the lottery! Out of all the people getting on the twin prop, all five of us, I got picked to have my checked luggage checked. The fella fished through my dirty clothes, declared them a little smelly, but generally safe to be put on the plane.

Second, I did the usual security check to get into the terminal. Of course, I set off the beeper, so it was off to the side and off with the cowboy boots.

And last, I was the lucky one of five to get another hand search before boarding the Beechcraft. Again, off with the boots.

Now I'm glad we're making the airspace of eastern Montana safe from terrorists and I'm happy to cooperate with all the extra security. I just wish they'd have some bootjacks to help us cowboys with the search process.

Train travel

Limited routes, limitless amusement — Dec. 16, 2002

I like to travel, and when I can accomplish the goal without gripping a steering wheel, so much the better.

That's why I like trains. All aboard! You settle in, sit back and, without even pushing the gas pedal, you're on your way.

The unfortunate thing about train travel is that your routes of travel are pretty limited. I'd like to take the train from the ranch south to Bismarck, N.D., but it just isn't in the cards. Same with Billings, Mont., or Spearfish, S.D., or Denver, Colo.

But if I want to get to Havre or Cut Bank or Malta, Mont., I need only climb aboard the Empire Builder at our station in Rugby, N.D., and I'm on my way.

Working the high line

I've taken speaking jobs in places like Cut Bank and Chinook and Havre,

Mont., just so I could ride the train out there. Well, maybe I was influenced by the speaker's fee I collect, but train travel was a nice bonus of the job.

This winter, I was invited to speak to the Montana Area Conservation Districts state meeting in Lewistown, Mont. Now Lewistown isn't on the Amtrak line, but I mentioned my penchant for train travel and, before you know it, I had an Amtrak ticket to Malta and a rental car in the works for the 100-mile traverse to Lewistown.

On the way to Malta, I took a snooze, did some reading and visited with a fella I barely knew who lived only 30 miles from the ranch.

I went to the dining car for lunch. One of the best things trains do for the betterment of mankind is fill every table in the dining car. So, even if you go in there alone, you get seated with another traveler, or, at supper, another three travelers to fill the seats.

During lunch en route to Malta, I had the pleasure of eating lunch with a young lady who was a Congregationalist minister in Massachusetts. She was off to the backwoods of Washington state for a two-month sabbatical. I sent her off with a copy of "A Collection of Cowboy Logic" to lighten up her sabbatical meditations.

Detrained and on foot

The trip to Malta isn't a long one, and by early afternoon I had "detrained" and was looking for my waiting rental car. The only car at the train station parking lot was an early '70s model Grand Toronado.

The Toronado was a little short on paint, the stuffing was coming out of the seats, and there wasn't a hubcap to be found on it. I never know what the budget might be for my speaking clients, so I tried the dented door in the chance that this might be my waiting rental.

The door was locked and I spied a sign in the windshield that said the car belonged to an Amtrak traveler who'd be back to retrieve it in a couple months. That's the kind of people I like to travel with, not those first-class jet setters paying $20 a day to park their Mercedes while they're away.

My rental, a 1996 Ford Taurus, did show up, and I made the drive to Lewistown to do my deal. The next day, I was back on the train and back to enjoying my trip.

Dinner in the dining car with a Montana farmwife, a retired military man and a Wisconsin real estate agent. An across-the-aisle visit with a Twin Cities architectural artist who had made an alternate party run for mayor of St. Paul and now traveled by train to his primitive homestead cabin in northern Montana every other week.

Yes sir, train travel. There's just nothing like it.

Author's Note: One of my astute readers from Malta, Mont., read this column and solved the mystery of the semi-abandoned car that I described in the Amtrak parking lot. The car was called "Big Red" and was owned by a writer at the Phillips County News who left it there when he jumped a train for Aurora, Ill., to play Santa Claus at a big shopping mall for a couple of months. I think I would've enjoyed riding the train with this Montana Santa who maintained an affection for well-used cars.

Globally positioned

Plotting property under the satellites

Sept. 8, 2003

Ranching isn't generally known for cutting edge technology.

We still ride horses and string barbed wire. Horses have been around about as long as dirt, and barbed wire was invented in 1874. We like tradition.

One piece of technology that has caught my eye, though, is the global positioning satellite receivers.

Farmers have been using GPS to guide their field sprayers and plot their yields as they harvest. They say they're pretty accurate, amazing when you consider the information is coming from satellites in outer space.

Travelers use GPS quite a bit. I was in a rental car once with a talking GPS receiver that could take you from the Minneapolis airport to the Metrodome and never miss a single exit!

Geocaching has a lot of regular folks out and about with their GPS units looking for hidden treasures. It's quite a craze and websites direct people to different caches as they travel on their family vacations or make day trips around the region.

As of yet, I don't have one of these global positioners, but I have gotten to take one for a test drive.

Global fishing

I was at my uncle's one day when he handed me a little black thing that looked like a cell phone and said, "here, see if you can get this to work." What he handed me was a GPS receiver, and, kind of like inviting a grandson over to set the clock on your VCR, he was hoping I could figure the gadget out for him.

He had important business to do with his GPS. He wanted to mark his favorite fishing spots.

I fired up the receiver and got excited as soon as it showed my location at 48 degrees 12 minutes north latitude and 100 degrees 18 minutes west longitude. I've always liked geography – I've been a member of the National Geographic Society since 1986. This was right up my alley.

I wondered what I could experiment with to get proficient with my uncle's receiver.

In some of the drought years, I could have used GPS coordinates to mark the rounds in the hayfield. But the hay wasn't that thin this year. I could tell the difference between hay that was cut and wasn't cut without satellite help.

I thought about using the receiver to find all the tools I've lost around the ranch. I've been geocaching fencing pliers, wrenches and ear taggers for years and didn't even know it. Unfortunately, I didn't have any of the coordinates marked of where I lost them, so I couldn't use the GPS for that either.

But I could use some GPS help marking property boundaries down on the hay meadow.

Satellite sections

Our property lines are pretty loose. It comes with living in an area where land isn't worth too much. But we still like to have a post or two to sight by when we're striking out a field.

Property lines can make for interesting sport. Dad says there were a couple of old codgers in the neighborhood years ago who had a square surveyor's stone marking their property line. By the time those two neighbors got done rolling that stone back and forth trying to get a little of each other's land, it was plumb round!

Once I got the unit switched from nautical miles to miles and I figured out how to convert latitude and longitude to the corners of sections, I set up some pretty good lines.

The sky was clear and the satellites were putting out a strong beam. The unit showed an estimated error of zero feet. I was going to let the receiver plot my route back home when, all of a sudden, the screen went blank.

All this advanced technology, and there I stood with a set of dead batteries.

Lucky for me, I had a non-globally positioned prairie trail to lead me home.

Telemark Taylorson

Rediscovering Norwegian roots

Dec. 15, 2003

People wouldn't expect a cowboy with an English surname to be very Nordic, but, the truth is I'm three-quarters Norwegian by blood.

So along with my penchant for horses and cattle and my British accent that's been watered down by 300 years of living on this side of the pond, I find myself with some pretty strong desires that can only be explained by my Norwegian roots.

I have the explainable old-country appetite for foods in various shades of white smothered in butter. I don't really mind cold weather, snow, ice, long summer days or long winter nights. And, since an early age, I've been quite comfortable with having my feet strapped down on a pair of long, thin boards.

I remember when I was about 12 years old, my full-blooded Norwegian mother brought home a pair of cross country skis and boots for me from a sporting goods spring clearance sale. The skis were a little long and the boots a little too big, but she figured I'd grow into them.

I did. North Dakota is a good place to cross country ski with a lot more places to go cross country than downhill. During high school, I would ski a couple miles every day while I checked my trapline for the fur pelts that funded my youth.

After a few years of kick and glide cross country skiing I was able to head to the mountains and start in on some downhill skiing. It struck a chord. Maybe some genetic memory of the fjords that Grandpa went careening down back in Norway.

Legend has it my grandfather was a pretty good skier in his younger days in Hallingdal, Norway. There's even a trophy cup in the family that he won in a ski jumping competition.

Another Norske in our flat land neighborhood was very famous in the old country for his skiing ability. Sondre Norheim is buried in a country church cemetery just 15 miles or so from our ranch.

He was just another Scandinavian homesteader around here, but, worldwide, he's recognized as the "father of modern skiing." A competitive, prize-winning skier, he immigrated from Telemark, Norway, to Denbigh, N.D. His ski and binding modifications and telemark skiing style were the model for popular recreational skiing today.

Recently, I was in Banff, Alberta, for a speaking job, and I took an extra day to spend at the ski slopes. I figured it would be a good time to honor my Norwegian ancestors by trying the classic telemark style of skiing.

I rented a pair of "teles" with the free-heel binding and the boots that flex. It's a pretty loose system compared to the more popular fixed-heel alpine skis.

When you're telemarking, every turn requires you to drop down on one knee while thrusting your other knee forward. It's a somewhat prayerful looking position. Most of us are praying that we'll be able to stand up straight again after we're done turning and that our legs will still function at the end of the day.

I had a little experience with the telemark turn from cross country skiing, and, along with a few pointers from another telemarker on the mountain, I made a pretty good go of it.

After ripping one particularly good run down the mountainside, I felt especially Nordic. Folks at the ski lodge must have figured that tall, lanky carver coming down the hill was surely Ole Olson or John Johnson or Thor Thorson.

After that good day of telemarking, I'm ready to renew my heritage. I'm asking for a Norwegian ski sweater for Christmas, one long enough to cover up my big cowboy belt buckle. I'm going to slip a little more Norwegian brogue into my talk and stray from my perfect Queen's English.

It'll be a complete transformation from Taylor to Taylorson. God dag.

Home on the winter range

Where the deer play and stay and eat

March 22, 2004

Our home where the buffalo roam, where the deer and the antelope play, is a little short on antelope, but the buffalo are roaming and the deer are playing in numbers large enough to make us wonder whose home this really is.

I hate to reinforce the image that North Dakota isn't real cosmopolitan, but a few weeks ago, we had to chase some buffalo down the road on our way to Sunday morning church. I'm not trying to cast a stereotype of the Great Plains as a Buffalo Commons; I'm just telling it like it is.

This herd of bison was migrating toward us when we got them turned around and heading back to our neighbor's ranch where they were supposed to be.

Like Roger Miller said, you can't roller skate in a buffalo herd. And, truth is, they're not real easy to drive a car through, either. It's best to just chase them from behind.

It's not every churchgoer who gets to chase a thundering herd on their way to worship. It was an easy chase since the buffalo didn't care to leave the road to wallow in the ditches with snow up to their beards. Luckily, they remembered to hang a right at the first intersection and found their way home.

The snow-filled ditches and snow-banked road edges have made both buffalo and cattle chasing easier this winter.

When one neighbor's heifers made an escape, all another neighbor had to do was toot his horn once and follow them back into the yard. They never strayed an inch from the roadway. Pretty easy cowboying on our snowy trails.

Deer dodging

If we're heading into town in the evening these days, we have to budget an extra five or 10 minutes in case we get caught in a deer jam, too.

Without fail, we'll find ourselves running late and driving 30 miles an hour behind a bunch of whitetails running as fast as they can, tongues dragging, sides heaving.

We don't dare get too aggressive in trying to pass them for fear of damaging the plastic bumpers and fiberglass fenders on our modern vehicle.

Finally, they'll either find an intersection or, in desperation, hit the snowy ditch, break through, roll, struggle and be on their way. By then, we're late and we have to use the caught-behind-some-slow-moving-deer excuse. But everyone around here understands.

Deer have gotten downright verminous in our neighborhood this winter. We never used to have that many, our hay was never good enough for them and we didn't spill enough grain by our feed bin.

Then I bought some pretty nice second-cutting alfalfa hay bales. I think some of the deer followed the truck all the way from the farm where I bought the hay 20 miles away. The rest must have heard about the fine alfalfa through the hungry deer network.

We're now a four-star choice for about 30 deer to stay and dine. I did get the alfalfa pretty well protected from them so they've diversified their diet to include a little bit of everything else in our feedyard.

I don't know how to get them to move on from our home on the range.

Maybe some of those antelope that live a long way from here could invite them down to play.

Weather watchers

Darn cold and proud of it

Anything worth suffering in is worth bragging about

Jan. 18, 1999

North Dakotans take a lot pride in their winter misery, and the last few weeks of frigid temperatures have had quite a few bursting at the seams with pride.

The other day, our thermometer registered 22 below zero. And just like we do after a summer rainstorm, we called one of the neighbors to compare notes.

Sure enough, their mercury had dipped even further – a boastful 28 below! It wasn't a big surprise, though. Their rain gauge always shows at least 10 hundredths more rain than we ever get, and I bet their bottom-bouncing thermometer came from the same manufacturer.

Braggin' or complainin'?

The tough thing to figure out is why we tend to brag about something that we really ought to be complaining about.

I can see the boast in getting more rain out of a rain shower – rain can bring a little prosperity to a farm or ranch. But why would we want to get more cold out of the cold front? Cold weather's not good for much of anything except turning the trunk of your car into that extra freezer space you needed for the deer you shot last fall.

Then I realized it's not about being better off, it's about being worse off. It's a pain thing, like the masochistic fella who kept beating his head against the brick wall because it felt so good when he stopped.

North Dakota doesn't get much play in the national news – I guess we don't have enough bad stuff going on to warrant the attention. But we will get a small piece of the spotlight in the winter when windchills dip to 60 or 70 below.

Like everyone else, I was proud when the recent cold snap made the morning news. What upset me, though, was that they chose to highlight Bismarck with its paltry 18-below-zero temperature.

It was a full 10 degrees colder at the Taylor Ranch! With such a mild temp making the headlines, I fear that the rest of the nation will begin to think we're getting soft up here on the American Arctic!

Comparative conversions

I finally figured out the North Dakota mentality toward cold weather when a friend e-mailed me the "temperature conversion guide." Here's a few of the highlights:

When it's 35 above, Italian cars won't start; North Dakotans drive with their windows down. At 32 above, distilled water freezes; Bismarck, N.D., water gets thicker. At 20 above, Floridians wear coats, gloves and wool hats; North Dakotans throw on a T-shirt.

When it's zero, New York landlords finally turn up the heat for their shivering tenants; North Dakotans have the last cookout before it gets cold. At 10 below, people in Miami cease to exist; North Dakotans lick flag poles. At 80 below, polar bears begin to evacuate the Arctic; North Dakota Girl Scouts begin selling cookies door to door.

When it hits 173 below, ethyl alcohol freezes; North Dakotans get frustrated when they can't thaw the keg. At 297 below, microbial life survives on dairy products; North Dakota dairy cows complain of farmers with cold hands.

And, finally, the one that goes to prove just how cold things might get this winter: At 500 below zero, hell freezes over; North Dakotans watch the Vikings win the Super Bowl!

Badger Day?

Move over Punxutawney Phil

Feb. 8, 1999

Another crucially important holiday, Groundhog Day, has come and gone. It's good to live in a country where even a lowly rodent has his very own day in the sun, or shade, as the case may be.

The good news is, of course, that Punxutawney Phil, the famous Pennsylvania woodchuck, was in the shade this year. Not seeing his shadow, the bucktoothed forecaster promised us an early spring.

Thanks, Phil. You can go back to bed now.

Groundhog-less

The Taylor Ranch is home to most every species of menacing critter capable of digging up a pasture, but somehow we've missed out on the groundhog.

Being groundhog-free has made it tough for us to really get into the spirit of Groundhog Day and celebrate Feb. 2 with gusto.

The next best thing we have south of Towner is a neighboring farmer whose birthday is on Feb. 2. We like to give him a call and see if he sees his shadow that day and then ask him what he thinks the weather is going to do for the rest of the winter.

Of course, every North Dakota farmer knows that shadow or no shadow, we can bank on having another three or four months of cold and snow.

We'd be elated to have winter end on Feb. 2 just because a groundhog didn't see his shadow. Heck, we'd be elated to have just another six weeks of winter because he did see his shadow! We'd settle for either of those woodchuck told fortunes. It'd be a real win-win for us Americans on the northern tier.

Workin' the woodchuck

The real win/win is for the communities who've capitalized on their local groundhogs.

The folks in Punxsutawney, Pa., are watched by the entire world on Feb. 2. It's a real economic boost for the town of 6,782 (plus one groundhog) northeast of Pittsburgh. You can buy T-shirts, salt and pepper shakers, stuffed Phils, ceramic Phils, and you can even get your honey a pair of attractive groundhog earrings (and just in time for Valentine's Day, too).

And even if a town's groundhog wakes up dead, it can still be turned into an event. In Wiarton, Ontario (population 2,313), their woodchuck, Wiarton Willy has made his last weather prediction. But they didn't let his death put a damper on their holiday. They threw a pretty wild wake and celebrated his passing with a party.

It seems like Groundhog Day celebrations tend to go on in fairly small towns of 2,000 to 6,000 people. I don't suppose there's enough bare dirt in the bigger metropolises to harbor any earth-dependent wildlife like groundhogs.

I think North Dakota is missing out on this chance at small-town fun, fame and fortune. I'm of the opinion that we ought to put on a holiday of our own to celebrate spring. The most appropriate earth digger we could use to rally around would have to be the badger.

Sometime in April we could declare Badger Day. Anyone sighting a badger out digging in the pastures or hayfields would know that spring had sprung because the ground had finally thawed out enough to let the ferocious little diggers go to work.

Badger Day would be best celebrated in some of our smaller Class B towns whose names start with a "B" as well. I can see the lineup of world famous badgers now – Bowman Bob, Bottineau Buck, Backoo Bill and maybe even Barney Barney.

White is overrated

I'm dreaming of a brown Christmas

Dec. 13, 1999

The last December of the millenium looks like it'll be one we'll talk about well into the next.

"Remember back in 1999?" we'll say to anyone who'll listen. "I was digging fencepost holes in my shirtsleeves on the 6th of December."

I've already heard folks practicing the pet stories they're planning to take into the next century. Farmers are out cultivating, ranchers are out building corral and digging in water lines, and I even heard of one fella who was haying on Dec. 2.

I think the haying was mainly ceremonial and done to clean up some old windrows, but, all the same, he was able to make hay in December, a time when we're usually several weeks into the feeding part of our annual hay season.

I heard a weatherman say that November 1999 was only the second in recorded history where we didn't record so much as a trace of snow. North Dakotans are starting to feel like Southerners, except without the drawl.

Every 63 years

I think the weatherman said the other snowless November was in the 1880s, but a few of my elder friends say 1936 was the one to remember for sunshine and warm temperatures in the month of December.

It must have snowed in November of 1936 according to the weatherman's records, but it must have melted, according to my friends who tell of a brown December in that year.

Brown is a good color if you're hoping to winter graze cows, but rabbits and weasels would probably prefer white, especially if they're trying to wear their white camouflage coats.

My uncle said rabbit hunting went pretty good in '36. White rabbits on a brown background were profitable pickings for a kid with a new single-shot 22 caliber and a 14-cent box of shells. Stark contrast greatly improved the accuracy and the earnings at a nickel a rabbit skin.

While he was hunting, a few neighbors were plowing ground that December. Probably cultivating a future for the Conservation Reserve Program, I'm sure. And some relatives on my mother's side were building a new hip-roofed barn on my great-grandfather's ranch.

It had to be pretty mild for a bunch of my relatives to sit perched atop a beam 40 feet in the air. If it was 20 below with a stiff breeze blowing, any relative of mine would have been in the house sipping a hot cup of boiled coffee. They were Norwegians after all.

Now, 63 years later, we're finally getting another nice December. I know comets that come around in shorter intervals than that.

White-less winter

Christmas is just a couple weeks away, and looking out across the brown prairie, I'm starting to realize what my friends in Texas and relatives in

California get to experience every year.

Granted, a thick, white blanket of snow makes for a more Currier & Ives-type Christmas scene, but, in cattle country, it also makes for a more hay and diesel fuel and extra chore time-type scene.

Plus, every day my cows can graze means another $120 worth of hay gets to stay in the pile. That's more money for holiday joy and Christmas presents.

When explained that way, most ranchers and their children especially would probably say that they're dreaming of a brown Christmas, too.

Trail breakers

Real leadership out on the range

Nov. 20, 2000

Looks like winter is setting in for good. We're all grumbling about the recent snow and cold like we've never seen either phenomenon in a North Dakota November.

Memories are short in the north country, especially after a couple of abnormally warm, open winters that we've tried to convince ourselves were normal. Everyone was hoping for a kinder, gentler North Dakota as we entered the new millenium.

Just when we think we can count on a little global warming, our greenhouse freezes up like it always has.

Search and rescue

I was hoping for another month of good grazing on the Taylor Ranch. A foot of snow, winds, drifts and begging, bellering cows crushed those hopes.

So I gathered up the cows and broke into the hay pile. I nearly forgot that I still had my bulls a couple miles from the ranch. I picked a cold, windy day to search them out.

I rode the pasture from stem to stern – no bulls. After losing the feeling in my fingers and toes, I decided to call it quits and resume the rescue the next day.

I saddled up and rode to the pasture again the next day. The lane leading there was belly deep on my half-broke colt who bucked, lunged and churned his way through the snow. It was well over the ears of my ambitious, but short-legged border collie buddy, Jess. She crawled down and in, up and over, the tracks of my horse, smiling all the way in anticipation of some cattle herding.

I remember chasing cows down that same lane several years ago in October when an early snow had trapped 50 cow/calf pairs with drifts more than 4 feet deep.

I couldn't get our toughest two-cylinder John Deere through the snowdrifts, so I saddled up a horse and grabbed the aluminum scoop shovel. No front-wheel-assist tractors and front-end loaders, just a forearm-assisted scoop creating a tidy little path 18 inches wide.

I got the cows started down the path that was partly shoveled and partly broke with horse hooves. They marched home single file like well-trained soldiers.

That worked well for the cows back then, but last week, I wasn't about to hand shovel a path for 10 bulls that I spent most of the year cursing anyway.

Bully determination

A sweaty horse, a tired cow dog and a cold rancher finally found the bulls in a neighbor's pasture. One drift of snow had paved the way for them by flattening a barbed-wire fence in a low spot.

I looked 'em in the eye and told them to go home.

I couldn't help but notice that one big, white bull turned, took the lead and further busted my path for his comrades following in single file. He did that all the way home, even when the snow got shallow, the troops continued to follow his lead.

They say if you're pondering your position as a leader, look behind and see if anyone is following you. If there is, you're a leader.

Sadly, many of today's politicians look for a group heading in a particular direction, then run like heck to get in front of them to take credit for their efforts and get a good photo for the papers. They could take a lesson from a bull who just got out in front to break a path in deep snow, doing the work needed to get a herd home.

As Teddy Roosevelt would say, "Bully!"

Shoo fly

Or better yet, drop dead bug

Oct. 8, 2001

The coming of fall in Dakota is always preceded by some real visible signals.

The leaves on the poplars turn orange and gold. The grass dries up and turns brown. The geese start heading south. And every doggone fly in the state starts heading into my house.

According to my neighbors, a few flies are trying to get into their abodes as well, but I'm sure the lion's share of the neighborhood fly population is buzzing around my screen door.

It's tough to blame them. After all, we do call them house flies. They're just trying to fulfill their named destiny.

On the hunt

I'm not generally a bloodthirsty man. But I brandish my fly swatter like a man possessed as I flail at the little six-legged enemies parked on my ceiling.

If I'm not within reach of a swatter, I'll go one-on-one, man-on-fly combat. I stalk them until I'm in reach, hand resting on the table they've made their landing strip.

Then we stare at each other like a couple of gun slingers facing off at high noon in Dodge City and I make my move. Quick as a cat, I make my swipe – fingers apart to let the air through, then closing the gap as I make my grab.

Sometime this works and I actually capture one of the little buggery bugs. Other times I unclasp to take a little peek and see if I got one, and off they fly. Catch and release. Most times it's a complete clean miss.

The biggest drawback of swatting and catching is that it's slow going. It may give you some personal satisfaction, but doing them in one at a time just doesn't cut it when you're trying to eliminate your house's fly population.

Chem clean

When the flies outnumber the minutes I have to hunt, swat and catch, I reach for some toxic help. Sprays, fogs, fumigators, you name it. I like natural biological controls of most pests and weeds, but I think flies deserve the best compounds available from the world of science.

Drug 'em, drop 'em, sweep 'em up. But no matter how good a job you do, they keep on coming. From where I don't know. I'm sure no one misses them in the place they vacated, though.

Just when I'm about ready to give up and live a life where flies sit on my food, put specks on my windows and crawl on my nose while I'm napping, I'm saved by a greater force: The start of a North Dakota winter.

Yup, if you can't crush, catch or poison those flies, sit back and enjoy the effects of a good hard "killing frost."

I know life gets a little more challenging when you have to fight freezing temperatures, deep snows and days with more darkness than light, but it does have its benefits. Not the least of which is the elimination of creepy, crawly pests.

It's almost enough to make me glad I don't live in one of those tropical paradises where the living is easy. The living might be easy, but the bug wars have got to be hard.

Winter of guilt

Suppressing our feelings of climatic inadequacy

March 11, 2002

The snow is falling. The wind is blowing. The thermometer is dropping. Whew! I feel better already.

It's been a really difficult winter in North Dakota. Especially difficult for those of us who take pride in suffering bitter cold and tough conditions. It's been so difficult because it has been so nice.

We've had hardly any snow. The temperatures have been mild and warm day after day after day. The roads have been clear and we've had mail service all winter long.

If I were still 4 feet tall and going to school, I would be really ticked about the lack of storm days to sit at home, drink hot chocolate and watch television game shows. How's a kid supposed to get a little R&R without some well-spaced snow days?

Yes, the winter of 2001-2002 will have to go down in my journal as a real disappointment. It's been plumb disgusting.

Heavy conscience

All across the once-proud northern plains, I talk to people who feel just the way I do – guilty.

We catch ourselves apologizing to southern visitors. "We're sorry, it's been a really nice winter. Not at all normal for us this time of year. It's usually a lot colder and snowier."

At the very least, we owe our winter guests some sub-zero windchills, or, better yet, a good windy ground blizzard. We're letting them down.

A friend of mine from Kansas was up a few weeks ago. His shuttle driver from the airport to the hotel in Bismarck, N.D., told him the current temperature was "34 above." "Above," he said, "what do you mean? Could it really be 34 below?"

It was nice of my friend to give the shuttle driver an opportunity to reminisce about the good, ol' days of 34-below temperatures and glowingly discuss winters past when men were men and boys moved south if they couldn't hack it.

We need those chances to defend our reputation, otherwise our conscience is unbearably heavy with feelings of an easy, unchallenged existence.

The big wait

The nagging feeling of inadequacy is matched by the uneasy feelings we've had all winter as we watch the forecast, scan the horizon and look back over our shoulder to see if we're about to get hit with the "big one."

We've been waiting for the other shoe to drop ever since we celebrated a barely white Christmas.

"Yup, nice day today, but I bet we'll pay for it with some big spring blizzards," we say with a hint of masochistic hopefulness.

Somewhere in our warped homesteading pioneer psyche, we've convinced ourselves that good fortune needs to be followed by an equal or greater sum of bad luck. It's the twisted prairie version of yin and yang.

So maybe this is it. Payback time. As I write this column, it's snowing and blowing outside, there's some nice pillow drifts piling up on the east west roads, and the weatherman even promised us some below-zero windchills.

We could do it all tonight – break our disgusting streak of warm winter weather, erase the cloud of guilt hanging over us, and relish in the storm (we knew it was coming) sent to punish us.

We could only be so lucky.

Shocking experiences

Drawbacks of the dry season

Feb. 10, 2003

In my part of the country, the winter season is a pretty dry season.

We see some pretty cold temperatures in the winter, but like we say, "it's a dry cold." We figure 20 below zero on the prairie is more comfortable than 20 above along the ocean.

It's the equivalent of Arizona's summer bragging rights about their "dry heat." Because, as we all know, "it's not so much the heat as it is the humidity." It's what makes 100 degrees in Arizona a lot more tolerable than 100 degrees in Florida.

Even with the comfort advantages of an arid atmosphere, there're times when a little humidity would be welcome.

Desert drawbacks

Dry winter air makes for a lot of static cling. Ladies' dresses and men's slacks get a little more form fitting in the static season.

Kids can stick balloons to themselves without even rubbing them on their hair first. If you aren't careful, you'll find yourself toting around that odd sock or dryer sheet stuck to your back side.

In the dry season, "nose bleed section" doesn't mean the top row of seats in the stadium. It can be just about anywhere. Bloody noses surely aren't caused by alpine elevation here on the Dakota plains, it's just inland winter atmosphere.

The carpet on the floorboards of the cars makes for some nice static electric charge when matched up with dry air, leather shoe soles and a little friction. It can make a person downright jumpy.

I've had cars where I'm afraid to even touch the door after I get out. Like Pavlov's dog, I can make the connection between stimulus and response. After being stimulated by static shock the first couple hundred times, I figured out it was easier to shut the door with an insulated elbow or a swing of the hip.

I've been in motel rooms in the winter that would exceed the Sahara Desert for aridity. I remember walking across the carpet in one Sahara-dry motel room and getting such a shock on the metal door knob that I quit answering the knock at the door. It cost me a pizza delivery, but I was too gun shy to grab iron.

In some places, I like to bring in a humidifier and let the machine duke it out with the electric heater. If you can keep pumping the water to the humidifier, it will get ahead if the motor doesn't burn out.

Electrical conversion

A couple weeks ago, I had one of my more interesting experiences with static electricity.

I was asked to help serve the sacraments at my church on Sunday. When it came time for holy communion, I took my place behind the minister with the tray of wine. It's a solemn ceremony and I'm honored to be part of the distribution.

The first altar full went fine, but after walking back across the carpet to serve the next group, the parishioners got a little more than they bargained for.

As I handed them the small glass of wine, I said, "Blood of Christ, shed for you," then Zzzzztttt! They got a full charge of static electricity when our fingertips touched around the little plastic cup. Once I thought I saw a blue spark jump between us.

I didn't drop any of them to the ground, but I think they went back to their pew with a little more respect for the power of the spirit. Yes, God was with us.

Fall frost

Time to bundle up

Sept. 22, 2003

It's hard to admit that summer's over and fall is upon us.

Every year, I live in denial for a good month or so, unwilling to accept the frosty fact.

I continue haying and pretend that the days are still 16 hours long and sunny. I'm usually "done" haying by the first week of September, but, like my

Dad, I don't usually "quit" haying until the first week of October.

Done haying means you have your easy acres put up or you've piled together enough hay to make the winter. Done haying can also mean that your help is back in school or off to college.

Quit haying means you've finished picking away at all the dried-up sloughs, unused pastures and road ditches, or you've been froze out, snowed out or just plain worn out.

Quitting haying can come when you wear yourself out or you finally wear your equipment out. When something major breaks in the hayfield in the fall, you just turn the key off, park it and head for home.

I remember fall haying days with Dad back in my youth. I'd get off the school bus, change clothes and head for the field. He was always glad to see me; haying's a pretty lonely business come autumn.

The days were short, cold and damp, less-than-perfect haying weather. I'd be wearing my yellow fuzzy chore gloves, a jean jacket buttoned all the way to the top and, when the haying went really late in the year, I'd be sporting a wool cap and drop the ear flappers.

If the breeze was just right, I could catch a little heat from the exhaust of the tractor. The day we quit haying and drove the equipment home was a happy day.

Wishful thinking

Last weekend, I jumped off the haying tractor and headed out for a speaking job in Rapid City, S.D. I took my bride and we swung through Billings, Mont., on our way home.

No matter which way you turn the map, central Montana's not really on the way home between western South Dakota and north-central North Dakota, but there was a horse sale pulling us that direction.

I figured since we were still haying, it must be warm enough to go tenting. We pulled into a Billings campground and staked down the frugal rancher lodge. We blew up our air mattress and gathered under a sleeping bag and a quilt with every stitch of clothing we had still on our back.

We went to bed early and, within 12 long, cold hours, we'd racked up about five or six hours of fitful sleep. I wished I had a ski mask to sleep in to keep my nose and balding forehead warm. As it was, we tucked our noses under an extra jacket and ran the risk of suffocation.

It seemed awful chilly, especially for haying season, and I did note a thick layer of frost on the windshield of the Buick when I stuck my head out the door of the tent.

I guess it's time to quit haying and admit that summer's over. And once I do that, I can feel justified to turn on the heat in the house, too.

Either that, or I'll have to get out from under the 200 pounds of homemade quilts and find a ski mask for my frosty snoot.

Early starts

Getting ahead on the season

Nov. 3, 2003

I'm not usually one to get a head start on things, but once in awhile I break out of the blocks and get out ahead of the pack.

Winter decided to get a little head start here in North Dakota. We got our first snow, a 5-incher, on Oct. 29. Although we'd just as soon put this off until Thanksgiving or later, it doesn't surprise us to have a white Halloween.

I drove through the falling snow to speak to a group of ranchers in Maddock, N.D., and, on the way home, I got a headstart on winter driving mishaps.

Slip sliding away

I had just poured a Styrofoam cup full of coffee as I headed out the door of the meeting hall. I was steering with one hand, drinking coffee with the other and visiting with my passenger bride about the meeting and the people we'd met.

We discussed the 5 inches of cold snow on the warm road and whether we should put the vehicle in four-wheel drive. I was frugal with the four high and left it in two-wheel slide.

I was picking up speed as we headed out on the highway. I guess I was accelerating like it was Oct. 28 autumn instead of Oct. 29 winter. All of a sudden, we were heading down the highway sideways as I gripped the steering wheel with my left hand and my coffee cup with my right.

We were still in a horizontal pitch when she slid right down the ditch. Not just any ditch, one with a pretty muddy bottom.

We came to a standstill. I still had two wheels spinning and half a cup of coffee in my hand, but I was in no mood to drink it. You'd have thought I was raised in Florida the way I handled that skid.

The good thing was it happened close to town. An easy walk to get a pull from those left back at the meeting hall. The bad thing was it happened close to town. It was easy for everyone to see my foolish predicament.

It took a little doing to pull it out since it was pretty icy. It felt good knowing I wasn't the only one experiencing a lack of traction.

From then on, I slowed up, put it in four-wheel drive and kept both hands on the wheel.

Thinking positive

My wife came up with the "look on the bright side" thought that it was nice to get our one allotted ditching out of the way early in the season. She had a point.

I've used the same logic when I've lost a calf to pneumonia early in the calving season, or had the first cow down the chute come up open at pregnancy checking, or lost a bearing or gotten a flat tire on the first day of haying season. It's kind of comforting, in a twisted sort of way, to get the bad luck out of the way right away.

I'm just not sure if one ditching will get us through the winter season of ice and snow. One of my neighbor's wives hit the ditch two or three times one winter on her way to work in town. And her car didn't just slide into the ditch; it would roll over onto its roof. Luckily, she always fastened her seat belt.

It got to the point where her son recommended she mount her cell phone antennae on the underbelly of the car instead of the roof. Figured it would improve her reception when she called him for help. Family can be so understanding.

Hopefully, my winter ditch quota is already filled.

Push and play

Deep snow and big toys for big kids

Jan. 12, 2004

For a fella who hates snow, I have to admit I kind of like it.

It's not just the winter sports made easier by snow that I like, it's the satisfaction of pushing it around and piling it up that bring me a little cold-weather joy.

After years of training in pushing around the dirt in my sandbox as a lad, I was ready and willing to make the switch from my Tonkas to some grown-up equipment. I relished the idea of getting behind the wheel of a big tractor and loader.

On the ranch, the next closest match to the sandbox dozing and pushing seemed to be the day's clean up activities after a healthy snowfall.

I've been through a variety of snow-pushing equipment on the ranch – the two-cylinder John Deere with a grapple fork loader that leaked more snow than it pushed, a newer old tractor with a canvas windbreak and similar leaky loader, an even newer old tractor with a cold leaky cab but a less leaky loader bucket, and, now, our newest old tractor with a tight heated cab, a radio and a joystick-controlled 8-foot bucket, no leaks.

I could push snow all day and be plumb happy in that rig. Unfortunately, I have to take a little time out from pushing snow to feed the cattle. Livestock continue to get in the way of the fun on the ranch.

Fun and function

It seems a little early, but my snow piles around the ranch yard are getting pretty big already. My nephews will be pleased to see that when they come to visit. It's hard to beat a good pile of steep, hard snow just feet away from Grandma's hot chocolate and toast.

The snow piles can be useful, too. I've seen a few guys bank a little snow against their house to increase the insulation and the R-value. I like to do a little snow insulating myself around the water tanks and pump shacks when the mercury dips and the water quits.

When the temperature dropped to 32 below zero last week, I hadn't spent enough time playing in my tractor and piling up snow around the pump shack that waters our house.

It's pretty depressing to turn on the faucet on the coldest winter night and get nary a drip out of it.

I suspected some frost in the pump shack or somewhere close to it. I plugged in an extra heater in the shack and went to work pushing and piling.

Once the hydraulics warmed up, I had that loader running smoother than a city snow crew in a shopping mall parking lot. I turned that pump shack into a pretty nice snowbank. It must have been insulated to about R-200 and been hotter than a sauna on the inside.

It wasn't long before the water was running again. Toilets flushed, showers ran and dishes got washed.

I guess we're lucky to get both snow and cold here on the northern range. Without the snow, I'd need a lot more store-bought insulation and something else to push around to satisfy my Tonka tendencies.

Off the ranch and on the run

Sellin' drugs

An over-the-road corporate cowboy

March 22, 1999

In my ongoing quest to meet interesting people, learn new ideas and build equity in a ranch that eats up money quicker than I drink coffee, I've joined the ranks of the wage earners.

Last month, I accepted a job as territory manager for Fort Dodge Animal Health, selling vaccines and pharmaceuticals to veterinarians and dealers in North Dakota. Yup, I'm a drug pusher.

A lot of farmers and ranchers work off of the place to make ends meet. Some have their spouses working in town to bring home the bacon, the health insurance and a good portion of the operating money for the outfit.

Being spouseless, I had to find my own job to land some health insurance and some operating money that I didn't have to pay interest on. And, of course, I need a little extra operating money to pay the hired hand who's doing the chores that I would be doing if I wasn't out working to earn the money to pay him to do the work that I'm not doing.

Mighty lucky

I'm not complaining, though. I'm mighty glad to have a good job with a good company, working with some really sharp people. I'm lucky to have one of the best hired hands a rancher could ask for, and I am able to create enough extra income to make the payments on the cows and machinery, and eventually on the land.

Driving around North Dakota visiting with veterinarians, animal health dealers and ranchers should give me some new material for this column. I'm quickly discovering that there's a wealth of cowboy logic around the coffee pots at the vet clinics and dealerships that I visit.

As a territory manager, I get to drive thousands of miles on the front roads and back roads of North Dakota. Luckily, the job comes with a reliable vehicle. You may not recognize me in such a new rig, but inside the outfit is the same self deprecating cowboy who'll be just as surprised as you are at the vehicle he's in.

Being on the road so much, I feel kind of like reporter Charles Kuralt, looking for the best in local culture, interesting old-timers and the finest of fare in the small-town cafes and restaurants.

North Dakota may not have the world's largest ball of twine, but we do have the world's largest cow, buffalo, walleye and turtle driving a snowmobile. My goal, as I drive around the state, is to get my photo snapped in front of each of them in true tourist fashion.

I'm actually campaigning my company to create the world's largest bottle of vaccine to help immunize the world's largest Holstein cow.

Considering her importance to the state's economy and tourism industry, it'd be in our best interest to keep her healthy.

Along with the exciting travel and the new column material I'll gain with my new job, I'm really looking forward to the things I'll learn by working for such a large company.

I'll be a true corporate cowboy with voice mail, e-mail, cell phones, faxes, files and memos. I'll know every corporate cliché, keeping everyone in the loop, giving them a heads up on situations out in the field, thinking outside of the box and pushing the envelope as I balance my new, complex lifestyle.

Author's note: I used this little column to let my readers know about my new job away from the ranch. I also learned how wide the readership is for Cowboy Logic, or at least how well a corporate clipping service can pick up on something when a corporate name is mentioned. It got the attention of the chairman and CEO of then American Home Products, the $12 billion parent company of Fort Dodge way out in New Jersey. Word came down the chain that I better watch what I write. His query was something along the line of "who the hell's this Ryan Taylor?" I grew sales in my territory by 42 percent that first year. They figured out who I was.

Look up for landmarks

Straight lines and square corners

March 13, 2000

Like all men, I pride myself on a strong sense of direction. Not necessarily accurate, but strong.

I've always done well on the wide-open prairies. One good landmark – that solitary tree or that lone farmstead – and I've got it made. I know where I'm at and where I'm going to be.

It helps that the people who platted out the prairie laid out the townships with straight section lines and square corners. No matter how lost you might get, you know you're heading one of four directions: north, south, east or west.

There're lots of curvy, crooked places in the world where you could be going south southeast, looping northwest and turning west southwest. There's no telling where you might end up.

Big city compass

Not long ago, I was in Chicago, bumbling around the big city. I sidled up and down the streets with ease. I always knew, roughly, where I was and how to get back to where I started.

I'm usually a little nervous about the mazes of the metropolitan areas. It's hard to spot the sun, you're always in the shadows of a bunch of tall buildings, and, at night, there're too many street lights to ever see the north star.

But the grid in Chicago was pretty square with the world. As long as I walked north or south on the streets, and east or west on the avenues, I knew about where I was on my mental map.

The Chicago skyline kept me straight, too. At any given moment, I could quickly spot the Sears Tower and go from there. Kind of like that solitary tree out on my prairie home.

It's good for a man to know where he is, because he isn't about to ask for directions anyway.

Fargo fog

You'd think that a guy who could navigate Chicago would be able to get around Fargo, N.D., with ease.

Traveling in Fargo last week, I did what I usually do when I peel myself out of the vehicle after a long drive. I kicked off my boots, strapped on my Nikes and went for a run to work out the knots and kinks. I figured two or three miles would do the trick.

It was getting dark, but Fargo's a modern city with electric street lights and everything. I took off at a steady clip and I was feeling good. I hit my second wind, got in "the zone" and decided to keep going.

The road curved around a golf course and some residential circle drives. There weren't any tall landmarks to guide me, but my strong sense of direction told me that the dark, curvy road was curving back toward my hotel. I was sure of it.

A mile later, I was beginning to wonder as I wandered. Another mile and I pondered my particular point on the map. One more mile and I spotted an unfamiliar Amoco station. I thought I'd swing in for a Gatorade and gather my bearings.

But I had no pockets, no cash and, in a thirsty state of exhaustion, I weakened and asked the attendant where I'd ended up. I was nowhere near my hotel.

Pointed in the right direction I kept running. Finally, I limped into the hotel lobby, cursed the lack of an elevator and walked the stairs up to my room.

The next day, I drove the route of my evening run and checked the odometer. My two-mile jog turned out to be a six-miler, a real 10K.

And maybe that's how the marathon was invented. A man, out for a short jog, got lost, wouldn't admit it, and went 26 miles. Thanks to his testosterone, an athletic pioneer.

Tough days

The life of a lifestyle tweener

April 24, 2000

They say you shouldn't shop when you're hungry. And I guess you shouldn't write when you're sad. Reckon I'm guilty of doing both.

I'm sitting at a laptop computer, room 331, Super 8 Motel, Williston, N.D.

I was having a pretty decent day. Doing what I do as an over-the-road sales rep for an animal health company. Visiting veterinarians, talking to ranchers and other animal-type folks about vaccines and pharmaceuticals. Seemed like the feedback I was getting was good.

Then I got a little feedback from home.

Incurable incident

Back at home, my parents, the hired man and a neighbor were gathered around the kitchen table for a cup of coffee after an afternoon of covering for my absence. They heard a whinny and saw our pregnant mare fussing in the pasture across the road. She turned, and everyone saw what the fuss was about. She'd failed to foal and, now, most of her insides were on the outside.

Mares are powerful creatures. So when the colt didn't come, her intestines did, right through the rectum.

They hooked up the horse trailer and got the poor thing loaded for the trip to the vet. The hired man had to get to his other job in town, the neighbor had to get back to his job on his ranch. Mom called another neighbor who agreed to drive my pickup and trailer and mare to town.

Dad doesn't usually feel good enough to go to town for his own doctoring. But, Parkinson's disease or not, he was going to get in the pickup with the neighbor and see that mare to town.

The vet confirmed what we didn't want to believe. There was nothing that could realistically be done for her at this point. They brought her back home, took her behind "the hill" and shot her.

Absentee tweener

Like most Norwegian Lutheran ranchers, I maintain a strong sense of guilt. Guilt for not being home to care for the mare. Guilt for not getting a certain stud colt castrated a lot sooner last year before he bred his half sister mare that now lays dead behind "the hill."

But, we make choices. My choice has been to spend more time off the ranch to help earn my living and fulfill my life. Earlier this week, I was off the ranch again, speaking to an adult farm management group in Stanley, N.D. I enjoyed it. I thought the speech went well, and the feedback seemed good.

Before I spoke, they discussed some national trends in agriculture. We need to gross more than $200,000 to make it on today's farm. Those big farms are growing in number.

Smaller farms, "lifestyle farms," are also growing in number. Lifestyle farmers make most of their living off the farm, so efficiency and profit margins aren't as crucial.

However, those in between the big outfits and the little lifestylers are becoming extinct. Economists call this endangered group the "tweeners."

I'm a tweener. Our ranch will never gross more than $200,000 unless I start buying out all my neighbors. And, working off the ranch, I'm also a lifestyler.

And I'm not a lot unlike dozens of my friends who are doing the same thing. I do feel lucky that I enjoy everything I do – ranching, representing animal health products, speaking at banquets, writing a column.

But even when you enjoy the things you do, there are times devoid of joy. And then you just write down your thoughts about a dead horse and go to bed. Room 331. Super 8 Motel. Williston, N.D.

I made the hill

And the five miles before it

May 22, 2000

There's a few things cowboys aren't supposed to do, like wear tennis shoes and expend energy for no apparent, tangible reason.

But when you're a cowboy who's knocking on the door of 30 years of age and trying to extend that youthful feeling, you break a few rules in the old cowboy code.

So I've been strapping on my sneakers and running down the road. Not because I need to get anywhere faster than a walk – I usually just turn around and run back – but because I'm trying to build up my stamina for an October marathon.

A marathon's a darn long way, 26.2 miles to be exact. So to warm up to the idea of racing that far, I thought I'd try something a little more manageable like 10 kilometers, or 6.2 miles for us metrically unenlightened.

Bismarck bound

Esteemed road racing counselor and cow doctor, J.D. Rowe, D.V.M., put me on to the "I Made The Hill Road Race" in Bismarck, N.D.

Dr. Rowe was looking for a new road racing protégé since his last victim, I mean disciple, came up lame. Cowboy poet Rodney Nelson was medically coached through a five-kilometer run by Dr. Rowe. He survived that but fell lame when he broke a leg coming off of a green horse this spring.

So I become the new apprentice in the Rowe Running School. Rodney moved up to the role of trainer. His main job consisted of parking his car halfway up the mile-long hill and shouting encouragement to the cow doctor and the cowboy as they sprinted to the peak.

The rest of my "training" for the race had been self-inflicted. I'd been running for a month or two, a few miles every other day or week.

I didn't mind the physical anguish of training, but the mental strain has been tiring. The main mental strain is trying to sneak in a run on our gravel roads without getting caught by the neighbors.

You hate to get caught exercising by a rancher. Once they realize you're not broke down and in need of a ride, they wonder why you're wasting the sweat and sore muscles on exercise and not work.

"Say, Ryan, as long as you're running down this road, why don't you put on a harness and pull a road grader behind you," or "Hey, Ryan, why don't you jump in and come unroll some barbed wire for me. You can run backwards and unroll it. Just don't let the barbs catch your pretty, white tenny shoes."

It ain't easy being an aspiring runner out in the rural reaches.

Part of the pack

On race day in Bismarck, I gathered with the other 508 runners and walkers to get registered and elbow my way to the starting line. This was a little different crowd than what I usually see at the calf workin's or around the coffee pot at the vet clinic.

These were people who were as comfortable wearing spandex in public as ranchers are wearing coveralls to the grocery store. There were guys who jumped right into the group stretching session and moved to the music with no inhibition. I've two-stepped and jitterbugged in front of others at the dancehall, but I just couldn't aerobicize with people I'd never met.

Despite my lack of spandex and my shy stretching strategies, I still made it to the top of the hill in decent enough time to get second in my age category, and, yes, there were more than two runners in my age group.

And even though I didn't accomplish any real work in that 46 minutes, I did get a free T-shirt.

The runnin' rancher

Off to the races for big 26.2

Oct. 23, 2000

Tell enough people you're going to do something, and you just about have to follow through. Most politicians don't feel that way, but I do.

I kept telling people that I was going to run a marathon this year to mark the new millenium and celebrate my 30th birthday. Oct. 22 is the day I follow through on my vow to run 26.2 miles.

I'm writing this while I'm packing my bags for Chicago and the LaSalle Bank Chicago Marathon. I'll be one of 25,000 or 30,000 other runners who also must have told a lot of people that they were going to marathon this year.

Seven of the 10 fastest men in the world will be there, along with one of the 10 fastest cowboy joggers in Smokey Lake Township. Last year's Chicago Marathon was a real horse race between a Moroccan fella named Khannouchi and a Kenyan named Tanui.

They'll probably be there again this year. The chances of a Dakotan named Taylor getting in the pack with them and sprinting toward the finish line is probably pretty slim.

There is some good motivation to try and catch them, however. First-place prize money in the Chicago Marathon is $75,000. If you're an American, it doubles to $150,000. They throw a little more cabbage at you if you're over 40, from Illinois or if you break a world record.

I didn't see any prize money offered for high-placing ranchers or runners with the knobbiest knees. Prizes drop off precipitously with 10th place raking in just $2,000. My goal is to finish in the top half and bring home a free T-shirt.

Cowboy training

When I first pondered running a marathon, I did a little research into the activity.

Participants told me it involved a lot of mental anguish and physical misery. Having been in the cattle business all my life, I felt uniquely prepared for the task.

They also told me that when you finish a marathon you feel a real sense of accomplishment and peace in having achieved the ultimate goal. Kind of like a rancher feels when he saves a calf in a blizzard or sends that last semi out of the yard with a good-looking load of steers.

Even though I felt like I had a jump start on the anguish, misery and accomplishment end of the marathon training, I decided it would be wise to do a little running beforehand, too.

So I've been following a regimented training schedule that's taken me from two-mile runs to 20-mile runs. It's saved me some gas in the pickup and reduced hoof wear on my horses as I've been able to check some of the cows while I'm training.

On days when I'm scheduled to "cross train," I just do what I'd usually do on the ranch. A little strength training with the salt blocks, a little balance training with the green broke colt, a little speed training as I sprint to beat the cows to the gate that wasn't shut.

So I'm ready to run this marathon. I'll do it to accomplish something that's out of the norm for most ranchers, I'll do it to celebrate the new millenium and my new age bracket, and I'll do it for that sense of physical and mental accomplishment.

But, I'll also do it so I have something to write a couple of columns about. So plan on catching the results in my next installment.

Race day

Shoes by Nike, body by beef

Nov. 6, 2000

I got up pretty early on Oct. 22. Like 29,074 others in Chicago that day, I was working on my pre-marathon jitters.

After logging 764 miles in training runs since March, I was ready to run the 26.2 miles of the LaSalle Bank Chicago Marathon that I'd been working toward.

I started race day by eating some carbohydrates and by putting on my protein-promoting tee. My race T-shirt had "Beef Builds a Better Body" written across the front and "Ryan the Running Rancher" on the back. One has to work to stick out in a crowd of 29,000 skinny, obsessive people.

Lining up 29,000 runners is no small task. Getting to the start line, I optimistically lined up in the 8-minute-per-mile area, which put me ahead of about three-fourths of the other runners. Even beginning from there, it took me three minutes to get across the starting line from the time the gun popped.

I didn't lose that three minutes from my race time, though. Like a can of soup at the supermarket checkout line, I got scanned when I crossed the starting line. That's when the computer chip Velcro'd to my shoe started my official time.

From there, it was just tuck in and run the course in the middle of the mob and enjoy the 1 million spectators who lined the streets. There were a lot of supportive folks along the route. A few even picked me out and shouted, "Go beef guy!"

Bands were playing, people were cheering. I hardly had to burn any of my own energy; I just used everyone else's.

Around town

We got quite a tour of the city. We traveled concrete canyons between the downtown skyscrapers, the high-rent district, the low-rent district, Little Italy, Chinatown, Greektown, Little Mexico, the lake front. I was waiting for a Little Norway and the smell of lutefisk, but no luck. I had to settle for Mexican mariachi bands and dancing Chinese dragons.

So I kept on running and enjoying it all. After about 20 miles, my feet got a little tired, but I was focused on finishing. Mile 21, 22, 23, 24, 25, I just kept plugging along, eight minutes per mile.

It was everything I thought a marathon would be – physical misery, mental anguish, a euphoric sense of accomplishment. And the marathon offered things I hadn't expected – it was the most fun I've had in a long time, and it had more spectator support and curb-side encouragement than I could ever imagine.

At mile 26, my pit crew handed me my cowboy hat, and with newfound energy, I sprinted to the finish like Forrest Gump. The crowd literally erupted with a roar and the announcer even picked me out of the field and announced my name and hometown.

I clocked in at 3 hours 31 minutes and 40 seconds. Enough to put me in 3,814th place out of 27,956 finishers, or in the top 15 percent of the competitive field.

The champion Khannouchi and five closely trailing Kenyans came in at a little over 2 hours 7 minutes. The last-place male crossed the finish at 8 hours plus but probably felt the same sense of accomplishment as the winner.

Being in the top 15 percent earned me a finisher's medal and a free T-shirt. I celebrated with a big ol' steak.

Chalk one up for the power of beef and the running rancher.

On course

And with the right attitude

July 16, 2001

Stay the course. That's the best advice we can sometimes come up with when times get tough. Stay the course.

Seems simple, but it's a pretty good idea. I'm trying to practice it.

I'm still on the course of my national "Beef Builds a Better Body" running tour. After my debut as "Ryan, the Running Rancher" in last fall's Chicago Marathon, I decided to take my animal protein promoting message to a couple more of the nation's urban consuming centers.

I guess I wanted to do more for beef promotion than just chip in my buck-a-head beef checkoff. I got my message to a million spectators while running 26.2 miles on the streets of Chicago last fall, plus a few more when

ESPN zoomed in on me.

Hard to believe, but I really enjoyed that morning of physical strain, mental anguish and beef promotion. So I set my sights on another urban marathon. New York City. The big run in the Big Apple.

But everyone wants to run the New York City marathon. So I did what people do when they find themselves in a crowd of people who all want the same thing. I took a number and waited for them to call my number.

I entered the lottery to run the race, along with nearly 50,000 other people. They had 30,000 slots to be drawn June 27.

Now if they were going to draw 30,000 names out of barrel full of 50,000 to win a million dollars, I'd probably be in the losing 20,000. But drawing 30,000 names out of 50,000 to experience pure muscle and mental exhaustion – yeah, I got that kind of luck.

So I made the cut. One of the 30,000 chosen. One of 11 North Dakotans drawn from the 21 who entered. And, come Nov. 4, I'll be lining up with the rest of the lucky ducks to see a little of Staten Island, Long Island, Queens, the Bronx and Manhattan, up close and sweaty.

Warming up

Even with those odds, getting drawn was the easy part. Now I have to train. Get my body and mind in marathon shape.

So there's lots of running. Training, of course, is fueled with beef, the tasty brain food that helps build healthy muscle. And I like to run the occasional race to test my progress.

Last week, I ran the 10K in the Prairie Rose State Games in Minot, N.D. I started strong, maintained a good running rancher pace and was feeling pretty good. I was staying the course.

Then about halfway through, the leader of the pack I was running in took a left turn. He thought he was staying the course. Another runner and I followed him, thinking we were staying the course, too. The dead end we hit proved all three of us wrong.

After a little running in circles, we doubled back and got back on course – the right course. It was then I learned a little lesson in life and running.

I shrugged off the frustration, got back in the race and picked up my pace. The fella I followed in to the dead end, spent a fair bit of time cussing, fussing, fuming and hollering at one of the race volunteers for not marking the course well enough.

The result was that the guy who smiled a little more and blamed a little less, finished the race a minute faster. A small test but one I'll be keeping in mind in New York this fall.

Stay the course, and do it in good nature.

A race to remember

Five boroughs, 26.2 miles, one cowboy

Nov. 19, 2001

I had my doubts about going to New York City to run the marathon on Nov. 4. A lot had changed since I started training for the marathon back in June. The whole world seemed more dangerous, more vulnerable, less free.

But I'm not one to back away from a challenge. It was a stroke of luck that I even got drawn to run the New York City Marathon. More than 50,000 people wanted those 30,000 slots for the race.

By going, maybe I could dispel my thoughts that the world was more dangerous, more vulnerable, less free. If I didn't go, I guess it certainly had gotten less free.

So I made my last leg limbering run on the gravel road that runs past our ranch early on Nov. 2 before heading to the airport.

It was a picture perfect morning. The sun was peeking above the horizon in the east and this big beautiful prairie moon shone still bright in the west. I raced a small flock of geese cruising south and watched the horses run and buck in the pasture.

I wasn't trying to be maudlin, but I told myself that if this was my last morning on the ranch – if my plane fell from the sky or some nut blew up the Verrazano Bridge while we were running across it or dusted us with anthrax at the starting gate – then it was a pretty good one. Hoka hey, Lakotas, it's a good day to die.

So, I struck eastward. It was dark when we landed in Newark, N.J., and I remember looking out the window toward lower Manhattan. Where the twin towers of the World Trade Center used to stand sentinel, I saw only twin floodlights, shining brightly to illuminate the grisly work being done on that now vacant spot.

When I've run other races, you think about the race, your shoes, what to eat, what to drink, how to get to the start. At this race in New York, there were a lot of other thoughts and concerns.

I did go to the runner's expo with my brother who came in from California to cheer me on. I did the usual carbo loading the evening before the race, joined by the friend of a friend who was taken from us on Sept. 11. And I did get up early on Sunday to lace up my shoes, don my "Beef Builds a Better Body" running shirt and catch the bus for Staten Island and the start of the marathon.

Mayor Rudy Giuliani fired the starting cannon, and I gave Rudy a wave as I passed. I spotted the snipers posted high on the Verazzano Bridge, admired the helicopters patrolling our air space and looked down into the harbor to see if I could spot the Navy submarine that was there to help guard the

30,000 runners on their vulnerable run across the bridge.

The spectators were spectacular in their support. From Staten Island to Brooklyn to Queens to the Bronx and Manhattan, we ran to remember the victims and heroes of New York City.

And in the midst of all that support and emotion, I ran pretty well. I crossed the finish line in Central Park in 3 hours 15 minutes and 37 seconds, a new personal record and in the top 5 percent of the race's 30,000 entrants.

They broke the course record that day and crowned the U.S. national marathon champions. But, even more inspirational, there were people with just a month or two of training who ran in the place of loved ones who were entered but were killed on Sept. 11. There were New York City policemen and firemen running in memory of friends and colleagues lost. All around, it was a race of champions.

Any doubts I had about going were a distant memory by the end of mile one. No doubt about it, I'm glad I went.

Starting anew

Heading fresh into 2003

Dec. 30, 2002

I like the idea of a fresh start. I even appreciate fresh snow for the way it'll clean up a landscape. I appreciate freshmen, whether they're in high school, college or the legislature, for the energy and the honest reflections they provide.

That's why I like to celebrate New Year's Day. It's just a day's difference on the calendar, but in my mind, it's as exciting as that first fresh snow. And depending on how we behave on New Year's Eve, some of us need that fresh start worse than others.

If New Year's Eve is about looking back – the year in review, the biggest news headlines, the year's top of the Top 40 songs – then New Year's Day is about looking forward.

I have to admit, I have a lot to look forward to.

Look out, 2003

The new year brings with it some new responsibilities.

To start with, it'll bring a new wife. Actually, I never had an old wife, so the new one will be a first, I mean, an only. I'm not so good with the terminology, but I really hope to be a good husband in this new year and all the rest to come.

It also brings new responsibilities for me as a state senator. Yes, a freshman senator, as the old guard would say, and I wear that badge with honor. I look forward to adding a fresh perspective in that historic and honored hall at our state capitol.

And, after our legislative session, I'll get to see more new life on the ranch with more new time than I've had in years. This new year, I'm going to calve out our cows and not feel like I should be anywhere else.

This new year, in light of my engagement and election and my jampacked schedule, I decided to leave the full-time sales job I've held off the ranch in the animal health business the last four years.

For four years, I've driven an average of 1,000 to 1,200 miles a week, stayed in hotels at least two or three nights each week and eaten more restaurant food in more obscure places than you can shake a stick at. Despite all that, I still liked the job, and I liked the deposit it put in my bank account every two weeks.

But I like other things more.

The good stuff

I like the idea of spending more time with my folks. At 81 and 70 years old, I know they're not going to be with me forever, and I'd like to use the days I can wisely.

I like the idea of being home on the ranch and eating supper with my new wife and not in some restaurant and motel 200 miles away.

I like the idea of being a better neighbor, one who can help his neighbors back after they've come over to help you. I'm going to like saying, "yes, I can come lend you a hand," and not, "no, I'm already booked that day."

And I like the idea of helping out in my community, as a legislator, as a young fella with a strong back and a willing mind.

No doubt about it, I'm going to like the new year. My sincere hope is that you do, too.

Change of pace

Homebound and happy

May 19, 2003

Last week, Monday was a pretty sweet day for me. It was the first Monday in more than four years that I hadn't packed a suitcase and hit the road to try to supplement my income on the ranch.

For four years, I worked a sales job in the animal health industry that had me traveling a thousand miles a week, staying in motels and eating in restaurants while I worked the veterinary clinics and animal health dealers of the state. I left that job at the end of the year and went right into four months of session in the North Dakota Senate. Again, it was a hotel and restaurants.

Now, life on the road did have its advantages. Hotel maids made my bed for me everyday and I always had a clean towel. I didn't have to buy a lot of shampoo or soap while I was traveling either.

Restaurants brought prepared food right to my table – no shopping, no cooking, no dirty dishes to wash. And, with all that time I saved, I could enjoy a big dessert.

But, it wasn't home. Many was the day I'd have traded all the fine hotels and nice restaurants for my unmade bed with its rumpled-up homemade quilt and a dish of hamburger hotdish on the table next to my piles of mail.

Busy as ever

Luckily, I do have a home and ranch to come back to.

Despite my absence, I was able to keep things going with a later calving season, some custom haying and a hired man to help feed and fill in the gaps. I managed the operation from a cell phone and a laptop computer, and Mom and Dad would call and inform me of the latest ranch crisis.

Still, a lot of things slipped through the cracks.

My old fences didn't get much updating. The old wire is rustier than it was four years ago, and now, even my splices have splices in them.

There wasn't much maintenance on my machinery. I kept the regular suggested maintenance intervals, but I put an extra zero on the end of the hours.

No one cleaned the shop while I was gone. I used to be able to park four vehicles in there. Now, you can maybe squeeze in one if you kick a few things to the edge and slope up the piles on the sides.

So there's plenty for me to catch up on now.

Important stuff

But it's not the fence or the shop or the machinery that really matters. It's getting to spend more time with my parents as they age and battle their ailments. It's being able to help my neighbors more when they need an extra hand.

It's getting to be a full-time husband after our July wedding. I'd hate to start off a new marriage as a weekend husband who comes home road weary, hands his new wife a bag of dirty clothes and scurries off to catch up on a week's worth of ranching in two days. I don't know much about marriage, but I bet that would go over like a lead balloon.

The big void in this new idyllic lifestyle is the monthly paycheck and benefits I left behind.

I remember talking to another salesman about the admirable size of our paycheck. I asked if we were being paid so well for our technical knowledge, our communication skills, our ability to meet a customer's needs? No, he said, we're paid well to be away from our home and families. That's the trade.

It made sense – the explanation, that is, not the trade. Maybe that's why ranching is such an underpaid profession. We trade poor pay for a life where we get to spend our time at home working with our families.

That's the new trade I'm anxious to make. I won't miss my Monday morning packing ritual, and I'll gladly stick that suitcase back in the closet.

Writing the range

Rancher, writer, book publisher

Just in time for Christmas, A Collection of Cowboy Logic

Nov. 9, 1998

Once again, I've ignored the advice of the wise person who said, "You can't beat a man at his own trade."

Most of my loyal readers know of my past "successes" in being my own mechanic, veterinarian and computer upgrade expert. I rely on the same self-sufficient, but ignorant, confidence when I'm doing my own carpentry, plumbing and electrical wiring.

It seems like most of my forays into others' "own trades" are highly dependent on the availability of adjustable tools.

In my vet work, I get to work with adjustable syringes, adjustable calf chains and adjustable squeeze chutes. Mechanically, I rely on crescent wrenches, Vise-Grips and plain ol' pliers. Same tools I use for computer fixin'.

Plumbing has really gotten rancher friendly since the advent of plastic PVC pipe. Plastic pipe, some glue and a hacksaw is an adjustable man's dream. Mess up? Just saw it off and start over. And if I ruin the whole section of pipe, I'm only out 78 cents.

I feel qualified to do a lot of the ranch electrical work because of my expertise with that black tape. I can make adjustments with my trusty cutting pliers, and I can get out of most any bind I'm in with a quick splice and some of that black tape.

Self-published

All my years of amateur success in everything from computer mechanics to plumbing have prepared me well for my latest adventure – book publishing. It's been an adjustable project as well. I didn't get to use my adjustable wrenches, but I did get to use my adjustable deadlines.

At first, I thought about getting a book of my columns out last winter. But before you know it, Christmas had come and gone and I'd missed the big holiday shopping season.

So I figured I'd get a real early start on it for this Christmas. I figured I'd have it out by Oct. 1. Well, maybe Oct. 15. Then it was "heck, as long as I have it off the presses before Thanksgiving we should be all right." Right now, the book is ready to go.

Like all my learned trades, I began by buying a book on how to publish a book. It sits on the shelf next to "Plumbing Made Easy" and "Advanced Home Wiring Projects."

The result is "A Collection of Cowboy Logic, A Look at the Lighter Side of Going Broke, Raising Cattle, and Living on the Prairie," nearly 300 pages of homegrown philosophy and columns from the past four years, complete with some catchy cartoons drawn by award-winning cartoonist Steve Stark.

Along with the cartoons, I did swallow my self-sufficient rancher pride and force myself to seek some outside expertise in editing and graphic design. If you'd like to have your very own copy of the book, you can send me a check for $14.95 plus $2 shipping and it's yours. Make it out to Sandhill Communications, 1363 54th St. NE, Towner, ND 58788.

I think the book turned out way more professional than the last bit of plumbing I did, and, on the subject of plumbing, I think the book is printed on soft enough paper that you can go ahead and leave it in the outhouse.

The book-peddlin' cowboy

Retailin', wholesalin' and barterin'

Dec. 14, 1998

So much for Christmas being one of those meaningful seasons of peace, hope and sentiment. With a few thousand books of Cowboy Logic on hand, I'm realizing what everyone else in the retail business already knew — Christmas is about getting inventory out the door.

Symbolically, the new year represents a clean slate and the excitement of starting fresh in a new calendar year. But, to us hard-core capitalist retailers, the new year represents another 11 months of slow sales before the next Christmas shopping rush.

So I'm hitting the book-peddling trail pretty hard. And despite the long miles and lack of sleep, it's going pretty good. Before you know it, I'll have most of the printing bill paid.

Being gone from the ranch is never easy, but so far most of the cattle are still alive. I'm lucky enough to have a friend, sometimes referred to as a hired hand, to feed the cows for me while I'm gone and he's as good as they come.

Although I hate to be gone so much, it's actually a double benefit to the ranch. First, when I'm out on the road, I'm creating some much-needed cash flow. Secondly, the more I'm gone, the less money I'm spending.

Sure, being on the road will cost you some meals, gas and lodging, but that's nothing compared to what it costs to have me at home breaking stuff. It takes a lot of high-dollar repairs to keep a guy like me around.

Plus, I save a lot of money because, when I'm gone, I'm not tempted to start any expensive ranch improvement projects. The less you're around, the less you think about the need for the $1,000 stretch of wind break, the $200 barn door or the $400 water fountain.

My absence more than covers the cost of having a friend come out to feed the cows.

A trail of books

Last week, I had the state of North Dakota pretty much covered, traveling from Towner to Fargo to Rhame and back home. I was easy to track, though, leaving a trail of books in my wake. I was doing farm shows, holiday showcases, speaking engagements and cattle meetings, promoting my wares like a pyramid scheme marketer on speed.

I could hardly stand going through a town without stopping at the book stores, gift shops and ranch supply outfits to see if they'd like to put a little Cowboy Logic on their shelves.

Whenever I stopped at a café to eat, I'd pop up a little "books for sale" sign right next to my coffee cup and stack a few volumes by the salt and pepper shakers.

And to help move some inventory, I've even done a little bartering. As a matter of fact, I traded one book for a haircut at a barbershop in Mandan, N.D. It was a pretty good cut, too.

This week, I've got a book signing at Barnes & Noble in Fargo on Dec. 18 at 7 p.m. and another one at the B. Dalton's store in Minot on Dec. 19 at 1 p.m., so maybe I'll see you there.

And if you see a fella in a cowboy hat on the road between those two towns, driving a blueish-colored Buick with a sagging rear end and jam-packed with book boxes, flag me over. I'd love to sell you a book and lighten the load.

9/9/99 still fine

No rest for the writer

Sept. 13, 1999

I wasn't really planning on having to write this week's column. I was counting on a Y2K warm-up tragedy with the magic numbers 9/9/99 to save me from this week's deadline.

I was looking forward to my first week off from the column biz in the last five years. After 260 weekly ramblings, I was looking forward to a week free of writing down my ramblings. Probably a few of the readers were looking forward to a week off, too.

I was banking on a predicted computer meltdown on Sept. 9 that was supposed to be caused by the digital disaster of 9/9/99 when some computers would want to turn to 0/0/00 and call it a century.

It wasn't predicted to cause near the global mayhem that Y2K is supposed to this winter, but I was hoping it would at least give me a little break in my weekly responsibilities.

Ready, set…

I was completely ready to handle a 9/9/99 shutdown of services. Along with having not written my 9/13/99 column in expectation of computer failures, I had ignored paying bills that were due on the 10th of the month and I didn't bother resetting the clock on my VCR since it would be blinking 88:88 again in no time.

The cows weren't wasting any time getting ready either. Afraid that the power would go out and that the electric water pumps would start leaving the water down in the ground, they pushed over a cross fence and automatically rotated themselves into a pasture with a big fresh water lake.

The cows probably had a little help getting 9/9/99 ready from our growing mosquito herd. When the cows were contemplating a break toward an energy-free watering source, I could see and hear a black cloud of skeeters herding them toward the cross fence that they needed to crash.

Apparently, the mosquitoes were also quite concerned about a power failure and cows with no water. No water, no blood. No blood, no nutritious meals for a young, growing mosquito.

I hear some people are worried about nutritious meals for themselves, too. Afraid that Y2K and/or 9/9/99 and/or any other hype-riddled day of the year will leave them without the necessary basic staples of life, they've taken to ordering those things in nice airtight 5-gallon buckets to get them through an entire year, figuring we'll have things straightened out by 2001.

Of course, I never realized that the necessary staples of life were considered to be dehydrated banana chips, storable powdered meat substitutes and sprouting seeds for growing our favorite fresh sprout salad. And I never realized until I read a brochure written for folks living in fear, that you could get a 365-day supply of bucket-sealed food powder for a mere $1,500.

No, it looks like my fence-crawling cows were more prepared for any 9/9/99 glitch on grass supplies than I was, but their preparation and fence busting was all for not.

The 9/9/99 catastrophes didn't pan out and this hastily written column should be all the proof you need that I really believed the day would darken at least a few of the world's computers.

Oh well, maybe we'll all get a little break next January during Y2K. But I think I'd rather have to write a column than break lake ice for 200 thirsty cows.

The lutefisk circuit

Researching a directory for the love of lutefisk

Nov. 8, 1999

Another day, another dollar. Another year, another annual Lutheran lutefisk supper under my belt.

I've written of my adventures as a server of the holy cod in this column before. I still get a lot of joy and satisfaction from the annual flounder fundraiser for Zion Lutheran Church and, along with that joy, I get a big ol' belly full of that wonderful lye-soaked, wiggly fish.

One thing I've noticed in my years of flinging lutefisk is that the patrons come from far and wide. When you feed 500 people in a town the size of Towner, you know that you've attracted a few out-of-towners.

Word travels well amongst lutefisk lovers. Aside from a few posters and a couple of sentences in the church bulletin, the news is spread by word of mouth. It's really kind of an "underground" activity. Like prisoners tapping to each other on their jail cell walls, fish-loving Norskies pass along the whens and wheres of local lutefisk suppers.

Now, though, I say it's time to go public with our eating habits. I think it's time someone take the initiative to publish a lutefisk lover's guide to suppers held across the upper Midwest. Maybe someone who, a) likes lutefisk, and b) has a way to gather information through the media, should put together the directory and accompanying road map.

I asked a few of my friends in the media business if they'd like to tackle the project, but they just didn't have the stomach for the job, or the lutefisk. So I've decided to do it myself.

Calling all suppers

Here's the deal. If you know of a good lutefisk supper, write me a note and give me the specifics — when, where, why and any other interesting points on the supper's history, record-breaking eaters or other interesting sidebars.

More than likely, you've already held your supper, so give me the date for next year's or tell me an approximate date the supper is held every year, like "the third Sunday of October" or "as soon as Olaf, chairman of the cod committee, gets the fish ordered in early November."

Tell me where you hold the supper, like a Lutheran church basement or in a tent that is burned immediately afterward to rid the community of the smell.

Tell me about the usual menu — lutefisk, lefse, meatballs (for the weak-hearted non-lutefiskers), enough coffee to fund the retirement of Juan Valdez and enough melted butter to drive up the world price of dairy products.

Tell me anything that makes your supper really interesting. And tell me how long you've upheld this prairie tradition.

My plan is to compile all this data and create a guide that will bring some order and organization to the lutefisk supper circuit. I think a map might be in order as well so that folks who really want to maximize their fall fisk intake could plan their trips efficiently.

Or, better yet, we could design a bus route and charter a Greyhound for the hard-core enthusiasts. Like mountain climbers aspiring to climb the "Seven Summits," the highest point on each of the seven continents, lutefisk eaters could aspire to the "Fourteen Flounders," hitting the 14 major lutefisk suppers on the prairie.

I'm not sure what 14 would make the list — maybe Towner, Almont, Park River, Bottineau, Minot's Norsk Hostfest — but if you send the specifics of your supper to Ryan Taylor, Attn: Lutefisk Circuit, 5435 13th Ave. NE, Towner, ND 58788, you'll at least have a fair chance at it.

Author's note: This project has yet to leave the desk. I'm still taking submissions on favorite lutefisk hotspots, but in the meantime the best place to discover lutefisk and other church and community suppers on the plains is at writer and historian Tom Isern's website, www.plainsfolk.com/suppers.

Change is good

Making time for the millenium

Feb. 28, 2000

Memorable moments. Forty one years ago last week, my father married my mother. Twenty years ago last week, the United States beat the Soviet Union in Winter Olympic hockey. Six years ago, I got a letter back from the American Quarter Horse Association that said they liked the way I write.

My folks gave me the genetics and upbringing to achieve many things. The U.S. hockey team showed me that you can beat the odds if you work hard enough. The letter from the AQHA admitted cowboys do know how to use complete sentences. The AQHA liked an essay that I had written well enough to place it in the top 10 of a stack of entries more than a thousand deep. There were some nice prizes.

But the longest-lasting prize was a phone call I got from Ann Bailey, a writer for the Grand Forks Herald. She thought their Sunday edition could use a feature on this essay-writin' rancher who was punching both cows and the keyboard.

A couple of months after the story ran, I got a call from Agweek magazine, a publication of the Grand Forks Herald, asking me to write some hard news and features for them.

A few months into the job, I tried my hand on the editorial page with a little something called Cowboy Logic. I've written it 283 times since then, every week, 52 times a year, without a break.

Next week will be my first break in nearly six years.

Weak weeks

After 5 1/2-plus years, my column ideas are getting a little scant.

And rather than sit down and write something just for the sake of filling a page, I asked my editor, Kevin Bonham, if I could start writing Cowboy Logic every other week.

Kevin probably suspected that my column inspiration was waning when my Tuesday noon deadline slipped to Thursday afternoon week after week. He said he'd look around for someone to write a column and relieve me on my weak weeks.

Next week, Ann Bailey, the same person who opened the door to Agweek for me, will begin writing a column on farm life. It'll give me an extra week to get inspired, i.e. a tractor to break down, a cow to roll me, a fence to fall flat. And it'll give Agweek readers a chance to read the writings of a very talented woman. I know you'll like Ann.

Free time

There're plenty of takers for the time I'll be freeing up in the new column off weeks. Things have changed some since I started writing in 1994.

I'm still a rancher, but the ranch has had to move over for a full-time career in the animal health business. I've warmed myself up for this lifestyle, working off the ranch on and off the last few years.

When I started writing in 1994, no one was asking me to speak and entertain at their banquets and meetings. Nowadays, I'm doing about 25 storytelling, rope-twirling gigs a year.

I never had a book to market six years ago, and the "Collection of Cowboy Logic" takes some time out of my day, too.

But the real target of my newfound free time will be staving off my premature mid-life crisis. I turn the big three zero in July, so I've got some things to do. Run a marathon, travel the world, buy a good horse, learn another language, play the saxophone again.

I'd like to thank everybody for putting up with me these last 284 weeks. Take a break, I'll see you on March 13.

Rural Christmas Elves

Delivering toys to a fellow young farmer

Dec. 18, 2000

I sometimes wonder what I'm going to write my column about when it's around Christmastime. When I got the following e-mail from Ty Zimdars in Brockview, Mont., my wondering was over.

"Ryan – I have read you column for quite a while and most of it hits right home for all of us in eastern Montana and western N.D. I read of your marathon and it was quite a feat to accomplish that. We are going through a marathon of our own now and thought you might be able to help me by helping out my 10-year-old nephew Tyrel Bain.

"Sunday, November 26, at 2 a.m., he and his family lost their home to fire getting out with only the clothes on their backs. Tyrel, being a hobby farmer and rancher, lost the John Deere collection of HIS lifetime and informed me he had just increased his cow herd to 50 head of plastic critters.

"So, now that he is out 60 to 70 tractors and implements, and 50 cows, he is ready to start over like a typical hard-headed cowboy. I thought only I was that hard headed. I was wondering in your travels if you would have an idea of how to start a toy tractor drive or cow drive to help him start over."

An idea!

Yes, Ty, I do have an idea of how to start a tractor and cow drive for our young farming friend, Tyrel Bain, and this column is it.

I'd like to ask the folks reading this column if they could possibly send a green tractor or some desktop-sized cows to a fellow rancher down on his luck.

I called the Zimdars and got the details on how to get these things to Tyrel. His address is: Tyrel Bain, 762 Road 431, Richey, MT 59259.

I don't know a lot about the Bain family, but Mary Zimdars told me that Tyrel has two older brothers, that his dad is a truck driver and that his mom and dad also do some foster parenting.

She said the community support since the fire has been heartwarming. It would warm my heart if our larger community of farmers, ranchers and others who read this column would shower Tyrel with little green tractors and black, brown, red, white or even blue cows to get his operation back on track.

Consider this an opportunity to promote your breed to a future producer. He could probably even put a red, orange or blue tractor to use if you just can't bring yourself to send a green one.

If we go way overboard and fill the family's new temporary quarters to the rafters with these items, I'm sure we can find good homes for the excess.

On its way

I know of at least one toy tractor making its way to Richey, Mont. I took this event as an opportunity to spend some special time with my 6-year-old nephew and ponder the things we should think about at Christmas.

I told my nephew about Tyrel's situation, about the fire that put them out in the cold with barely any clothes on their backs and certainly no toys in their hands. He looked at me with the seriousness only a 6-year-old can muster and told me we ought to go to the Tractor Supply store and see what we could round up for "that kid."

He picked out a nice tractor with a loader (handy for moving the snow we'll be getting this winter) and even wrote Tyrel a Christmas card in his best handwriting.

It's all in the mail heading your way, Tyrel. Have a merry Christmas.

Job satisfaction

The good days of being a columnist

Feb. 25, 2002

Some readers will remember a column I wrote just before Christmas a little more than a year ago. It had to do with a young man from Montana who'd recently lost his home to a fire.

Losing his home was bad enough, but he also lost all 10 years worth of his toy tractor collection and all his other toy farming necessities, from implements to livestock.

I asked readers to devote a little of their Christmas giving to this upstart farmer who'd fallen on some hard luck. Well, it worked, and the following is a letter I recently received.

Thanks, readers!

Dear Mr. Taylor,

It has been a little over a year now since our house fire that took my collection of toy tractors. I would still like to thank the many people who have sent me generous gifts of their collections and pieces they purchased because of my loss.

The first time I saw the piles of packages under our mail box I did not know what was going on. At that time I found out that my uncle had contacted you concerning my family's loss. It is amazing how a computer can generate such a reaction in a time of need.

I received everything from tractors to clothing and bibles. We are so thankful. It has been interesting to see where all of the packages came from. California to Canada, North Dakota to Nebraska, we appreciated them all. I hope to meet some of these great people someday and thank them for their gifts.

Sorry this is so late, we are just now moving into a home of our own. Thank you and God Bless. Because of my uncle's love of farming and ranching, I would like to give him a special thanks for sharing that love with me. I hope that when I am as old as my uncle Ty there are still farms and ranches. Sincerely, Tyrel Bain and Family

Chance to meet

It was really nice to hear from Tyrel and find out how well our toy drive went. I got to see a picture of a very happy young farmer surrounded by rows of toy tractors and machinery that the readers of Cowboy Logic so generously sent his way.

Even better than that, I got to meet Tyrel and his family when I was in Baker, Mont., to speak at a chamber ag banquet. They drove an hour and half from Richey, Mont., to see me, and it really made my day.

Tyrel and I became fast friends and he even helped me do a little rope spinning in my after-dinner speech. He showed me more pictures of the new tractor collection and told me about coming home to a mailbox surrounded by hundreds of boxes from around the country.

He had a box full of letters, notes and cards that accompanied the gifts. With his mom's help, they had a notebook listing everything they'd received, who sent it and when it arrived. I could tell by the care they took with those letters that everything was truly appreciated.

It warmed my heart to see firsthand the generosity of fellow farmers, ranchers and column readers from around the continent, coast to coast. It made me proud to be part of such a wonderful group of people, and I felt a deep sense of satisfaction in the good things that can come from a few published words.

It felt like Christmas in February.

Empty-handed

The no-column column

June 18, 2001

This is a column about not having a column. Hopefully, by the end of this non-column, a column will have magically appeared to get me out of my "no column to send an hour before the deadline" situation.

In my seven years as a columnist, this is the first time I can remember having completely blown a deadline. It's Friday afternoon and Agweek goes to press in a few hours.

Today's "where's your column?" phone call from Grand Forks caught me completely unaware. It was like I forgot I even wrote a column. I should've known it was my turn since I saw Ann Bailey's column in this week's issue.

There're times when I know I'm pushing my deadline, but at least I know I've got a deadline to meet. I'll have pondered an idea or two for the column, and maybe even have a couple hundred words started on my computer screen. A couple hundred words is way better than zero when it comes to reaching my bi-weekly 550-word goal.

The editors would love me if I could get these words for page seven to them by Tuesday — one less thing to worry about when everything else is hitting them later in the week. They won't love me, but they will tolerate me if I can get my column e-mailed by Thursday. Occasionally, they get a Friday morning e-mail from me. I'm sure no one's smiling about that, but they've been good enough to put up with it.

Now I'm scrambling to get some words on the screen and get it shipped off after an hour or two of forced creative imagination.

Nothing

Jerry Seinfeld made a television career out of his sitcom that he billed as "a show about nothing." My writing career is somewhat similar, based on my "column about nothing." But today's column is really about nothing, nothing at all.

People ask me if it's hard to come up with things to write about on a regular basis. The answer to that question is yes.

There're always things to write about, but to write about them in a way that is interesting or entertaining or, at the least, informative, is the hard part.

This week, I could've written about my Monday plane trip into Minneapolis through lightening, a hail storm and a not-so-distant funnel cloud. But when that plane landed, I was just glad to be on the ground. I was thinking more about the fine print on my life insurance policy than I was about the print I needed next week for Agweek.

I could've written about my cousin, a Wall Street CEO and author, who's speaking in Minot, N.D., next week about his book and Social Security reform. But his talk isn't until next Tuesday, so I need a few more days to get my material.

I could've written about last night's Miss North Dakota High School Rodeo Queen contest in Bowman, N.D. Somehow I got wrangled into being one of the five judges for the contest. I think they needed a male on the committee, or else they had a quota to fill for absent-minded columnists. But we won't know the results of our scoring until Sunday, and I'd hate to write about the contest without knowing who got the title.

There're a lot of other things I could've written about, but, dangit the computer is telling me that I just broke through the 550-word threshold.

But don't feel cheated, it was really nothing.

The big screen

Trying to make it in the movies

Feb. 23, 2004

I've always been intrigued by the movie business. I even figured that if I couldn't make a living in ranching, writing, sales or business, maybe I'd take up movie acting as a career.

The trouble with that idea is there aren't a lot of movie opportunities in North Dakota. I'm not interested in moving to Hollywood or New York City or even Vancouver. So here I am, a budding actor without an outlet.

Then one day a couple of years ago, I'm walking down the street in Medora, N.D., when someone says, "Are you going to audition for the movie?" Sure enough, North Dakota's very first movie production was about to be filmed in the scenic badlands.

It was going to be called "Wooly Boys" and star Peter Fonda, Kris Kristofferson and Joe Mazello. Although they had some big names, they needed a few little names like Ryan Taylor to play "Man walking down street" and "Restaurant customer No. 4."

It might have been my one chance to make it on the big screen. But, alas, I had a lot of other irons in the fire. I had a ranch to tend to, an off-the-ranch job with a busy schedule and a calendar that just wouldn't allow me to be on call for two weeks straight for some demanding director.

So I passed on the auditions.

Paper star

Even though moviegoers won't see me on the screen with Kris and Peter, a friend of mine in the book business suggested that I leave a copy of my book as a possible prop in some of the scenes.

So I left the prop folks a copy of my "Collection of Cowboy Logic" and went on down the road. Now, a couple years later, "Wooly Boys" has been released to theaters in North Dakota with a potential wider distribution to follow.

I went to the movie to see if my book got a cameo appearance on the screen.

First off, it was a good family movie. A little hokey at times, but, hey, it's a movie. There were some great panoramic shots of the North Dakota badlands and the story about two cantankerous old sheep ranchers taking one's overprotected Minneapolis grandson out to a western North Dakota sheep ranch was pretty amusing.

For the record, everyone should know that there are more cattle than sheep in North Dakota and more cowboys than wooly boys, but sheep ranchers need a little big screen recognition, too, I guess.

If it gets to a theater in your area, give it a shot and support North Dakota. If it doesn't get to your movie theater, you can probably rent the video someday.

And if you're watching "Wooly Boys," I want you to pay particularly close attention to one of the first scenes where Kris Kristofferson rolls out of his sheep wagon, goes to the saddlebags on his horse, grabs a book (yes, a book!), rips out a couple of pages and heads down to the brush to take care of a little personal outhouse-type business.

It may not be the big-screen debut for my book that I was hoping for, but I think that book in his saddlebag just may have been "A Collection of Cowboy Logic."

I always said the paper was pretty soft. Just ask Kris.

Faith, family and friends

In the right wrong place

Blizzards don't care where you need to be and when

Dec. 28, 1998

I rolled down the car window and looked for the yellow line. Supposedly, I was going south down Interstate 29 between Grand Forks and Thompson, but it's hard to tell where you are when you can't even see your hood ornament.

Blizzard Clint was taking its toll on my usually high level of driving relaxation, not to mention my ability to get to the Barnes & Noble book store in Fargo, N.D., for a Cowboy Logic book signing.

It took me an hour to cover the 12 miles from Grand Forks to Thompson, so I decided to pull off the road for awhile. I holed up at editor Rona Johnson's homestead, and, although Rona was still in Grand Forks, her husband was there to greet me and get me in out of the wind.

But after an hour and a half of forced idleness, I decided to make another try at getting to Fargo for the book signing. I'd already packed my winter survival gear, so I pulled down my earlappers and hit the road.

There wasn't much traffic – probably because the highway patrol had already closed the gates at Grand Forks.

I was sure that I would drive out of it if I kept going south, though. I plodded along behind one other fellow blizzard driver in a sport utility vehicle at a rate of 5 to 10 miles per hour.

Then the SUV stopped dead in its tracks on the middle of the interstate. The driver came back to my car and told me it wouldn't move and wouldn't start. We couldn't even roll the locked-up vehicle to the side of the road. In no time at all, the dead vehicle was ice cold.

I invited the stranger into my warm car and told him we could use my cell phone. We learned a couple things on the phone – no tow trucks were dumb enough to risk coming out, we should stay with his vehicle to keep others from hitting it, and we shouldn't be driving anyway because the interstate was closed for a reason.

So we sat there idling time and idling the motor of my cozy, heated car. My newfound companion was a businessman from Minneapolis and we spent a couple of hours learning about each other's lives and careers. Then the storm seemed to start clearing and moving south, so we turned around and headed for Grand Forks.

In the spirit of the Christmas season, we discovered there "was no room at the inn" in all of Grand Forks. But, luckily, Rona had reserved a room for me. I offered the extra bed to my blizzard buddy.

As I think about it, I know that I shouldn't have left Thompson to try and make it to the book signing in Fargo, but if I hadn't, it could have been a real tough night for at least one traveling stranger stranded without any winter gear or a cell phone.

Judging from the block of ice in my traveling coffee mug the next morning, cars don't stay too warm without a running motor and a heater. And, in that storm, I know it would have been pretty tough for a semi to see his vehicle in time to keep from rear ending him if he was forced to sit in that cold vehicle in the middle of the road.

So maybe I wasn't supposed to be in Fargo peddling books that night. But, in some coincidental, Christmas sort of way, I think I was supposed to be on I-29 in the middle of that storm.

Parts person

Breaking down just won't be the same

June 21, 1999

There aren't many positive angles to breaking down in the hay field.

But, in Towner, we had one thing to look forward to when the wobblehead on our mower exploded or a bearing decided it couldn't bear another day of our hard labor – we could look forward to jumping in the pickup with our collection of steel fragments and going to see Nancy, a.k.a. "the parts lady."

Breaking stereotypes

If someone asked you to paint a picture in your mind of a person behind a mechanical parts counter, you might picture some burly, grumpy guy in a sleeveless snap-front shirt with a five o'clock shadow and a 4:55 p.m. attitude.

You might imagine hearing him growl, "What do you mean you don't have the part number? You expect me to waste 15 minutes looking up your $2 tube? I got better things to do. Why don't you go buy some new equipment that won't break down so I can take a break and get back to reviewing my 1984 baler babes swimsuit calendar!"

That may be a stretch, but we've probably all run across a parts man that resembled at least portions of that stereotypical description on certain days.

Nancy blew that stereotype right out of the water when she got into the parts and repairs business. She was a regular ray of sunshine in a dimly lit world of broken down machinery.

She could cheer up the grumpiest of frustrated farmers and cranky cowboys. Her attitude was contagious and, before you knew what hit you, you'd forgotten about the hay that was down, the rain that was coming and the dirty, greasy job you had ahead of you.

Nancy's business was a place where you kinda liked to spend a little time in reflection and small-town conversation. It had a good long parts counter with comfortably cushioned stools for sitting customers and lots of leaning room for those who preferred to stand and visit.

She could find your part, with or without a number and a detailed description, as good as anyone in the business. And she could do it in a way that made you wish you'd broken a few more pieces so that you could give her a little more business and help support one of the last businesses in a dwindling rural town.

Prime of life

One day I was in at Nancy's to pick up some grease or anti-freeze when the conversation turned from the weather and the farm markets to something that made thunderstorms and the cattle on feed report look like the most trivial topics in the world.

"They found cancer in me," she said as I sat next to her counter drinking a Styrofoam cupful of coffee. I tried to handle the news with a trait common among folks in agriculture – hope.

We both talked of the hope that the doctors could remove it, treat her and that we could add her story to the list of successful fixes made at Towner Parts and Repairs. The whole community shared in that hope.

Last summer, our community held a funeral for a 58-year-old lady who made breaking down and going to town for parts a pretty positive experience. I wish I knew what the part number was that we needed to help repair a cancer. I wish I could have looked it up, gone to the shelf and gotten her back in the field.

Days to remember

Making war and making hay

Aug. 9, 1999

My birthday has come and gone, but the Monday when this column runs will be Aug. 9, my father's birthday.

I can't say I've had any historically significant birthdays up to this point. Sure, I've seen the usual milestones that a Generation "X" member sees – reruns of "Cheers," the falling of the Berlin Wall and years of relative peace and a strong economy for everyone but the nation's farmers and ranchers.

My dad, on the other hand, has seen some things that really shaped the world and the century that we're about to close out. Just looking at him, you wouldn't realize that this lifelong rancher had seen much beyond the Dakota prairies where he made his life.

But, in early August, in 1945, he saw things on the other side of the world that were far removed from the hay meadows in Smokey Lake Township where he spent every August after that.

The "big one"

Before Dad dedicated his summer birthday to two-cylinder John Deeres putt putting across an ocean of grass, he spent one on an LST floating in the Pacific Ocean heading to Japan.

Dad was a part of the 8th Army in Northern Luzon, Philippines. The 8th Army would have likely been one of the sacrifices made in a potential invasion of Kyushu, Japan, an action that held the potential for a million American and Japanese casualties.

In early August 1945, he was camped at San Juan La Union. Like many soldiers from the land of plenty, one memory that sticks out in his mind had to do with hunger in a land of little. Local children were so hungry that they fought over the food in the camp's garbage left over from the G.I. mess kits. Guards had to watch over the kids to make sure they didn't hurt each other.

More memorable than the hunger of the Philippine children was the news that the U.S. had taken an unprecedented action of war – it had dropped two atom bombs, one on Aug. 6 on the city of Hiroshima and one on Aug. 9 on Nagasaki. The two bombs took 240,000 lives.

The plutonium bomb, nicknamed "fat boy," dropped on Nagasaki on the same day that a certain skinny young cowboy private from North Dakota turned 24. After spending two years in the South Pacific and preparing for what was certain to be a suicidal invasion of mainland Japan, he was probably pretty glad to be alive on that birthday.

Tokio Bay

From San Juan La Union, the birthday boy took a train down to Manila and shipped out at Subic Bay in one of 50 LST's that were headed to Tokyo.

His birthday cruise was a little rocky. In a storm off of Okinawa, they had to get below deck and three of the LST's hit mines that had broke loose. He never heard if anyone survived the hits.

Like most ranchers, he talked to a neighbor to get the exact weather report. A fellow hometowner, the late John Burckhard, was on Okinawa when that storm was blowing in the ocean. He said they clocked the winds at 150 miles an hour on land, probably worse on the ocean.

But they made it through. And his birthday cruise had a pretty nice ending. Pulling into Tokyo Bay, they could see the battleship U.S.S. Missouri where the surrender was signed. The just-turned 24-year-old could look forward to peace and a trip home to his sandhills and hay meadows.

Quite a birthday for a ranch kid from Towner.

Harvest pride

Bringing in the grain

Aug. 30, 1999

Harvest season is rolling along and wrapping up on the northern plains.

The annual gathering of grain from south to north takes place every year like clockwork, or as close to clockwork as can be considering the heavy dependence on the whims of nature.

Only a month ago, I was traveling to Pierre, S.D., when I saw the big custom combine crews out in the fields cutting the crop by the section and township. The big green machines were a marvel of modernness as they did the initial grind and shake that would continue until the grain was ground, shaked and baked all the way to the dinner table.

I could admire the combining activity, but only from afar. Having spent my entire life on a strictly cattle and hay outfit, I was a little aloof to the joys of threshing grain, as my father's generation would call it.

A glean scene

My cowboy search for crop combining experience wound up in a western North Dakota oats field. Since the oats were being harvested for cattle feed, it wasn't quite a full fledged farming-for-nothing experience, but it was close enough to give me a taste of grain shaking.

I didn't want to take too big of a step into the era of modern machinery, so I was glad to see that the ol' Gleaner in the oats field wasn't quite as tweaked out as the outfits I saw on the custom cutting crew in South Dakota.

I felt right at home in the 1978 model silver grain shaker and straw maker. We made a half dozen rounds while the truck went home to unload, discussing the progression of farm equipment and farm communities.

Harvest wasn't quite as social as it used to be in the days of neighborhood threshing crews that brought everyone together, my combining companion told me. After the combine came out, everyone had their own way to thresh and the farms got larger while the towns got smaller.

Along with the air seeder, the four-wheel-drive tractor and a full slate of other cropping technology, we learned how to feed the world and the economies of every community but the farm community.

Meanwhile, the ol' Gleaner kept on gleaning at a rate of 1.5 miles per hour in its Dunn County field.

Prairie pride

Regardless of how cynical and jaded a person can get when he's contemplating agriculture, there are still some very inspirational moments that can put you back in the right frame of mind.

One of things that put me back on track is the sight of an American flag flying high atop a prairie grain elevator. The elevator co-op might be going under, the farmer who delivers his grain there might be flat broke, but we still have enough pride in who we are and what we do to set that flag on the highest point we can find.

The elevator flag paled next to what I saw a week ago, though. Driving at dusk between Turtle Lake and Underwood, I saw a farmer out reaping the seed that he had sown while the sun began to set. A small green machine and a cloud of dust moved up and down the golden field.

But his old combine had some non-standard equipment. On a pole above the cab flew a full-size North Dakota state flag in all its royal blue splendor.

All I could mutter as I drove by was, "damn right, buddy."

Thanksgiving gave out

Looking for the bright side on a dim morning   Nov. 29, 1999

Thanksgiving Day is supposed to be one of those days where we bathe in the warmth of good feelings and gracious appreciation.

I was fine with that, and I was ready to start the day by counting my blessings and letting the thanks flow. That lasted about five minutes.

That's when I walked into the corral and found that my darling, freshly weaned calves had spent the night stampeding around and had flattened about 80 feet of what once was a pretty respectable fence.

I wasn't feeling too warm and gracious at that point. But I did have a blessing to count, and I was thankful that the calves had only broken into an empty pen and hadn't gotten mixed up with the cows.

Then my Thanksgiving day got pretty thankless. Right after noticing the flattened fenceline, I found a flattened bovine. Well, maybe not quite flat, she was starting to bloat up and get kind of round looking.

It looked like she had gotten inside the bale feeder, got stuck when she tried to get back out and had somehow tipped the feeder over on herself and died a miserable death on an otherwise pleasant Thanksgiving eve.

After finding that, every ounce of holiday happiness I might have had disappeared.

Bright side?

I spent the rest of the day trying to find the bright side of this dim situation.

I thought of the old, "Well, at least it wasn't one of my really good calves," line to try and cheer myself up.

But the fact was she was one of my best replacement heifer candidates. Of course, every cattleman knows they're always the ones you lose. The worst disease, pestilence, bad weather and hard luck imaginable will never kill the runty, no-good calves in the herd. Like they say, only the good die young.

I thought that maybe the sight of their fallen comrade would forever deter the rest of the calves from trying to crawl in the bale feeders. But a person should never credit cattle with any kind of learning ability. Calves continued crawling in and out of bale feeders like kids in a fairground fun castle.

I tried to think about how glad I was that my only calf loss had been an unavoidable accident and that it was better than having a bunch of sickness or disease.

But when you lose a calf to sickness, you're kind of braced for it because you've been doctoring it and have mentally prepared yourself for its usually inevitable death. In a way, even that's better than finding them dead in a bale feeder.

So my dark cloud was doing a pretty good job of blocking out any silver linings.

Truly thankful

I concluded that the calf episode looked pretty depressing from all angles. With that decision made, I decided to go on with Thanksgiving.

As it turned out, my two nephews didn't let one less calf ruin their Thanksgiving at our house.

My 5-year-old nephew said grace and he never even mentioned that calf. He just said thanks for the food, the day and Grandma, Grandpa, Mom, Dad, brother and even Uncle Ryan. No one could really say for certain, but I'm sure the noises coming from my 7-month-old nephew resembled "Amen."

I decided that maybe the two little people at our dinner table had the right idea. Forget the calf and be thankful for the food, the day and the people. And that's really probably the right way to step into the Christmas season.

Remembering

Sept. 24, 2001

Like many people around the world, I've had only one thing on my mind the past two weeks.

Tuesday, Sept. 11, I was doing something pretty common for me. I was drinking a cup of coffee and watching some morning news. Newscasters were innocently trying to understand why one of the world trade towers had been hit by an airplane. A failure in guidance, air traffic control perhaps?

As I watched, a second plane slammed into the second tower. There was no more guessing about what was happening.

A few weeks earlier on the evening of Friday, Aug. 17, I was doing something a little less common. I was enjoying a visit with an old friend and high school classmate who had moved away, his girlfriend who I'd first met more than a year ago, one of her friends and co-workers who I met for the first time that night, and another good friend, my classmate's brother, who still lives in the area.

It was more than a good visit. It was a great visit around a campfire on a cool evening on the rolling prairie. It was an evening complete with the singing and guitar playing of my talented friend and classmate. An evening of roasting marshmallows on our prize skewers recently whittled from a nearby thicket of poplar trees.

It was laughter and conversation with two interesting and intelligent young women. One raised on our country's west coast, the other in London, England.

It was an incredibly clear evening with a perfect view of the stars. We all spent a fair bit of time admiring those stars in the dark prairie sky. We even watched several of them fall and made our wishes upon them.

I shook my blankets out by the fire, slept a little and left before the rest of the camp was awake. I didn't get to say goodbye to my classmate and the two women who were heading back to their homes and careers away from North Dakota.

But I did send an e-mail to the personable Brit with the charming accent and received one back on Aug. 31. She said she had a great time in North Dakota, and she described her experience of watching the sun come up from a hill by the campsite as "eerily quiet, but beautiful."

And she finished the e-mail with, "See you in November for the big run, we'll be here rootin' for ya!" The run she referred to was the New York City Marathon that I'd entered. The two women I sat with around the campfire lived in the Big Apple and worked in Manhattan for a company called eSpeed.

Not knowing what part of town they worked in, I e-mailed her that Tuesday, Sept. 11, to ask if they were OK. After sending the e-mail, I went to the Internet to look up eSpeed's address – it read 103rd Floor, One World Trade Center.

That e-mail came back as undeliverable with "non-fatal errors." That wasn't right. That e-mail was undeliverable because of an attack that was extremely deliberate, and it was very, very fatal. And it was, I'm afraid, fatal for my two campfire friends who are among the more than 6,300 missing.

I only knew Kristine and Suria a short time – one for a little more than a year, one for just a few weeks – but I am so sad to think that they are gone.

I try not to think of their fearful final moments on those floors above the impact of the first tower hit. But I do. I hope and pray that there was some source of comfort found in those last desperate moments.

And, as beautiful as our view was of those stars in the heavens several weeks ago, I believe that their view is even better tonight because they are so much closer now.

Saving grace

Country churches struggle in the country

July 15, 2002

I like to think that people who live at the end of gravel roads are some of the better people I know. Maybe that's just because I live at the end of a very long gravel road.

I've also come to believe that churches next to those same country roads are pretty special, too. No, they're not any more sacred, or holy, or directly hotwired to the heavens. Every church out there should stand on equal footing with the landlord upstairs regardless of their size, shape or location.

But, in my eyes, those white-steepled, clapboard guardians of the prairie are a cut above their urban counterparts. And I say that as someone who's always gone to a brick church in town on a paved street.

I've been in country church country, though, and spent some quality time in those short church pews where the farthest back row is still only 20 feet from the pulpit. You feel pretty bad if the preacher catches you sleeping through the sermon when you're that close to the action.

You're so close to the weddings in those churches you can see the sweat roll off of the groom and hear the bride whisper orders to her new husband. At the baptisms, you might catch a little splash and be rebaptized yourself.

At funerals, it's tough to reserve pews for family members when there're so few pews to start with. Of course, in the small communities served by the country churches, everyone's related anyway, at least by marriage. Reserved or not, every pew will have family members sitting in it.

At some point, unfortunately, these proud rural churches began holding more funerals than weddings and baptisms. A 1998 survey of North Dakota's 2,000 historic church buildings showed that at least 400 of them had been abandoned.

The National Trust for Historic Preservation put rural churches on the endangered list last year.

Sell or celebrate?

Two of our local country churches are facing the trend. Both are closed. One recently had their annual summer heritage service, the other had their last service of sorts – an auction sale.

I attended the heritage service at Norway Lutheran Church, a church hidden away along the Mouse River on a peaceful hillside. It's on the National

Register of Historic Places.

The service was also attended by a writer for the New York Times. Her July 7 story on the demise of rural congregations said the beautiful Norway Lutheran was "on a road so isolated that the only person who can admire it is the mail carrier." And, I suppose, the local ranchers going to and from their pastures and fields. Not much random passing traffic, for sure.

There were cars and traffic for the summer service, though. Old members like to get together when another former member is able to return from Iowa and play the 1912 Packard pump organ for the reunion service.

The other local church was Berwick Lutheran Church, forced to hold a sale, not a service.

I got an unofficial report from the auction – the pews brought $250 a piece, the altar and pulpit $450, the organ just $150. The church itself had been sold earlier, but the deal fell through.

The shocker of the whole deal was the sale of the church's outhouse privy. It brought $180, $30 more than the church organ! It seemed almost sacrilegious. At the least, overly practical and pragmatic.

But I suppose if one were looking for quiet spiritual moments and some silence for self-reflection, an outhouse could be assigned more value than a noisy organ.

In all places and at all times, He is with us. I wish those country churches could've stayed with us, too.

Musical encouragement

National Symphony reaches deep in the plains May 5, 2003

Feed the cows, eartag a few newborn calves, fix some fence, clean up and drive into town to hear the National Symphony Orchestra. It's a bit of a contrast, but it was all in day's work, and pleasure, for this rancher last week.

North Dakota, 1,600 miles and a world away from the Kennedy Center and Washington, D.C., was the 12th state chosen to host the NSO's American Residency Program.

It was a rare opportunity to hear our national symphony just 60 miles from the ranch.

Encouragement

Out here, we're best known for "never is heard a discouraging word," but along with that void, we need to hear some encouraging words. The NSO brought lots of encouraging words and sounds when it reached out to young people and schoolchildren across the state.

Kids need a lot of encouragement, and I'm just getting to an age now where I'm really starting to appreciate the encouragement my parents gave us.

Mom's our original musician. She's an accomplished fiddle player and can sit at the piano or pick up a guitar, mandolin or banjo and strike the right chords and sing and play by ear. We had it pretty good when it came to bedtime lullabies in our house.

Mom and Dad paid for my sister's clarinet and my alto saxophone that we played in school bands for seven years.

Mom drove the 17 miles into town every week, and baby-sat my piano teacher's two children for an hour while I was downstairs taking piano lessons at the age of 9 and 10.

They borrowed the old upright piano to our minister and his piano-teaching wife that I took those lessons on. And they helped carry it down into the parsonage basement. I can only imagine the cuss words that were swallowed as they struggled down the preacher's stairs and squeezed around the corners with that piano.

Then there's my brother, our family's musical pride. He can sing, play every woodwind instrument made plus a few more and listen to music and write it down note by note.

He majored in music at college, and I remember making the road trips to hear him play and sing with all the Concordia College music groups.

Once, Dad, Mom, my sister and I loaded up in the 1960 three-quarter-ton black Ford pickup to drive 140 miles to hear him play in a symphony orchestra concert. The temperature was way below zero and the roads were snowy, but Dad had a full load of feed on the back of the pickup to give us a little two-wheel-drive traction.

Those drives were Dad's contribution to the music of our family. He never played an instrument, but he loved to hear us play ours. He never had a four-wheel-drive pickup, or a tractor with a cab or a decent shop, and Mom never had a nice kitchen, or a fancy car or a leather couch, but we had band instruments, and pianos, and music lessons, and two people who'd drive a lot of bad roads in old vehicles to hear us play.

I'd imagine the 100 musicians of the National Symphony Orchestra have 100 interesting stories on how their talents were supported while growing up, too.

I got part of one story from a nice visit with one of the cellists during the concert intermission. He told me he grew up on a 60-cow dairy farm in New York state. I smiled at the thought of cows being milked to the music of a cello.

Yes, musicians can grow up in most any environment, and with a little encouragement, they might someday find themselves in our National

Symphony Orchestra with others of outstanding talent. And those of us in the audience, from D.C. to Dakota, all get to benefit from that early encouragement.

Deer day

Putting meat on the table

Nov. 17, 2003

Hunting seems suspiciously recreational, and, like most farmers or ranchers, I try to keep my recreation time to a minimum. So when I do hunt, I have to hunt fast. There're lots of real jobs waiting at home, you know.

For the most part, I've been able to complete my deer-hunting duties on the first day of the season. I generally get a gratis landowner's license, I generally know where the deer are, and I'm generally happy with a buck smaller than trophy size. It all helps me get in and out of the field in a jiffy.

I remember my first deer hunt when I was 14 years old. I headed to the hills by myself with a rifle I borrowed from a neighbor.

Season opened at noon, and by 1 p.m., I saw a nice little buck walking toward some trees. I finished my season right there, and drove home with the deer, guts and all, to surprise the folks. They were surprised I didn't gut it. And they were pretty proud of my first hunt.

Since then, I've learned to field dress my game, leaving a little something for the coyotes and magpies. I've even learned how to process the deer – take off the outside, take out the inside and eat what's in between (minus the bones).

I know hunting isn't something accepted by everyone in society. I respect everyone's opinion, but I've never considered the respectful taking of game and the feeding of that bounty as cruel. Sure, I saw "Bambi." It was a cartoon.

I'm glad that I learned how to hunt. I like the activity – the outdoors, the challenge of the hunt, the satisfaction of eating something you put on the table.

I also help feed and provide habitat for the animals we hunt. I put out some grain for the deer in the winter, I have partridge and grouse that hang out in my hay yard and wild turkeys that roost in the trees that we planted.

I realize, though, that game populations can't grow unchecked. Car fenders realize it, too.

Learning how to shoot a gun was an important part of growing up. Both Mom and Dad took the time to teach me about guns and safety and how to use them. There're kids in inner cities who learn about guns, too. Unfortunately, they get the wrong lessons and they end up shooting each other.

This year's deer hunt was typical. I got a nice, smaller buck on opening day and took it home to begin boning out the meat. I worked away in the shop with a sharp knife and a pair of happy dogs awaiting their scraps.

I took the liver and part of the loin in to Mom and Dad. I took a tenderloin home for me and my wife. It tasted good and we gave thanks for it.

I remember my mom talking about caring for her mother as she was dying of cancer in the 1950s. There wasn't much more the doctors could do. The best the family could do was keep her comfortable in her last days.

When asked what she was hungry for, she told my mother and her sister that she'd like to have some fresh venison. The two farm girls went out and brought back a nice fall doe for their pioneer mother.

They fried up the venison, and Grandma ate way better than usual, despite her sickness. A few months later, the cancer overtook her and she was gone.

I think my mom and aunt still consider that their most worthwhile deer hunt.

A thoughtful Thanksgiving

A lot to ponder

Dec. 1, 2003

As I write this column, it's Thanksgiving Day. We polished off a prime rib – no holiday turkey on this cattle ranch.

Besides, we can't risk turkey's tryptophan-induced sleep. Gotta stay awake and play cards till our eyes cross. And we know beef is a proven brain food, lots of choline to sharpen our minds. It didn't help my canasta game, though. I should've had another helping of prime rib, I guess. Maybe pinochle would've made better use of my finely tuned, beef-fortified brain.

With beef on the table, we're not tempted to demote the name of Thanksgiving Day to "Turkey Day." It wouldn't fit. Plus, we ought to remind ourselves that this is a day to give thanks and not just a day for flaunting fowl and gluttony.

This year, I did a lot of thanking. I also did a lot of thinking. I have a lot to be thankful for, and many of us in North Dakota have also had a lot to think about.

Hard holidays

This holiday is going to be a very hard one for some.

Last Saturday, a 9-year-old boy was killed in a tragic farm accident near Streeter, N.D.. His father was a college friend of mine. His boy had a real love for farm life and all the things to do on the farm.

Yesterday, the day before Thanksgiving, they held his funeral. I can't begin to imagine the pain or the sorrow that his parents are feeling. I can't imagine the empty feeling at their Thanksgiving table today. As a friend, and even as a writer, I don't have any words to console them. All I know to do is pray for them.

Saturday was a tragic day in another part of North Dakota, too.

In Grand Forks, N.D., a 22-year-old female college student left her job at a shopping mall and has not been seen since. She was talking to her boyfriend on her cell phone when he heard her say, "Oh my God" or "Oh no" and the phone disconnected. There's been a massive search for her ever since.

I know her family desperately wanted her back for Thanksgiving. The last newscast I heard said she had not yet been found. Another tough Thanksgiving for another family.

Although they haven't found her yet, they've found a lot of care and concern in the community for her well-being.

More than 1,300 people volunteered to help with part of the search on Tuesday. More than 450 possible tips had been phoned in to the Grand Forks Police department by late Wednesday. Local landowners are searching their property for any possible signs or clues.

Maybe those are the things we have to be thankful for on this kind of Thanksgiving Day.

Thankful for the outpouring of care and support and prayers when a precious little boy is taken away from this life too early.

Thankful for the genuine concern and tireless efforts of an entire town and region when a beautiful young girl is abducted and cannot be found.

We need to be thankful for our faith. It's sometimes all we have.

While many of us are saying thanks for turkey or beef or televised football or a decent deal in a card game, let's remember to say thanks for our family and our friends. And let's remember to think about and pray for at least two other families in the days to come.

I know I will.

Author's note: Sadly, the body of the young lady, Dru Sjodin, was found April 17, 2004. The convicted sex offender accused of her kidnapping and murder awaits trial.

Christmas crash

One cow wrecks lots of cowboys

Dec. 29, 2003

Christmas seemed a lot merrier before I listened to the news on Dec. 23.

One cow 1,200 miles away has tried to steal my Christmas joy.

Christmas week started with everything looking pretty good on the ranch. I had our entire calf crop weaned and on feed. I had all our cull cows on feed and gaining weight. The market was the highest in history.

Newspapers across the country ran stories on record beef prices and the "enormous" profits being made by cattlemen. Profits aren't enormous until the cattle are sold, though. If you're going to die rich in the cattle business, you have to die on the right day.

Our cattle weren't sold. I was trying to do the right thing – wean the calves, get them started on feed, make sure they're all healthy and straight before selling them to a feedyard. Doing what the experts say to do on the cull cows – put some easy weight gain on them, increasing their value and hitting a market when fewer cows are traditionally sold.

I was starting to think about the things a rancher could do with a decent paycheck. Not an exorbitant, beyond-mathematical-comprehension paycheck like news reports on the booming beef market would lead you to believe. Just one that would compare to other businesses with million-dollar investments. One that would pay all the bills, support a family and allow you to have a few of the nicer things like people who work in the cities.

I thought about adding on to the house. Since getting married, my one-bedroom, one-closet bachelor quarters could use some expanding. Hoping to raise a family that would at least staff a small haying crew, it'd be good to have a few more bedrooms.

I thought about becoming debt free and maybe putting some money away for the future.

But it doesn't look like I'll have to worry about those things. One cow diagnosed with bovine spongiform encephalopathy (I refuse to join the media in their sensational, non-scientific terms of "madness") has closed our export markets and put our domestic consumers on guard. The markets will go down faster than they'll ever come back up.

It will give us more empathy for what our Canadian neighbors have experienced this past year, and it will make things even worse for the entire North American beef industry.

Many of us with cattle to sell will kick ourselves black and blue for not selling in that record-high market when we had the chance. Quite a few of us went to bed on Christmas Eve feeling like we had failed, missing the chance to give our families a taste of prosperity.

But wait. It's Christmas. How can we let something like money and cattle markets bring us down? There's a birthday to celebrate, a gift of life and salvation to give thanks for, a day to count our blessings. And our blessings are much greater than the downside of next week's cattle market.

So, I say "bah, humbug" to this cattle market. Fear may have knocked at the door, but faith answered and nobody was there. Christmas should be the best time of year to muster up our faith.

I have faith in the safety of our beef supply and faith that all our customers, domestic and foreign, will keep looking to our product for tasty, wholesome nutrition when the dust settles. And I'll feed my calves to finish and take them to those customers 1 pound at a time with a guarantee of its safety if that's what it takes to weather this storm of reactionary perception.

So, Merry Christmas! Really. And let's get to work to make the new year both happy and prosperous.

Memorial Day address

Towner Memorial Day service

May 31, 2004

Good morning friends, guests, honored veterans. I'd like to thank Sam Thomas for inviting me to speak to you today. As a matter of fact, Nikki and I were discussing our plans for Memorial Day and attending this service when Sam called and asked if I'd speak. It kind of cemented our plans on attending when we saw my name printed on the program in the newspaper!

I'm grateful that I was raised in a family that fostered an appreciation for Memorial Day beyond its status as a three-day weekend, the official start of summer or the point in time when we could expect gas prices rise even further (if that's possible) as demand increases for the summer vacationing and driving season.

I grew up knowing that on Memorial Day weekend we would pack up and go to the Union Cemetery with plants and water and garden tools in the trunk of one of our big, old, four-door cars to tend to graves of our family and ancestors. As children, we learned early on about honoring not only our family who were veterans, but others who were mothers, grandmothers, uncles or aunts.

We would tend to the grave of my Uncle Reinhart, an army veteran who died in a car accident at the young age of 27, the man who became one of the namesakes of my son, Marshall Reinhart, born just 3½ weeks ago. Reinhart worked as a medic on a hospital ship between Japan and the United States, transporting some of the servicemen back to America who had "wounds we couldn't see." His kindness and understanding fit well with the job of working with soldiers suffering from mental scars received in the war.

I learned the stories of Smith and Fay Taylor, sons of Alex Taylor, who homesteaded where Dale Kuhn's farm is now four miles east of town. They were men of education, athletic ability and service to country. Both UND graduates, they served in World War I. Fay is buried in our Union Cemetery, dead at the age of 26 from injuries and poison gas received in the Meuse-Argonne offensive of the "war to end all wars." He was gassed on Sept. 27, 1918, but actually died of the complications from the gas in New York City on May 10, 1919. I'm reminded of the song "The Green Fields of France," where the singer stands by the grave of "Willy McBride" and asks, "I hope you died quick and I hope you died clean, or Willy McBride was it slow and obscene?" I'm afraid that Fay's death was slow and obscene in its seven- or eight-month duration.

Smith, a college football and baseball player and amateur wrestler, served in our North Dakota National Guard before World War I, getting in on the chase of Mexican rebel, Pancho Villa. He entered officers training at Fort Snelling, Minn., on his return from Mexico. Commissioned as a second lieutenant in 1917, he survived World War I to become a school teacher at various prairie towns and a store keeper in Surrey, N.D..

Thanks to an aunt's genealogical work, we have records of Taylor's volunteering and serving in every war since the Revolutionary War. We had family members on both side of the Civil War. Taylors lived in Dekalb County, Tenn., a county that sent 10 companies of soldiers to the Union Army and 12 companies of soldiers to the Confederate Army.

The history of Memorial Day dates back to the year 1868, just after that terrible Civil War of our history when brothers and neighbors fought and killed each other. We gather here on Memorial Day for an appreciation of the history of military service in our country. We come not to glorify war, but to honor our sons who never made it back home to continue their lives of teaching or farming or storekeeping. When our armies are put in places of extreme danger we don't know who will survive and who will die.

I am here today because one of Towner's boys survived his tour of the Pacific Theater of World War II. My dad, Bud Taylor, shipped out on the train from Towner in 1942. He was co-commander overseeing the troops trip from Towner to Fort Snelling with Slim Funk, another Towner boy who would survive service as a bomber navigator in WWII only to be called up in the Reserves for the Korean War and die in a watery crash in that subsequent war. Dad lost other friends, too, like Vernon "Bub" Starks, for whom our VFW Post is named. He wrote Bub a letter while in the Pacific and had it returned to him "deceased." A tough way for a soldier to learn of a friend's fate. He lost friend Max Rosencrans, who died on the other side of the world in the fighting in Italy.

Dad served in the Philippines, participated in the battle of New Guinea, provided support for the war efforts in the South Pacific and, on his 24th birthday, Aug. 9, 1945, he found himself on a landing craft, outfitted for "Invasion A," the massive land invasion of Japan, when Japan surrendered after the dropping of the atom bombs on Hiroshima and Nagasaki. He saw the USS Missouri where the treaty was signed on Tokyo Bay and stayed for the occupation of Japan until he was able to return to life as a rancher on a piece of McHenry County, N.D., on the other side of the world.

Not many 33-year-olds like myself today have had the opportunity to be raised by a WW II veteran, a member of what Tom Brokaw has called the "Greatest Generation." I have, thanks to my father's extended bachelorhood and his not having me until he was the ripe old age of 49. I've said it's kind of like being raised by your grandfather, and it's given me an outlook on life and the world that I've come to appreciate immensely.

I can talk to both of my parents about life in the Depression, about the sacrifices and service made for World War II, and the compassion and the selflessness that came from those experiences. They taught me not to take anything for granted.

Like a lot of veterans, Dad doesn't talk a lot about his experiences in WWII, a snippet here and there about certain people or places or the experiences of becoming a little more worldly as a small town North Dakota kid who'd never been farther than Yellowstone Park on an FFA trip or Miles City, Mont., to buy himself a saddle. We found a few of Dad's letters written home to his mother and brother, and reading them helped me realize that ranchers are still ranchers, even when they're in the army and half a world away. Of course, you couldn't write much about what you were doing or where you were and still get past the military censors, so his letters talked about the things at home like rain, cattle markets, a new bullrake, the want for a new hay mower, a calf that they'd written was sick and how they fared on selling the calves. He'd ask about the military service assigned to others he knew and mentioned on Christmas 1943 that maybe he'd be home for the next Christmas. He didn't see another Christmas at home, one with snow, until 1946.

I realized fully what my father knew about war when we were haying on our meadow one summer and Dad thought he'd smelled something that he'd not smelled for many years. Ranchers know the smell of death and decay, from livestock and cattle that expire on the ranch. But Dad was certain that he smelled something different, that of human death and decay. He had me saddle a horse and look to see if I could find anything. It may have been possible that a person had wandered off in the winter and died on our meadow to be discovered in the summer. I didn't find anything and, more than likely, the smell had come from another animal of some kind, or muck in a drying slough or maybe it was just a certain kind of day that triggered something in Dad's mind. He'd seen dead American servicemen stacked in body bags on the shores of New Guinea. It's a smell and a sight he said he'd never forget. And it still could be triggered 40 years later. One of those wounds that we cannot see.

It's important for us to remember that Memorial Day is not a day that we celebrate with fireworks, it's a day that we observe with prayer and remembrance. We are not here to glorify war. We are here to remember the fallen in our families and other families in this community. I am reminded by my own father and war veteran that wars are about death and dying, from the more than 400,000 who died in his war, to the 1 million Americans who've died in this country's wars since the Civil War when we began decorating graves and observing what would soon be called Memorial Day. We realize on Memorial Day that death goes beyond the duration of the wars they occurred in. For the families of the fallen, the void lasts their whole life.

I told Sam Thomas that I felt a little inadequate to be addressing this group on this day. I'm not a veteran; I've not seen the battlefield. As a matter of fact, by my age, I'm a member of what's known as the "me generation." What a description when you compare people of my age and younger to those in the "Greatest Generation" who experienced a depression, fought and won a war and built America to be the greatest of nations. After Sept. 11, our generation's idea of sacrifice was to keep shopping, keep spending, keep those credit cards humming, so that our economy would remain strong, or at least propped up on credit.

No, I would hope that the "me generation" and "generation X" and "generation Y" would do much more than that to become less self-centered and self-serving. I would hope that we would challenge ourselves to learn from our elders in the Greatest Generation. We need to learn their stories, ask their advice, and live their lessons before it is too late. And, as we know from this weekend's dedication of the WW II Memorial, 1,100 veterans of that war die each day, and with them the lessons we could have learned.

Eric Bogle, an Australian songwriter has a song called "And the band played waltzing Matilda" about the ANZAC battle of Gallipoli in Suvla Bay, Turkey, in WW I. It was one of the bloodiest slaughters ever seen in war resulting in the death of nearly 265,000 Allied troops as they tried to fight their way up an extremely fortified Turkish shore. The Australians observe the anniversary of that battle much like we observe Memorial Day with parades and remembrance.

I quote his lyrics, "And so now every April I sit on my porch, And I watch the parade pass before me, And I see my old comrades how proudly they march, Reviving old dreams and past glories, But the old men march slowly their bones stiff and sore, Tired old men from a forgotten war, And the young people ask what are they marching for. ..." It is our charge in the younger generations, myself and the youth essay speakers before me, Sam and Beth and all the others here today to know and understand what our veterans are marching for on Memorial Day, to respect and honor the sacrifices made by those with the flags on their gravestones that we'll see today.

Memorial Day is for remembering our fallen soldiers; Veterans Day is to honor all veterans, living and dead. But we ought to do both all year long. Gordon Lightfoot's song, Don Quixote, has a verse, "see the soldier with his gun who must be dead to be admired." We must admire our soldiers while they are living, and we have ample opportunities to admire our young men and women going to and from Iraq and Afghanistan.

Many speakers end this kind of a speech with the words, "God bless America." Yes, I hope and pray that God blesses America, but I think it is critical for myself and other believers to ask more of God than just to bless America and Americans. We must ask His blessings for others in our world, other nations, other peoples, and ask Him to show us how to be less selfish with the blessings He's granted us. Only then will our world find the peace that He wishes for His creation.

May God help us all in that task.

Bachelorhood to Fatherhood

Flower power

Going wild with wild flowers

July 17, 2000

I'm not much of a hippie, but I'm a firm believer in flower power. And flower power's even better if you've got access to wildflowers that are free for the picking.

I'm not sure how far along the grain crops are in the neighborhood, but I can say with certainty that the wildflowers on our hay meadows and pastures are headed out and in full bloom.

When the flowers' head out in my part of the country, the ranchers head out to gather 'em up to earn valuable points and prizes in the game of female relations.

Pickin' and grinnin'

With no organized flower delivery service to the rural reaches, ranchers are left to their own devices to get fresh flowers to the ladies in their lives. We're lucky to get UPS out here, much less FTD.

The trouble with the locally grown bouquets is that they're only available for a short burst of time. My favorite wildflower, the wood lily, is called a "June bloom" by some of my German Russian neighbors. The nickname helps them remember when to start looking for them.

I just call the red-petaled posy's tiger lilies and know that they'll be available some time after I know I should start haying but before I actually do. This year, the "June blooms" came the first week of July.

The tiger lilies can be picked while you're haying, and pickers have the satisfaction of sparing the little lilies from being mowed down, raked up, baled up and fed to some slobbery old cow with no appreciation for the plant's former brilliance.

No sir, the lilies clipped by the rancher's jackknife can look forward to a mason jar full of water, a prominent position on a sunshiny kitchen table and the adoration of mothers, wives and little girls for at least several days.

June and July end up being make-up time for forgotten birthdays, missed Mother's Days and Valentine's Days that unconsciously became just another day of doing chores and feeding cattle.

If they can just be patient, they'll get a chance to see our caring and thoughtful side. We just need to wait for the sun to warm us up to the idea of doing something nice.

Points of delivery

I've always been a big believer in picking a few flowers when you're out checking cows, fixing fence or making hay. The sentiment will help mend those fences back in the home yard.

I grew up picking bouquets for my mother, which is something I picked up on from my father. We'd be driving along, and, all of a sudden, he'd bale out of the pickup to collect a few long stems, tie them with twine and lay them on the seat between us for the trip home. It's a good investment for men who know that, "if mama ain't happy, ain't nobody happy."

Secretary's Day usually comes and goes without much attention. But I've had a few jobs where there're ladies who regularly do nice things for you, whether they're administrative types, receptionists or even front desk folks at a hotel. A few wildflowers in a mason jar will let 'em know you appreciate those nice things they've done.

And, of course, flowers are a staple of courtship. I've picked a few for different gals I've known, and they've generally gone over pretty well. The only trouble comes with the long-distance relationships where you need to rely on the U.S. Mail to get your flowers delivered.

Those spindly, little, wilted lilies aren't much to look at after two or three days in a flat envelope, but, like they say, it's the thought that counts. And it might be another year before that thought comes again.

Clear sailing

A lemons-into-lemonade conversion

July 29, 2002

"Surf's up!" It's not a slogan heard often in North Dakota. "Wind's up!" however, can be heard fairly regular.

We're not Wyoming, but we get some pretty stiff breezes here on the prairie. Windy days can be pretty depressing. A good steady gust can suck the energy right out of a person it seems.

But, as they say, if someone gives you a lemon, make lemonade. And if climatic phenomena gives you wind, make the wind your friend.

The wind has been a hard-working friend on our ranch. It's been good about running the windmills and helping pull some water out of the ground. Recently, it's been an innovative and ambitious companion, helping to drive the Prairie Winds wind turbines for our rural electric cooperative to generate some renewable electricity.

I appreciate the working wind's efforts, but I'm most excited about making the wind a friend for fun. Turbines and windmills are fine and dandy, but how about harnessing that power for some good times and recreation?

Cowabonga, dude. The (wind)surf's up in Dakota. Hang ten!

Sail away

Being three-quarters Norwegian, you'd think I had a lot of sailing experience. I guess I'm a pretty poor Viking. My ancestors must have rolled up the sails and buried the rudder after crossing the Atlantic and discovering America. We've been land lovers ever since.

Thanks to a friend, a wind surf board and the big waters of Lake Sakakawea, I'm getting back in touch with my nautical Viking roots.

Lake Sakakawea is no North Atlantic, but it's pretty good water for the prairie. It has more total shoreline than the coast of California, and it makes a wet spot of about 315,000 acres right in the middle of North Dakota.

After a solid five-minute lesson in sailing basics, I was up on the board, filling my sail and cutting across the water. If it weren't for my bowed legs and pale, white chest, you'd think I was born to be sailing in the sun and surf.

Winter winds

With some good recreation like windsurfing, summer winds might prove OK. But it's tough to find a bright side to the region's winter winds. Seems like they're good for nothing but setting record windchills.

One of my old Norwegian relatives figured out how to enjoy those winter gales in the late 1800s though. Cousin Thorvald stayed in touch with his Viking roots and built himself a snow sail sled with runners made from ash trees and a 10-foot sail made of muslin cloth.

He sailed across our prairie ocean of snow pretty efficiently back then before fences crisscrossed the country. His longest trips were from where he stayed to the Kongslie Farm, a distance of 30 miles. His best sailing day got him there in one hour flat.

Despite occasional breakneck speeds, time wasn't a big issue for Thorvald. He'd go there on a southeast wind and patiently wait for a nor'wester to bring him home. Apparently, he made good use of his time at the Kongslie Farm, as he later married one of the daughters.

I reckon that's one way to get in some extra courting. If the parents are pressuring you to leave and quit eating their food, all you have to do is check the wind direction and tell them you're marooned for at least another day or two.

I guess courting, like windsurfing and snow sailing, requires you to be persistent like the wind that got you there.

Cold kindness

Winter's a good time for warm favors

Jan. 13, 2003

There are times when a little kindness can go a long way. Winter is one of those times, especially in North Dakota.

I thought about this when I was scraping the ice off the windshield of my fiancee's car. After the scraping, I started the engine to give it a chance to warm up a bit.

It reminded me of something that my father always used to do for my mother before she got in the car to head to town in the winter.

Dad, like most stoic old ranchers, probably didn't tell Mom he loved her every morning or give her a kiss as he headed out the door. But he did take the time to do the little things that let her know, just the same.

Like scraping her windshield and warming up her car. I suppose remote car starters can replace the care of a husband these days, but I don't think they can replace the kindness.

Cool opportunities

People in warm climates probably find ways to lend a helping hand, but cold climates do seem more conducive to the activity.

While going to college in Fargo, it was pretty common for my friends and I to find someone spinning their car wheels in a snowy parking lot on a patch of ice.

A couple of strong farm boys could usually lean a shoulder into the back of the car and get it out and rolling. We were especially happy to help if the person in distress was a pretty young co-ed.

Icy sidewalks, parking lots and street crossings give Boy Scouts and anyone else with a heart the chance to help elderly people traverse the treacherous spots.

If you're handy with a scoop shovel, you won't have to look far to find a driveway or a walkway in need of some snow cleaning. And use the shovel, not the snow blower, it'll make you feel better about the good deed you're doing.

One sure way to cure the buyer's remorse of spending too much money on a big four-wheel-drive pickup is to keep a tow rope handy and an eye out for hapless motorists who've slid into the ditch. The warm glow of their appreciation will help ease the sting of that next big pickup payment.

Winter chores

I knew a fella who showed his love for his wife by filling the feed pails in the granary when she was set to do the feeding the next day.

I know, a real romantic would've put aside his other tasks or travels and fed the calves for her, but it's still a decent gesture. It's still more endearing than getting her a new pair of insulated coveralls for Christmas.

Another neighbor of mine bought a new hot-off-the-line front-wheel assist tractor, not for himself of course, but for his wife. As long as she was home with the baby and doing winter chores while he worked a job in town, he felt moved to get her a nice, dependable unit with a comfortable, heated cab. I reckon he kind of liked driving it on the weekends, too.

Ice, deep snow, tough winters, hungry cattle – they all give us a chance to be a little kinder. It's easy to understand, now, why Santa Claus lives on the North Pole.

Setting the table

Scattering a few fine chinas

March 10, 2003

I never gave much thought to what kind of dinnerware cradled my food, held it in place and kept it from slopping onto the table. Then I decided to get married.

I thought I had a pretty nice set of matching plates, bowls and cups. Nice for a bachelor anyway. They were blue-speckled enamel steel campware – affordable, unbreakable and versatile.

You could set them out for supper or throw 'em in a box and take 'em camping. They could be dropped from an airplane and survive the impact with nary a scratch. They were noisy, though. The clatter of forks and knives on steel plates was deafening if you were feeding a hungry crew. And it was best to eat quickly because food cools off fast on a tin plate.

The only decision I had to make when buying them was whether to go blue-speckled or red-speckled. Either would have fit in with my rustic ranch decor.

They were quite a step up from the paper plates I had preferred.

I remember when one of my other bachelor friends had rented a house that came complete with a pretty nice built-in china cabinet. Not one to waste such a fine showcase for his dinnerware, he displayed his finest Chinet paper plates in there on the backlit oak shelf. They were the heavy paper ones, too, certainly worthy of display.

Higher standards

Women have different ideas about dinnerware though. With a wedding date pending, I'm learning the ritual importance of choosing the china pattern. Yes, that's china pattern, not Chinet pattern. It's way beyond deciding if you want the three compartment plates, the no compartment plates, paper, plastic or Styrofoam.

You have to consider white or ivory, platinum or gold, floral or banded, bumpy edges or smooth edges. The cups come with little handles or really little handles. The china can be porcelain or bone, easy to break or really easy to break.

I guess it's alright to choose a china pattern and register at a department store so that a few of the plates match each other. I was hoping to pick a brand of tools and register for some matching sockets, but dishes will have to do.

I think it's fair to say a fella can pick out a set of plates in 10 minutes tops. We're well past the 10-minute mark and still looking at china patterns. I know she really wants my input. She just doesn't understand that I gave her all the input I had in that first 10 minutes.

One thing I noticed about china in my extensive studies is that it seems awfully fragile compared to my tin campware. I hate to even pick the stuff up much less think about washing it.

I suppose if I break a couple right off the bat, I can get out of washing the dishes when we use them. But if I break too many, she might quit feeding me altogether.

I guess if it comes to that, I can always grab my old blue-speckled tins and open up a can of pork and beans.

Wedding details

It ain't all garland and roses

July 14, 2003

Over the past several months, I've seen a lot of articles on weddings – tradition, etiquette, receptions, ceremonies and the duties and responsibilities for everyone from the mother of the bride right down to the videographer's cousin.

They did, however, completely miss at least one topic that I would like to write about and submit to the wedding industry press.

Pulling duty

My fiancée, now my wife, and her mother, now my mother-in-law, had worked like slaves planning their wedding. I was invited to attend and play the part of the groom.

I also helped with the invitations, and I lined up the band, the bar and the team and wagon to serve as our horse-drawn limousine. And, I was put in charge of waste management.

Having fed some cattle in confinement and having dabbled in the world of politics, I seemed uniquely qualified to be put in charge of the Porta-Potties for the reception and dance.

I happened to know a team roper who doubles as a Porta-Potty landlord. He's an expert on crap.

He recommended a potty per 50 potters. I told him we were expecting 400 to 500 head, but I figured half of them were men and there were plenty of trees in the vicinity. I decided to rent four mobile outhouses that came on two trailers.

The question was how to transport them the 90 miles to the job site. I decided to pull one. For the other, I consulted the list of best man's duties – carry the rings, sign the marriage license and, I decided, "pull the Porta-Potty to the reception."

I picked up my Porta-Potty on the way to the rehearsal. Before leaving town, I also picked up two dozen roses to surprise my beautiful bride. It made for quite a contrast. Roses in the front, outhouses pulled behind. Sweet and sour.

Back hauls

I didn't mind the trip so much. Granted, I got a few looks of yearning from some cross-legged kids as they passed me. Dad wasn't making many bathroom stops with the mini-van on their family vacation I guess.

I slowed down for construction zones, but I tried not to go too slow. Otherwise, I'd have probably had someone in an orange vest and a hard hat pop out of one of the potties when I got to the farm.

My best man, and the groomsman with him, weren't real thrilled with the job of Porta-Potty pulling. As bachelors, I think they figured it cut down on their cool quotient as they headed down the highway. Knowing the way women need to use the bathroom while they're traveling, it could have been a good way to meet chicks had they pulled over and declared themselves open for business.

The wedding, reception, dance and Porta-Potties were a resounding success. But, as I had feared, I was left with both Porta-Potty trailers to pull back. That, and a half dozen tuxedoes. Another contrast to haul back both the rented formal wear and the rented outhouses.

I saw that the first trailer I'd hooked up to had another ball hitch behind so a second trailer could be attached. Yes, like all the other big truckers on the highway, I had the ability to pull a pup, a Porta-Potty pup.

I hooked up to the whole train, and, luckily, I had a three-quarter-ton diesel pickup to pull the load. A long night of eating, drinking and dancing can make for some pretty full potties.

I was careful when I turned the corners and I drove gingerly. Hitting the ditch and rolling a couple of Porta-Potties would have been a real mess.

Sadly, some couples don't get into potty training until a few years after their wedding. I, however, got to experience my potty train the very next day.

Secret shopping

Trying to figure out Victoria's secret

July 28, 2003

I'm the kind of fella who feels comfortable most everywhere I go.

I can be just as comfortable in a fancy French restaurant as I am out in the hay field. I can wear my boots and hat to a punk rock concert and not even feel out of place. I'm a pretty good mixer and I don't embarrass too easily.

Of course, that was before being assigned to the duty of buying lingerie for my new bride.

Girl stuff

Friends and relatives held a couple of bridal showers for my wife-to-be ahead of the wedding.

Her girlfriends put on a shower for her, and, there, her bridesmaids gave her a gift certificate for some honeymoon lingerie at Victoria's Secret. And I was elected to do the shopping and use the certificate.

I've heard about Victoria's Secret. I've even walked by a couple of their stores at the shopping mall and taken a brief, sideways glance at the displays in their window as I hurried by. I'm always afraid to take too long a look for fear of being labeled a pervert.

Now I was supposed to walk right in that store and do some serious shopping.

I tried to pick a time of low mall traffic to dart in and do the deed. I chose a weekday morning and wore my least-conspicuous cowboy hat to keep from being recognized.

The sales lady took one look at me and knew I wasn't there to browse. "Can I help you, sir?" she asked, much to my relief. With a little expert help I could be in and out of there in no time flat.

I explained my predicament – the gifted gift certificate, getting married, shopping for a little something for the honeymoon, admitting to my status as a first-time customer.

When she heard honeymoon, she steered me clear away from the flannel long johns and took me to the sexy section.

Down to business

Like I said, I'm usually a pretty comfortable person. But standing there amongst all that underwear and stuff, I was as nervous as a nudist crossing a barbed-wire fence.

The sales lady did what she could to put me at ease. She showed me what was popular with other honeymoon shoppers and she even tried a couple things on – the mannequin, that is – for me.

Judging how one of those outfits would look like on a person by seeing them on a mannequin took all the imagination this imaginative cowboy could muster.

One thing I could never have imagined is the price tag on those skimpy little things. Those little lace contraptions were about the same price as a pair of insulated bib overalls! And I know some ranchers who'd prefer to see their wife in the overalls! But, being a newlywed, I opted for the satin and lace.

I took a few glances around the store to see if I recognized anyone while I was shopping. I monitored the flow of people outside in the mall as I tried to blend in with my surroundings. It's tough to hide a 6-foot-2 cowboy in a lingerie store.

Finally, the choices were made and we headed to the cash register. Thanks to a good sales person, we surpassed the amount of the gift certificate and I dug into my pocket for the extra cash.

I bolted through the door and nonchalantly merged into the flow of shoppers with my pink- and white-striped shopping bag.

The experience didn't scar me too much, but I noticed something that would have been pretty handy as I made my exit.

It was a mail-order catalog.

Valentine's Day deadline

What to get, what to do

Feb. 9, 2004

It's getting close to V-day, and if I don't come up with something romantic real quick, it's going to be D-day, as in, done missed the opportunity to impress my gal.

I heard a radio ad that said naming a star for your sweetheart was the perfect gift. A woman in the ad exclaims ecstatically, "Oooohh, you named a star for me!"

She was probably ecstatic at the idea of a bunch of suckers sending her company $50 for a 50-cent certificate proclaiming a star was officially registered and filed in their file cabinet.

I think my sweetheart would rather have the $50. We can always stand outside, look at the stars and call them whatever we want.

It's a tough holiday to come up with something that's both original and appreciated.

Valentine traditions

Chocolate is an old standby and one that most guys use because they actually enjoy eating the chocolates that they've gifted. It's well known that I'm the chocolate eater in the family; she'd see right through it.

Flowers are another old Valentine standby. It's well known that she's the flower lover in the family; there'd be absolutely no element of surprise. There's gotta be something else.

Some people give jewelry for Valentine's Day. Or at least some rich people do. Pre-BSE, I might have considered it. Post-BSE, it's just not possible.

There're always romantic movies, sappy poetry and candlelight dinners. All pretty passe.

In doing a little reading on some Valentine's folklore, I think I ran across an idea with some real potential for struggling ranchers.

It had to do with an old Celtic story about two forbidden lovers from separate warring villages. Under penalty of death, they were warned to never see each other again. They ran away to a forest above the sea.

In those times, Celtic villagers were identified by a colored stone engraved with their family name. The stone was supposed to follow them wherever they went. Upon their death, the stone was cast into the sea and the name on it would be theirs for eternity.

The two forbidden lovers in this story rejected those family stones and took a new, single stone and engraved it with both their names as a symbol of their love. After engraving their new stone, they took it to a bluff overlooking the ocean, cast it into the sea and spoke this verse, "May the names inscribed here be forever united in love and hidden so long as this stone hides in the deep waters. May those who seek to separate us find us not, as they can never find thee."

As the story goes, the stone sank and was never seen again, and neither was the couple.

Where I saw the story, it was suggested that modern romantics pick up the tradition by painting their names on a rock, having a picnic, making up their own little verse and throwing their rock into the ocean.

A rock and a magic marker seem pretty affordable to me. The cold weather will make for a short picnic, saving as much time as money. And although we're a little far from an ocean in North Dakota, our hay meadow has become a sea of snow this winter.

I can hardly wait to take my sweetheart out on Valentine's Day to cast a rock out into the snowbanks! She'll be so impressed. That's romance.

Hah, hah, hee

Birth breathing is no laughing matter

March 8, 2004

Last year, marriage proved to be both a good move for me personally and a good source of column material for me professionally.

This year, I'm on the cusp of another life-changing event. Fatherhood. I expect it, too, will be both a good move and a good source of column material.

As a matter of fact, when my wife told me about the local hospital's free prenatal classes being offered to expectant parents, I said, "Sign us up. That's gotta be good for a column or two!"

I missed the first class as I had the chance at a speaking job that might help us pay for the first month's diaper supply. My wife said I could be excused.

She went and said they went over several things including the signs of pregancy. The ladies present decided that yes, indeed, they were pregnant. This explained their substantial weight increase, their fashionable move from jeans to bib overalls and the regular doctor visits they'd been making for several months.

The next week, I got to go and we listened to a dietician talk about expectant mothers and eating right. Beef and dairy both got high grades for the nutrients they supply. I decided this dietician was OK.

We discussed a little physical therapy. My wife confided to the group that I was very supportive of her physical therapy activities during pregnancy. I let her carry feed pails to 200 calves everyday, and when the pregnancy demanded less lifting and more walking, I devised a complementary system for her to carry half pails with twice as many trips from the feed bin to the feed bunks.

I heard a few gasps from the others who were apparently quite impressed with my level of support and understanding.

At our last class, we really got into some fun stuff – breathing and relaxation. We even brought a pillow to class. It had been a long day on the ranch and I was looking forward to putting that pillow to use for a little nap. It turned out that the pillow was for the mother to use to get comfortable when we sat on the floor.

We learned some breathing techniques to get the mother through the pains of labor and, possibly, a natural birth.

We learned the "hah and hee" breathing rhythms. I grew up watching "Hee Haw," and, on occasion, have exclaimed "Yeehaw!", but hah then hee were new to me. I asked if it was similar to the commands of gee and haw used to steer mules left and right. I received an affirmative no.

Hah's are the short breaths taken in and hee's are the longer breaths exhaled. Used appropriately, it can help you breath away your pain.

So the lessons were mostly for the mother. The husband's just supposed to remind her to breathe, not scream, through those gut-wrenching contractions of labor. I can only imagine those unsolicited suggestions are met with a variety of responses.

I'm trying to take it all in, though. They say it helps to focus on your "happy place," to have some soothing music playing and to take long, deep, cleansing breaths between the contractions.

Even though I'm not the one going through the labor, I'm jotting down a few notes to get me through some of the pains of ranching – calf kicks, cow crushing, slipped wrenches and off-target hammers. In the past, all I've done was cuss. Now, I can breathe, focus and visualize.

And I have a feeling my new "happy place" to visualize will be the crib where my son or daughter sleeps – safe, healthy and content.

A happy Mother's Day

And a good start on Father's Day

May 17, 2004

It was quite a Mother's Day here on the Taylor Ranch.

In the days around the Sunday established to honor maternity, we had a plethora of parturition. A bunch of cows calved in my late calving season, one of the ranch cats had a batch of kitties tucked away in the hay manger of our barn, our pregnant mare foaled and gave us a nice wobbly legged filly, and, oh, by the way, my wife gave birth to a beautiful baby boy!

Like I said, it was quite a Mother's Day.

Proud only begins to describe my feelings. He's our first child. He's perfect. He's cute as can be. He's ours.

He's sitting in his little baby seat next to me and taking a snooze while I write this column. It's hard to get much writing done. I spend most of my time staring at him, watching his facial expressions, tracking his wiggles, admiring everything from the fineness of his hair to the size of his hands.

It's hard to imagine life being any more perfect. And I thought life was pretty good before the stork brought us this little bundle.

No comparisons

I'm of a vocation that considers itself to be pretty handy with laboring females. Ranchers figure all their years of supervising calving cows make them experts in the field.

As a writer, I make points with comparisons. I'm not too sparing in my use of metaphor and simile. The temptation would be to compare my experiences with the cow herd to my wife's birth of our son.

I'm here to testify, after experiencing both, there's no comparison. At least not in the way you feel.

Sure, I understand the mechanics of the deal. But watching your wife deal with the pain of delivery gave me feelings of sympathy I'd never known.

I've never considered myself to be squeamish. I've been around lots of needles and blood and tense moments. But my knees got pretty weak when I was trying to keep my wife still while the anesthesiologist was fishing around in her spine with that epidural needle.

But I had toughened back up when it was time for the delivery. I did everything I could to help this 8-pound 10-ounce boy into the world, which wasn't much.

But the new mom performed pretty well, and I learned that the sound of a wailing baby can be music to your ears.

It was nearly 3 a.m. when everything came together, but, in my mind, time had stopped at about 8 p.m. when we were driving to the hospital.

I've learned a lot of new things in one short week of fatherhood.

I've learned about changing diapers. I don't think I've ever changed one. I never volunteered to change the diapers on anyone else's kids. I do volunteer to change our son's.

I've learned that there's not much a father can do to satisfy a baby who's looking to nurse. You can sing, talk, walk, rock. It's best to just get him to his mother.

I've learned about precious cargo. Whether I'm just picking him up, carrying him or driving him home from the hospital, I've discovered a whole new level of careful.

And I've learned there's a place in your heart that you never knew existed until you've held your baby and looked at him in all his innocence and hope for the future.

I've also learned that, despite what you may have heard, cowboys do cry. Like a baby. For a baby.

I expect I'll learn a lot more in the years to come.